MOTHERLAND
GROWING UP WITH THE HOLOCAUST

Rita Goldberg

THE NEW PRESS

NEW YORK
LONDON

The photograph of Hilde (front cover and illustration 10)
appears courtesy of Monica Kaltenschnee of the Stichting
Annemie en Helmuth Wolff, Amsterdam.

The Nazi "transport" list (illustration 11)
appears courtesy of René Kok at NIOD.

Requests for permission to reproduce selections
from this book should be mailed to:
Permissions Department, The New Press, 120 Wall Street, 31st floor,
New York, NY 10005.

First published in Great Britain by Halban Publishers Ltd., 2014
This edition published in the United States
by The New Press, New York, 2015
Distributed by Perseus Distribution

ISBN 978-1-62097-073-7 (hc)
ISBN 978-1-62097-074-4 (e-book)
CIP data available

The New Press publishes books that promote and enrich public
discussion and understanding of the issues vital to our democracy and
to a more equitable world. These books are made possible by the
enthusiasm of our readers; the support of a committed group of donors,
large and small; the collaboration of our many partners in the
independent media and the not-for-profit sector; booksellers, who often
hand-sell New Press books; librarians; and above all by our authors.

www.thenewpress.com

Book design by Spectra Titles, Norfolk

Printed in the United States of America

2 4 6 8 10 9 7 5 3 1

For the grandchildren and great-grandchildren of Hilde and Max:

The Goldberg Harts

Daniel, his wife Ellen and sons Gabriel and Jamie
Benjamin

The Goldberg Brubakers

Heather, her husband Zach and daughter May
Melanie and her husband Robert
Michael

The Goldberg Ross Russells

Rebecca and her husband Riz, daughter Zawadi and son Simoni
Adam

And for all their future descendants

Contents

Acknowledgments

I HAVE BARELY started, and already I feel like an Oscar nominee fearful of leaving people out. First thanks must go to my mother's rescuers: Zus and Joop Scholte, in Amsterdam, and Robert Dupuis and family in the Ardennes of Belgium. Without them my mother would probably not have survived, and there would be no marriage, no children and no story. They should have been inscribed among the Righteous of All Nations at Yad Vashem in Jerusalem, but for some reason that never happened, possibly because of my mother's habit (so like my own) of jettisoning the past like a booster rocket on her voyage through life. I hope that this book will make some amends, especially to Kiki Scholte, the youngest daughter of the Dutch family, who has been a friend all these years.

I mention Yad Vashem, but other museums also appear quite a bit in this book, not only because people working there have kindly helped me with research, but also because museums make concrete what so many survivors' children have internalized. I would like to say, though, that my mother's life with the rescuers, and with other survivors during and after the war, was not museum-like at all: she drew emotional nourishment from their warmth, joy and sense of fun. Some of the postwar pictures included here give an inkling of their vitality, as well as of their heroism.

My closest friend, Ilene Neuman, should be thanked too, though she died of breast cancer long ago. Ilene knew my story from the inside. She was a year older and came from my hometown, Teaneck, New Jersey, though I didn't know her in high school. From the moment we met during my first weekend in college, we were nearly inseparable. Her father had survived the camps, and we had in common our recognition of the existential absurdity of our position. When things got tough, our mantra was always: "Well, at least it's not Auschwitz!" followed by explosive laughter (Ilene, like my mother, was an excellent laugher). When she was dying in Palo Alto, California, I called as much as I could, and visited a week before her death. At that point in 1995, the year she died at forty-seven, her cancer had metastasized to her brain and bones. She had constant pain and nosebleeds, though her intellect was intact right until the end. Her family, under the stress of her illness, was in disarray. "It's still better than Auschwitz!" she said. In a horrible way it was better, and she knew it. Auschwitz didn't even let her experience her own suffering fully. I miss her to this day and wish that she were here to celebrate this memoir with me.

Among the living, family and friends come first in the order of gratitude. My parents, Max and Hilde, are still living together in Teaneck and eager to see this apparently endless project appear in print. My sister Dot recorded long interviews with our mother in 1983, and the typescript of these became the basis for my own interviews much later on. Dot and my middle sister, Susie, have offered unwavering love and support from the beginning, when they read the first version of the memoir.

Oliver, Benjamin, Daniel and his wife Ellen and their two little boys, Gabriel and Jamie, are the delight of my life and have made me a happy writer even when the work has been sad. They (at least the adults) and other members of the extended family – nieces Heather Brubaker and Rebecca Ross Russell, and Becky's father, David Ross Russell – read the manuscript at various points. The entire clan, including cousins in Switzerland, Israel and the Philippines, has been a source of loving strength, and I recognize my good fortune in having them.

Special thanks go to two people whose intellectual support has been essential. My husband, Oliver Hart, has been everything writers usually mention at the very end of the acknowledgments. We have been married forty years, and he has been patient, loving, hilarious and generally adorable. He has also been a challenging reader and fastidious editor even when he had to grit his teeth to plow through yet another version of a chapter. Our son Benjamin Hart, who is a professional in these matters, has edited several versions of the manuscript down to the one now in print. His love of language and his grasp of structure and logic are amazing, and his comments have been astute and characteristically witty. He also gave me the title of my book.

Warm thanks as well to Myra McLarey and Steve Prati, who have been insightful readers, commentators, cheerleaders and beloved friends. I'm grateful for the help, interest and unflagging kindness of many people in Lexington and Cambridge, Massachusetts and abroad, only a few of whom I'll name here: Steven Cooper; my close friend, Pat McFarland, who died before she could see the published book, and her husband Philip McFarland; John Gledson; Ruthy and Elhanan Helpman; Linda Jorgenson; Eva Simmons; Esther Silberstein; Ali Butchko; colleagues at the Department of Comparative Literature at Harvard; and the now-defunct Porch Table writers' group in Cambridge, Massachusetts, the brainchild of Elena Castedo and of which Myra, above, Gregory Maguire (to whom thanks as well) and I were members.

I would like to thank the many archivists, historians and researchers who have helped me – some for years, some more recently. These include the incomparable Genya Markon, who as Director of Photo Archives first contacted my mother on behalf of the United States Holocaust Memorial Museum. She has, regrettably, semi-retired, though she still does work on behalf of the Museum in Israel. She gathered photographs and interviews for the Museum, where they are in safe hands, and she introduced my mother to other scholars. Dutch researchers from NIOD (the Institute for War, Holocaust and Genocide Studies) and from Dutch Public Television, both based in Amsterdam, the Netherlands, include Matthijs Cats, Gerard Nijssen, René Kok, René Pottkamp, Erik Somers, the late Eric Nooter (who worked in New York) and Ad van Liempt. Several of these historians also participated in making a television program about my mother that aired in the Netherlands in 2003. They generously shared major discoveries from their archives, and I have been able to use these in the book. Simon Kool, An Huitzing, and Monica Kaltenschnee, from the Stichting Annemie en Helmuth Wolff, recently discovered a cache of wartime photographs and out of the blue sent me three formerly unknown pictures. The cover portrait of my mother at eighteen, in her nurse's uniform, comes from that collection. An Huitzing in particular has become an invaluable and generous friend to whom I owe many new connections and discoveries.

Thanks go also to Elisa Ho of the Jacob Rader Marcus Center of the American Jewish Archives in Cincinnati, Ohio; to Lynn Fleischer, of the Annette Levy Ratkin Jewish Community Archives in Nashville, TN; to Reuma Weizmann (wife of the former president of Israel), though indirectly, because she sent her unpublished memoir to my parents; to David Delfosse, of Paris, who is working on a book that prominently features my uncle Jo; and especially to Megan Koreman, a brilliant historian who generously shared information about Jo and his underground connections in Belgium. Her meticulously researched http://dutchparisblog.com allowed me to find some information online, but she was generous with advice and further commentary as well. Karen Packard, Theresa Norris and Alicia Peters of Wales Copy Center in Lexington, Massachusetts, have helped me over many years with printing and illustrations in all kinds of complicated permutations. Judy Stewart, my copy editor, and Michelle Levy, the book's designer, have been a delight to work with and have taken care to minimize error and please the eye.

I should add that I'm not a historian, and that this is not an academic enterprise. Because I wanted to tell my mother's story as she told it to me, and to tell my own in relation to hers, I chose not to read other people's memoirs, or even to dip into the huge critical literature on the Holocaust. I didn't want to be too influenced or to be made more self-conscious than I already was, though I know many excellent books exist. I'm sure that my work joins others in the articulation of many shared ideas, but I have neither read nor borrowed from anyone else in that regard. On the other hand, I've tried to cite the historical and other sources that I do use, again by no means exhaustively, with great care. Because of my own linguistic limitations, I haven't been able to read most Dutch historical sources in their original language. As authors always say in these situations, any mistakes are my own.

Final thanks go to my peripatetic agent and friend, Andrew Schuller, who divides his time between Canberra and London, and to Martine and Peter Halban, who have also become friends as well as publishers.

Rita Goldberg
Lexington, MA
October 2013

Notes on the Text

I have tried to minimize abbreviations in this narration, but several recur:

AJDC – the American Joint Distribution Committee, also known as Joint. This is a Jewish relief organization based in New York and still very much in existence. It provided crucial assistance to Jews in Europe, especially immediately after the Holocaust. My mother was employed by the AJDC for the latter part of her time at Bergen-Belsen.

NIOD – the acronym for the Netherlands Institute for War, Holocaust and Genocide Studies. This organization has changed its name several times, but NIOD always refers to it.

UNRRA – United Nations Relief and Rehabilitation Administration, an organization that my parents, especially my father, were involved with for a couple of years after the war.

Because this story covers almost 100 years, it jumps around in time a bit. Many conversations with Jo Jacobsthal (my uncle), Joe Wolhandler (who was present in 1945, postwar, at Bergen-Belsen) and even with my mother took place in the mid-1990s and early 2000s, but are often retold in the present tense. I have tried to be clear about these distinctions in narrative time.

American Prologue:
Mother and Daughter

THE GRASSY FIELD in the middle of the hospital grounds ought to have been lawn, but it had been left wild and was known by now as The Meadow. Five substantial brick houses adjoined it, two on one side, three on the other. The houses had been built about three decades before in the Georgian style, with white-columned porticos and side wings lined with windows. Winter and summer, a path ran not quite straight across The Meadow from one set of houses to the other. In the spring, before the grass had begun its serious growth, it looked like a part inexpertly drawn through a luxuriant head of hair. As the summer progressed, the path diminished from a clear line to a trace to a mere fold in the waving grass, until it finally disappeared altogether, only to re-emerge from the snow and mud of winter once again. I remember lying on my back in that sweet-smelling nest, looking up at the summer clouds and listening to the scrabbling of small creatures.

This was in Rhode Island, in the mid-1950s, on the grounds of the state mental hospital where my father, Max, was a doctor. I lived there in episodes for a total of perhaps five years before I turned nine and we moved away for good. I have always identified so strongly with the little girl in the long grass that my habit of retreating there seems to define something to which all subsequent experience somehow referred. I wonder now whether the comfort I drew from being on my own in the buzzing silence of that miniature world, from relying on my own thought and observation, and especially from the idea of not being found, came from a deep part of my being, a part I dared not confront, really, until much later in my adult life. *Hiding in the long grass* became my shorthand for escape. Decades later, I think about the appeal of that hidden place. Something about hiddenness and surveillance, about the refreshing of identity in solitude, had meant a great deal to me and seemed to endow an ordinary experience of childhood with exceptional weight. The long grass was more than a safe haven. It was genuinely an escape, and the question becomes: an escape from what?

Sometimes I think that the escape was from the long reach of memory, that shadow over the sunlit lawn of my own little life, from infancy on; and not from my own memories, which were only beginning to take shape at that age, but from my mother's memory, from our family memories, even, it sometimes seemed, from the collective memory of the Jews. My father was a psychiatrist, a professional rememberer, but he spent more time analyzing than recalling, being a true disciple of Freud and Erikson. His sort of remembering was supposed, eventually, to bring you health. In fact he often protected my mother, Hilde, from remembering too much or too fast, but my mother on her own was not very self-protective. She talked freely about what had happened to her in the years just before I was born. I feel, sometimes, as if I had taken in her stories at her breast, before I had the power of speech. I knew the family history so early that I cannot remember a time before knowing. My dreams and waking life swarmed with frightful retellings.

By the age of three or four, I knew that it was pure chance that had saved me from the boxcars I had heard so much about, those trains which took terrified innocents, crammed together standing up and dying of thirst and exposure, to their deaths in the camps of Eastern Europe. I was born a few years too late, but I knew right from the start that my blue eyes, my blond ringlets, and my prattle would not have saved me. Children younger than I had perished. I had seen them in my mother's photograph album. At first I imagined myself in those boxcars. As I grew older, into womanhood and then into motherhood, I imagined my younger sisters on them, and then my children. The dream of deportation was a nightmare that could be adapted to all the stages of life, because it had been a reality, though not directly for me.

When I grew old enough to read, I was introduced to *The Diary of Anne Frank*. By the age of ten, I'd read it many times over. I don't think that was an unusual thing to do, since the book was a bestseller by a child, but in my household it had a special significance. Anne's father was my godfather, and I knew him very well. I had always called him Uncle Otto and thought of him as a blood relative, my favorite, in fact. One of my first extended memories from childhood is of Otto standing on his head in a shaft of sunlight pouring in from a window behind him. His smooth, benevolent face is getting redder and redder, but being upside-down on a warmly patterned Persian rug doesn't keep him from spouting delightful nonsense. I laugh and laugh – I have that body memory of laughter welling up from inside – and once Otto is upright again, his three-piece suit pulled to rights and his fair complexion recovered from the rush of blood, he gives me a British pop-up book full of tile-roofed houses populated by dolls who speak an odd sort of English and have fairy cakes for tea. It's like an afternoon in Ali Baba's cave. I already possess other treasures he has given me. The tiny antique silver eggcup, napkin ring and spoon slotted in a case of blue velvet and engraved with my name were given to my parents when I was born. All my memories of him in my first years are of laughter, play and affection.

By that time, Otto and his second wife, Fritzi, had settled in Basel, Switzerland, where his mother, sister and brother and their families had survived the war. Basel was the city of my father's birth, and of mine, too. My parents had seen a great deal of the Franks before our departure for America in 1950. The two families had lived around the corner from each other when I was born, and my mother took me to visit almost daily. In the next couple of years, we came back once or twice for visits we could ill afford, and when my father was drafted into the US Army and sent to Germany, we traveled back and forth: Frankfurt and Basel were not very far apart. My memory of Otto on his head comes from that period, when I was just under four. Otto and Fritzi came to us in the US quite frequently too, as the fame of Anne's Diary continued to grow.

In 1958, when I was eight and we were spending our last winter in Rhode Island, my mother sprang a surprise on me. She knew that Otto was coming on his way, or way back, from visiting Hollywood, where George Stevens was making the movie version of the play of the Diary, but she didn't tell my sister Susie and me. I went to school as usual, and as usual was daydreaming at my desk in the country schoolhouse where two classes were combined. The third grade was probably doing math, and I was probably half-listening to the fourth-grade geography lesson instead. I caught a glimpse of my mother's face and Otto's through the glass panel of the classroom door, jumped up squealing and ran into Otto's arms, breaking up both lessons. My teacher was evidently a co-conspirator. My mother introduced Otto to the class, and I was whisked off to spend the rest of the day joyfully at home.

But the book, the Diary, was another matter, and as I grew older I came to see the suffering that underlay my charming godfather's kindness. The Diary was his reality, and we, in our happy oasis, were an illusion. His heart had been broken, and there wasn't much we could do about it, not with all the affection and laughter we could muster. Every now and then the darkness peered out. I watched him in Manhattan a few years later, when some sculptor unveiled a bust of Anne and chattered on about the effects he had hoped to achieve, not recognizing that the legendary girl had once been flesh and blood, and that her flesh-and-blood father was sitting before him. But we noticed. We watched Otto's eyes fill with tears as he gazed at the likeness of his daughter; we heard his voice falter. He had made it his business to keep all the wounds of his past open. That was his tribute to his dead family, and his apology to them for having survived. He would not allow a scar to form over his shattered heart. His tears were not in the least contrived. He often seemed to be unaware of them, continuing to talk as they coursed down his cheeks.

My mother had known Otto since childhood. She had lost her parents in the war at the same time as he had lost his children. The two survivors became close after their postwar reunion in Amsterdam. They were naturally cheerful people, but an edge of sadness crept easily in. Otto could be brought to tears by the slightest reference to the events of his past, but my mother was more guarded. They had in common a way of floating through the events of daily life as if they were not quite there, like initiates of an ascetic religion who had attained a higher order of detachment from this life than the rest of us. At the same time they were energetically engaged in various causes designed to improve a world whose flaws they knew so well. Otto founded

the Anne Frank House in Amsterdam, and later the Anne Frank
Fonds in Basel. He devoted his life to the ideals he thought Anne
expressed in the Diary. My mother, when her three daughters
grew a little older, established day-care centers for poor children,
first as a volunteer, than as a professional. They were a mystery,
those two, survivors whose personalities abounded in rich
paradox.

At first, before the fame of the Diary began to sweep him into
orbits of celebrity where we could not follow, Otto gave us the
sense that we in particular, rather than the world in general, were
especially suited to inherit the paternal love he had left over when
he had lost his children. He had a stepdaughter and step-
grandchildren in England whom we had never met, but he had
not yet developed the constant international following of young
people that eventually made his house in a suburb of Basel into a
kind of ashram. In the summer of 1960, when I was eleven, for
instance, Otto and I walked alone in a high valley in the Swiss
Alps. My family was visiting my grandparents when we couldn't
afford to, as usual. He gave me a little leather-bound volume of
Greek myths retold by Roger Lancelyn Green. "Anne liked the
Greek myths at your age," he told me, as if I hadn't already
memorized everything about her from my many readings of her
book, "and I thought you might like them too, since you want to
be a writer. Anne wanted to be a writer, you know." I did know,
since I was already haunted: by the Diary, by my mother's
memories, and by Otto's very presence. At night, dream-troubled,
I talked in my sleep about Anne, my near-cousin, my idol and my
rival, who had died so horribly.

My Rhode Island classmates for the most part didn't suffer
from such night terrors. But they were never allowed to visit me
at home. Although most of their fathers were guards at the state
penitentiary for men, where they kept watch over the murderers
and rapists whose cells the families could see from their porches

overlooking the prison, the children's parents drew the line at our loonies. We were in an area zoned for the misfits of society, on the 19th-century principle that it was better for the mental and moral health of inmates if they served out their time in the countryside. In fact the hospital was attractive and peaceful, an area of handsome brick buildings surrounded by woods and fields that abounded with animals: meadowlarks, pheasants, rabbits, foxes. We got milk and fresh vegetables from the state penal farm on the other side of the woods, and enjoyed our rural comforts.

The parents of my school friends were not frightened by pheasants and rabbits. It was the patients who scared them – patients who could be seen sometimes shuffling like grey ghosts at the bus stop outside the hospital gates; patients who occasionally made the news when they escaped from a high-security ward. To the neighbors, the hospital was a graveyard where everyone had died of the contagious diseases of madness and alcoholism, addiction and grief, and the figures they saw on the street were the wraiths of another world, prophetic and disturbing.

For my sister Susie and me (our younger sister, Dot, didn't arrive until 1960), the containment of hospital life was one of its charms. By the time Otto had come to my classroom door on that visit, we had moved around a great deal. I told myself that I hadn't minded pulling up roots. Life seemed adventurous, its difficulties part of our interesting foreignness. My energetic, multilingual parents were always at the head of our expeditions, as dependable in our mobility as Noah and his wife on the Ark. Back and forth we went between my father's jobs and assignments, from Basel to New York to Rhode Island, to Texas and back to Rhode Island, to Germany and back, to Boston and back. Until our final move to New Jersey when I had reached the ripe age of nine, Rhode Island was the center of the yoyo, the home to which our spinning family always returned.

The task of adaptation was more pressing at some times than at others. The two years we spent in Frankfurt, Germany, from 1953 to 1955 when, at the suggestion of the American government, my father was drafted into the Army Medical Corps with the rank of captain, must have demanded a great deal from me, because I remember so much about them. I was becoming old enough to develop memories that had some narrative coherence, and Germany forced memory on me like it or not. My parents have always said that they had been pleased that, in the last gasp of the Korean Conflict, "we" had been posted to Frankfurt and not to Korea. Certainly it was a piece of luck that the family could remain together during my father's military service. He became a citizen because of the draft, allowing my mother and me to become citizens quite soon after. We left Rhode Island in our car, the only property my parents owned, and went first to Fort Sam Houston in Texas and then to New Jersey, where my father completed his military training and set sail for Germany.

In recent years my mother has been able to admit that the idea of returning to Europe, which she thought she had left for good only three years before, and especially to Germany, the source of all the suffering of her youth, had caused her to fall into a profound depression. My mother, my sister and I first flew to Holland slightly before my father left on his troopship. We went to see my maternal uncle Jo, then recovering from a combination of meningitis, polio and tuberculosis. Then we had to spend several months on our own in Stuttgart before we settled into the Frankfurt apartment where we would spend most of the next two years. In Stuttgart, my mother found herself alone with a four-year-old and a one-year-old. My father visited on weekends when he could. The parents of the little girl across the road, whom I played with regularly, turned out to be enthusiastic former Nazis. We found out when the little girl's older sister, who was about thirteen, informed my mother innocently that her father was in prison. He had been arrested by the Americans years before, she said, because he had worked in a *Lager* (concentration camp) with *Häftlinge* (prisoners). The two German girls, intrigued by their new neighbors, always appeared when we left the house, and my mother changed her routines to avoid them. She says now that she sank lower and lower, though she tried not to show it. She admits that she confided in me in her loneliness, and relied on me to help entertain my little sister, Susie. I must have felt the weight of precocious responsibility.

Whatever the reasons, whether they lay in the family, in me, or in the actual landscape, Germany took on a distinctive emotional coloring that irradiated events with special intensity. There was not much external color in those days. In Frankfurt charred ruins loomed on every corner, and great pits opened up where dinosaur steam shovels gobbled messily at the earth, jaws dripping rivulets of soil. The round tin roofs of the American occupiers' Quonset huts shone dully in the half-light of winter, and concrete-block apartment buildings rose like a child's city of upended wooden bricks. All of these structures were grey, grey as the central European sky. The greyness had been caused by the passions of the previous decade. The city had been burned, and bombed so often that the gigantic pockmarks on its face formed the most common landscape I knew.

I was sent to nursery school with the other American children. It was on the grounds of the American base and ought to have had the cheerfulness of conquest about it. I remember Santa Claus landing by helicopter, for example, and I don't think a German Santa would have been allowed such a spectacular arrival, but that is the only colorful thing I can recall. The classroom was as dark as any other corner of Frankfurt. We sat at heavy brown desks lined up formally with a central aisle down the middle. Here, again, I was caught between the folkways of conquered and conqueror. Language always exposed my true identity, no matter how I tried to disguise myself. I was already decidedly foreign, and had a funny, regionless accent in what was otherwise fluent American English.

Before long our teacher, Miss Mathilde, had discovered that I could speak German, I don't know how. She was a sour local woman, with severe cheekbones and grey hair pulled back in a bun. She spoke to the class in English, but if she had anything to say to me individually, she addressed me in German. I remember thinking this odd because it embarrassed me, but since German was as natural to me as English, I didn't question her. It soon became apparent to me that what Miss Mathilde said in German corresponded neither in tone nor in content to what she said to the other children. In English she was sweet and cajoling, in German, sharp. I was terrified of her. We were perpetually in the middle of some crafts project or painting. I couldn't draw well, or cut or paste with even average skill, and I was often slower and clumsier than the other children. She had ample opportunity to make me aware of my shortcomings, and it seemed to me that she never lost a chance to do so. I don't know if I ever understood that I was being bullied. I could see that her use of German isolated the two of us in a world that the other children could not penetrate.

One day the class was told to make Japanese lanterns out of construction paper. We were supposed to make vertical cuts in the paper, so that when the sheet was curved into a cylinder and a flashlight propped in its center, the light would shine out through the slits. I felt an urgent pressure in my bladder, and I raised my hand to ask Miss Mathilde if I could go to the bathroom.

"Not until you finish your lantern," Miss Mathilde replied in German.

"But I can't wait," I said.

"You must learn to wait, and don't talk back to me in that rude way."

"Please, Miss Mathilde, let me go."

"Obviously your mother doesn't know how to raise little girls," Miss Mathilde said with what I remember as a sneer, "or you would never think of arguing with your teacher. Not another word. Just finish your lantern."

I struggled to get my fingers back into the handles of my blunt-nosed scissors. I stabbed at the purple paper with increasing desperation, swabbed paste on the edges, and tried to get the lantern to stay stuck. It took forever. Finally, there it stood, full of dried patches of glue where I had dabbed hysterically at it, upright but dirty like a child with a day's unwiped snot on its face. I put my hand up again. The act of jerking my arm upward caused a few drops to leak out.

"May I go now?"

"Have you finished?"

"Yes, Miss Mathilde."

"Well, then," said my teacher, "just bring your lantern here first. I want to take a good look at it. Then you may go."

As usual, I had been the last to finish. My classmates had long since handed their work in to Miss Mathilde so they had plenty of leisure to turn and watch me make my way down the long central aisle. As soon as I stood up, pee cascaded down around my ankles. I was transfixed in a spreading yellow puddle in the middle of the floor.

"Shame on you, Rita," Miss Mathilde said to me in German. "You are a disgrace. You will have to help clean up your own mess."

To the rest of the class she said, "Stop laughing, children. Poor Rita just isn't very grown up yet. You should feel sorry for her and be glad you're not like her. I'll call the janitor to mop up. We will move on to a story."

That's how I imagine the scene, at any rate, on the basis of my memory of the puddle and my burning cheeks. I sat with my mother shortly afterward on the steps of our apartment building. The weather must have turned mild, or perhaps we were closer to spring than I thought at the time. I told her that I never wanted to go back to that place. My mother listened, our heads meeting confidentially as we shared an orange. Her beautiful long legs swept sideways under the circle of her skirt.

"Are you sure about this?" she asked, looking at me as seriously as if I were dropping out of college. I threw my arms around her and told her I was sure. I hated Miss Mathilde. The children had laughed at me. I wanted to stay at home with her and Susie.

That was how I dropped out of school at the age of four. I didn't learn until recently, when my mother and I were talking about those days, that there was more to Miss Mathilde. I hadn't invented her persecutions. I was the only Jewish child in the class, and the only one who spoke German. My mother says now that she guessed instantly from Miss Matilde's pursed lips and military manner that my teacher was a former Nazi who could be one again, given half a chance. There was no proof, only a feeling, maybe some whispers among the parents, but nothing substantial. With my last name, I was natural fodder for her sadism, and who would ever find out? If I hadn't told my mother, I could have suffered in that classroom for months. There were real dangers in Frankfurt. People could blow up in your face at any time, like land mines. I wonder how my mother had felt about putting her daughter on the front line like that, however inadvertently. She protected me by letting me cherish the illusion that I was making a free choice, and I protected her by behaving as well as I could, even though I had ended up as a nursery school dropout despite my best efforts.

Underlying all other experiences, memory haunted our years

in Frankfurt. I began to remember events and people rather than fleeting impressions, and it was there that I first became fully aware of our family's history. Perhaps it was that knowledge which greyed the city beyond its own greyness. The sun must have shone sometimes, after all; there must have been trees and flowers in the city somewhere, nearly ten years after the end of the war, but I remember everything outside our house as tinted with no more variety than newsprint. The murky horizon was etched with the skeletons of bombed buildings and buildings going up. At a certain stage of construction, it was hard to tell decay from renewal.

Still, my mother says, my parents were by no means downcast. My father had not been sent to Korea, and the family was together. Life in the American army of occupation was comfortable, and my parents, as always, were popular and made friends easily. I remember the parties in our little living room; people really drank then. The women sometimes bleached their hair. They wore dresses with sparkly circular skirts and had bare shoulders and high heels. Listening from my bedroom, I heard flirtatious squeals and bursts of laughter. Doubtless I had handed around the canapés earlier in the evening, so I had had plenty of opportunities to observe before the adults relaxed into their late-night selves.

But the carefree young Americans who met up in the PX with loaded shopping carts and on Saturday nights at cocktail parties hardly seemed real. They were like children dressed up in the tulle and sequins of a pretend world. There were other, sadder visitors. Otto came often, to our delight, and sometimes we went to Holland or to Belgium to see my mother's old friends there. English was spoken only intermittently. Again there was plenty of laughter, but the laughter had more joy in it and often ended in tears. There were always plenty of tears.

I have a vivid recollection of Lotte Pfeffer, the widow of the man who was renamed Dr Dussel, the dentist, in Anne Frank's

Diary. It seems to me that she visited my parents one night, screamed at them and left crying. But my mother says that Lotte never came to Frankfurt, and that such a scene never took place. Even when Otto Frank visited us, most of the conversations I remember occurred after dark, when we children were in bed. I must have overheard much in the dim hours when dreams came into focus, like an old-fashioned tube television set warming up, and the realities of everyday – curtain, bookcase, wall, coverlet, my little sister's heavy breathing – faded into sleep. At that moment, the inner life, suppressed most of the time even in children, bursts into color. It must have been during this time of openness to the two worlds of sleep and waking that I overheard the grownups, and overhearing, gave bodies to the abstraction of talk.

Yet Lotte Pfeffer remains so real to me that I can't believe that I conjured up her visit entirely. The grownups' voices must have risen in the living room like a wind, for that's how I think of her, as a whirlwind whose tears sprang from her in hot, scattering rage. My mother says that Lotte did visit, not in Frankfurt but in Amsterdam before I was born, and tried to enlist my mother's help in stopping the publication of Anne Frank's Diary. That must have been in 1946 or in 1947, the year the book came out. Lotte was not a Jew, but she had been married to her Jewish dentist, and had suffered greatly for her loyalty. The German racial laws made her an outlaw, someone who had committed the crime of *Rassenschande*, or miscegenation. When Dussell/Pfeffer came to the Secret Annexe to join the Frank family, Lotte had already been whisked into the countryside, where she, too, had to remain in hiding until it was safe to come out. My mother remembers her as having been unfailingly kind during the years before the Final Solution reached the Dutch Jews. She understood what a torment it must have been to Lotte to see Anne's work go out into the world containing a portrait of her dentist as a blundering fool. My mother wanted to see the Diary in print, and so she didn't take up Lotte's cause with Otto. Still, the friends must have felt haunted by the misery that they recognized so well. Lotte disappeared from their lives, but the banshee scream of her guilt and sorrow reached my narrow bed in the dark.

When we returned to Rhode Island in the spring of 1955, in time for my sixth birthday – my father having been rehired to begin his stint as Clinical Director at the hospital – I had grown both more American and more European. My father was now an American citizen. I had been listening to American children's records and to Rosemary Clooney, and I had become a TV-watcher like all the children I knew. Six months later, when we spent a year in Boston, I stopped speaking German around the house. I wanted to fit in, and I thought that this secret language was the oddest thing about me. My parents made no objection, and I thought that I had moved a step closer to being a real American child.

But I had lived among the ruined cities of Europe. I had seen the haunted faces of my parents' friends and family. I had noted the little clouds that troubled my mother's peace, the emotional fragility of certain evenings. I knew that the world was full of Miss Mathildes, people who were not benign and not kind, and sometimes didn't even bother to disguise that fact. And I had heard the story of my grandparents, the story that formed my sisters and me and meant that, no matter what we did, some part of us was rooted always in the tainted soil where their ashes lay. There and back we went, between Europe and America, between the past and the present, between our parents' love and the abyss we knew lay in wait – even after the pendulum of our wanderings had slowed.

Amsterdam:
July 1943, Dawn

THE MOTHER I have known all my lengthening life began her existence not when she was born but when her parents, Walter and Betty Jacobsthal, disappeared. The Nazis then occupying Holland came for them at their Amsterdam apartment during the night of July 23, 1943. My mother, Hilde, wasn't there. She was eighteen and had gone to explore a potential safe haven in the country that some neighbors had found for her. She had never wanted to go. The family had been looking around for hiding-places, and Hilde didn't want to be separated from her parents; but it was riskier to go Underground in a group than on one's own. This time her parents insisted that she investigate the opportunity.

All the same, it was exhilarating to sit on a train without her star in the company of Gentiles and look at the countryside. By then it had been three years since she had left Amsterdam, and a year since she had traveled anywhere by rail. Everything you could put in a sentence with a verb, practically, was against the law for

Jews: travel, exercise, going to a beach or a pool or a park or the zoo, all other kinds of entertainment, most kinds of work, appearing in public without the yellow star, eating or shopping in the wrong places at the wrong time. The laws against moving freely had been designed to increase the anxiety of the Jewish population, which had been subject to constant pressure and violence. The Jews were corralled in the big cities and then picked off. To this day, my mother remembers the couple of hours on the way to the hiding place as a tiny vacation, heightened by the danger of "passing" and by the general sense of flight.

Anyway she didn't like the people, a country doctor and his family, who were supposed to be her protectors. They were haughty and mistrustful. They said that she would be taken on as a servant, as she expected, but told her that she'd sleep in the kitchen, should never speak to the children, and never speak at all unless spoken to. She imagined that they would denounce her as soon as the slightest thing went wrong. She thought them so dangerous that she slipped out of the inn where her neighbors had arranged for her to stay the night (an infraction, ditto), walked to the station, and took the first train back to Amsterdam.

Hilde arrived in the city at five in the morning. When she made her way past the SS guards and their dogs at the Central Station and took the long walk home to South Amsterdam, she found the apartment sealed and her parents gone. She knew that they had been arrested. It had taken nine tries, and this time the SS had succeeded. It was the morning of July 24, 1943, a date well-documented in accounts of the period. The massive operation of the previous night had been the last raid but one on the Jews of Amsterdam.

Chapter 1

Berlin

HILDE HAD LIVED in Amsterdam since the age of four and considered herself Dutch. But she and Jo had been born in Berlin. Their parents, Walter and Betty, were German Jews who had made their way to Holland in 1929, largely for economic reasons and well before the larger migrations after 1933, when Adolf Hitler came to power in Germany and Anne Frank's family arrived in Amsterdam. To Hilde as a child, her Berlin life had been miraculously full of music and play. Betty was one of four Littauer sisters, all of whom were working women and only two of whom married. With the help of a well-to-do uncle based in Berlin who had brought them to live in the city for their schooling, they had been unusually well-educated for the time. They had some training in foreign languages and literatures, and loved music.

These aunts appeared at all the children's birthday parties with presents, treats and songs, and they came along on summer vacations at Travemünde on the Baltic Coast. Though the sisters themselves came from a little village called Polajewo, then in the

German province of Posen, now part of Poland, and were probably considered *Ostjuden* – Polish Jews – by the longer-established Jewish citizens of Berlin, they were German-speaking. (Yiddish was déclassé in those circles before the war.) They thought of themselves as Berliners, with all the attendant snobberies that entailed. They came of age when Berlin was one of the brightest artistic capitals in the world, during the last days of the reign of Wilhelm II and then under the short-lived Weimar Republic. They were full participants in the life of the city and were formed by its modernity. Hilde adored their liveliness and sense of fun and remembers many of her infant adventures in their company.

Her father, Walter Jacobsthal, was as playful as the aunts, only much taller. Betty had met him just before World War I at the ready-to-wear firm where they both worked, she as a secretary and he as a salesman. Betty, like her children after her, learned languages easily. She was an excellent organizer, and had made herself indispensable in the business. Walter traveled abroad six months of the year and didn't come to the office very often when he was in Berlin, so Betty hadn't encountered him before, despite having been at the firm for some time.

Walter was a hard man to miss. He stood six foot six, with a full head of shining black hair swept back from a dramatic forehead. He had an arched nose, a long, dimpled chin, big ears, and a small face. Women liked him for his elegance and his humor. He was high-spirited and fun to be around: my grandmother Betty liked to tell Hilde and Jo about the time he jumped over the back of an unoccupied seat at the opera to sit next to her.

A precocious sense of responsibility had been forced upon him when his father died suddenly at the age of forty-eight. At that time, Walter was sixteen and about to launch on his training as a painter. His talent had already been noticed by Max Liebermann, the pre-eminent German painter of the period, who had remarked upon a picture of Walter's at an exhibition of work by local high school students. Liebermann offered to teach the boy himself. But his father's death ended all that. Walter went to work to support his mother, older sister and younger brother.

The family had been well off at first. Walter's father had owned a textile firm and had lived rather grandly, but the money gave out soon after his death. Walter dissolved the family business and joined the same company where Betty had made herself so useful.

From the sound of it, the young couple bumped into each other at the events they both loved as much by accident as by design. Neither was a stay-at-home in that worldly city. Betty was used to being independent and had her three sisters – Paula, Herta and Jenny – for company, and Walter was often pressed into the role of escort to his formidable mother, Ida. Despite the diabetes that eventually killed her, Ida was an active and dominating woman. When the children arrived, she became *Grosse Oma*, Big Grandma, to distinguish her from the Littauer grandmother, tiny Ottilie. Under her severe skirts, Ida must have had the high waist and long legs of my grandfather, mother and uncle.

Despite Ida's unwavering opinion that a young man of Walter's standing could do a lot better, Walter proposed to Betty soon after they met and was joyfully accepted. By then there were bigger obstacles ahead than the disapproval of a prospective mother-in-law. In August 1914, war had broken out after the assassination in Sarajevo of Archduke Ferdinand of Austria, and Walter was soon drafted. He told Betty that he considered himself engaged to her, but that it would be rash to marry when he might be killed at any moment. She would be free to release herself from her promise to him during their separation, and he hoped she would marry another man if he didn't come back.

Walter remained in Flanders, sometimes in France, sometimes

in Belgium, for the duration of the war, almost five years. The anti-Semitism which German Jews took for granted in those days meant, according to my mother, that he was assigned to an all-Jewish brigade, where "real" Germans wouldn't have to rub up against Jewish soldiers in battle. He was promoted to the rank of lieutenant, an unusual honor for a Jewish soldier, but Betty knew that lieutenants led the charges and were the first killed. Walter was wounded, spent months in field hospitals and convalescent homes, and was returned to the trenches. When a house exploded and collapsed on him during a bombing raid, his left eardrum shattered and he was finally injured enough to be discharged, but by then the war had ended.

Betty, on her own in Berlin, lived in a state of torment. She had never taken life lightly, despite her ready laugh. Underneath, there was a dark anxiety about the rightness of things. She feared that her happiness would be snatched away before she had tasted it, that terrible things would happen, and that Walter's witty letters, complete with his drawings of life in the trenches and hospitals, would one day arrive to tease her when her fiancé already lay dead in the Belgian mud.

She tried to keep her fears at bay by working harder than ever. After she left her job at the office, with its greater demands and longer hours, she took to visiting her future sister-in-law, Walter's older sister Lucie, who had a baby, Marion. As food grew scarcer, the task of motherhood became more and more demanding. Betty traveled across the city to help Lucie, and often went out into the countryside to scrounge and barter for food. The contacts she established then helped her through the war and through the hungry 1920s, when her own small children accompanied her. Many years later, after the next war had brought Marion to Leeds in England, she told Hilde that she owed her survival to Betty.

Betty talked freely to her children about the war years when they were growing up, but she emphasized the public stories of national madness and of general suffering. She hinted at an inner darkness much later, when my mother was an adolescent old enough to understand. Once, in the mid-1930s, there was a mysterious solo trip to Arosa, a mountain resort in Switzerland. My mother speculates that this was a sort of emergency, and that Betty needed the break. Because their business didn't allow both of them to go away at once, Walter arranged the holiday for his wife. Did he want her out of the way because another woman had appeared on the scene? He didn't seem the type, nor did he need to use such a device, since he traveled such a lot. I suspect that depression, the shadow on my grandmother's happiness all her life, almost got her that time. She also suffered from the migraine that she passed on to my mother and to me, and I feel how she was harried by those vulnerabilities. She had her own front during the war, and there she fought without companionship as best she could.

Walter, on the other hand, enjoyed the company of his fellow soldiers, although he was frequently in combat. In a handful of photographs, he clowns with the shortest man in his regiment, who pretends to tower over my seated grandfather. I ask my mother if he ever talked about the war, and if he suffered from shell-shock or nightmares. She says that he didn't talk much about his experiences, nor were there lasting effects, at least any a small child might notice. He did tell the children that books by Erich Maria Remarque, the author of *All Quiet on the Western Front*, were an accurate rendering of trench warfare, and he particularly liked Remarque's *Drei Kameraden (Three Comrades)*. The novel is dark and pessimistic, full of the poverty and broken hopes of the young veterans at its center. Clearly there was much about Walter that his young daughter didn't see. Nonetheless, he had gotten along so well with the Belgian family upon whom he had been quartered that they corresponded for some years after the war. I react with disbelief to this news. Surely she must be romanticizing him, I tell her. He was the enemy, in an army of occupation. But my mother is adamant, insisting that she saw the letters in her girlhood. I try to reconstruct a man charming enough to befriend the people he was invading, and sturdy enough to be a good soldier, one who could survive four years of warfare. Did he ever kill anyone, I wonder? He must have, in four years. "He was at Ypres and Verdun," my mother says, "and I think at the Battle of the Marne too."

I look at the pictures again. Walter stands in a mock-heroic pose, arms folded across his chest, alongside Captain Rosenbaum, his superior officer. The men wear the tight, uncomfortable-looking tunic of the Kaiser's army, and tall tight boots, but they look like civilians all the same. "This is ridiculous," they seem to be thinking. Such thoughts don't make good soldiers; and all soldiers must transform themselves back into good civilians when the war is over. My grandfather seems genuinely to have managed the feat of being valiant in war and peaceable afterward, though his inner wounds must have made him suffer. He came back in 1919 with a medal, the Iron Cross First Class, and with an affection for the Kaiser which persisted long after the defeat. When Walter moved his family to Holland, where Kaiser Wilhelm had lived in exile after the war, he took the children to see the former Emperor's residence at Doorn. It was 1929, and my mother was four years old. She remembers it because they had to stand very still and be respectful.

In the end, Betty's misgivings about Walter were unfounded. He came back a war hero, only slightly damaged by his hearing loss. On August 7, 1919, the newly returned Walter Jacobsthal, *of the Mosaic religion*, married Betty Littauer *of the Mosaic religion* in a ceremony conducted, my mother was always told, by the leading Reform rabbi of Berlin (most likely Leo Baeck). Walter was twenty-nine; Betty was twenty-seven.

Chapter 2

Berlin and Amsterdam

MY MOTHER SAYS that her unusual talent for remembering relies on song. If she thinks hard, a song associated with a certain place or person will come back to her, and once she has the melody, she has the image as well. It has always been a joke in our family. "I know a song about that," she used to say, as we teenagers rolled our eyes. I admit with disbelief that I'm teased now for the same remark.

If her parents were singing in the ten years between 1919, when they married, and 1929, when they left Berlin for Amsterdam, it must have been to keep their spirits up, for that postwar period was full of hardship and turbulence. Revolution broke out immediately after the war, often with open street battles in the cities, especially in Munich, Berlin and such port cities as Kiel. Germany suffered from the reparations exacted as punishment through the Versailles Treaty by the victorious Allies. Food shortages and inflation led to political unrest, and would contribute eventually to the downfall of the short-lived Weimar Republic and the rise of Hitler in 1933.

In the photographs from the period, my grandmother Betty looks plump and tired, and generally older than her chronological age. My mother Hilde, born in 1925, looks too serious for a little girl, but Jo, born in 1921, seems fully at ease. I recognize his smile from those early photographs, but Hilde, with whom I associate a similar broad and ready grin, looks worried, rather like her mother. Perhaps Hilde had picked up some of the anxiety of those difficult years. Or perhaps her reserve had something to do with her older brother, who by all accounts was a handful.

My mother says that Jo was her parents' golden boy, handsome and temperamental. Both children were considered frail, after their precarious arrival during the hungry years of the 1920s. Jo got his own bread ration upon his birth in 1921, and the children were put on fattening diets to supplement the meager provisions meted out briefly by the state. Jo had to drink a pint of cream a day, despite the expense, and my mother remembers the ghastly concoctions they were required to swallow, including a cod liver oil for children which, though flavored with vanilla or orange, didn't fool them for a minute. These supplements were paid for by the garment workers' union, to which both parents belonged, but food was still scarce and expensive.

In the extended family of aunts and parents, there was constant discussion of the children's thinness. My grandmother got special permission from Jo's school for Hilde to join the class for free milk every morning, probably because she had rickets in the first few years of her life. Once or twice during the winter, wearing only their underpants and a pair of sunglasses, the Jacobsthal children had ultraviolet treatments administered by the family doctor, who lived conveniently in the apartment upstairs.

Betty took Hilde along on her expeditions into the countryside, lugging suitcases full of worthless postwar currency to pay for the fruits and vegetables they bought from farmers. The coins alone weighed a lot, being made of rough earthenware.

Hilde, a city toddler, saw her first potatoes, radishes and peas growing in the ground. Later, she "helped" her mother prepare the vegetables on the balcony of their apartment at Helgoländer Ufer 5, on the banks of the river Spree that runs through the center of Berlin. Those moments, she says, were especially sweet. They ate a number of the beans or peas before they ever reached a cooking pot, and chatted, and her mother held her close.

Children were especially valued in those austere days, when everyone was weakened by years of starvation, or near-starvation. There had been miscarriages before Jo, and there were more between the children. Betty counted herself lucky that she became a mother at all: there were many fertility problems after the first war among women lucky enough to marry. Serious health problems became real crises in those days before antibiotics. My mother still remembers seven-year-old Jo's infection after he stepped on a needle, which had to be removed surgically. Jo got what was known as blood poisoning and spent many weeks recovering, keeping his foot elevated and being coaxed to eat.

Still, my mother remembers the children's songs from that period in the context of a very happy early childhood. Her mother and aunts taught her the art of celebration, as my sisters and I learned it from her. On her third birthday, the aunts threw a fancy-dress party whose theme was cats, with an original musical revue. The dining room sliding doors divided the stage from the audience, and everyone had masks and tails. Hilde, the star, was too small to perform reliably, so she was cast as a kitten and allowed to meow at will. Birthdays were always a particular excitement, but there were also Sunday walks, picnics, parlor games and, above all, music: "A little rabbit slept in his burrow. Why can't you hop, bunny, are you sick?" Or the dance from *Hansel and Gretel* – songs that I remember myself, because they were passed on to me. On special days, Hilde was allowed to have hot chocolate from a special demitasse cup, pink on the outside, gilt inside, with lions' feet and a golden tail for a handle. In that household, according to her, special days were not all that rare.

This handful of memories centers on my grandmother and her sisters, the female society of Hilde's first years. My grandfather spent half the year abroad as a garment industry representative, viewing collections and making sales. There was one episode in the late twenties when there was a major train crash near Nuremberg in which scores of people died. Walter was on that train, and as a result of a back injury he was sent to a sanatorium. He came home after two months completely cured, and in excellent spirits. My mother wonders now whether he benefited from the glamorous social life there as much as from the medical treatments. He was away such a lot, with work that kept him constantly in the company of fashionable women. If he was unfaithful, not a word was breathed of it. My mother remembers my grandparents living lovingly together, though they did fight about money, which was always short.

Walter enjoyed the comforts of life: the theatre, wine, travel, good food. He managed his business efficiently and worked hard, but he wasn't practical, and financial restraint was not part of his nature. No matter how skilled a manager Betty tried to be, she always had to work to earn a bit extra. When Walter had the train accident, for example, Betty became secretary to an orthodox rabbi with many children. She took Hilde along to the rabbi's house where she worked, and even as a two-year-old, Hilde hated it there: it was noisy, it smelled, the place was a mess, and the children's mouths were perpetually smeared with jam.

My mother's account of her parents' first years together and of her own early childhood offers only a few insights into their lives, because her exceptional powers of observation have been occluded by survivor's guilt and by the passage of time. She is good at remembering, so good that she has had to protect herself against her own talent. There has always been an aura about her, a subtle remoteness. She has often told me that she *builds a wall* when things get difficult. Her wall allows her to attend memorial services or to speak about her past without disintegrating in public, but she always pays later, in her dreams. Her memories of her time in the war, her girlhood in Amsterdam, and then, further back, of her babyhood in Berlin, are deep and detailed. She can describe the dryness of a piece of cake she ate when she was a toddler, a cousin's characteristic glance, the long corridors –"good for scooters" – of the first apartment she lived in, and probably every song she's ever heard. But she can't remember quarrels, or doubts, or nastiness. What she has recovered has been carefully conserved, gone over in every detail and protected as if wrapped in velvet, like jewels recovered from a shipwreck. The stories from Berlin – of how her parents met, and how she and her brother grew in the early years – are, as in every happy family, the founding myths, the Genesis, from which the household springs. The children already know the outcome, for here they are! Any reversals or sorrows, however real they once were, become comic obstructions on the way to the happy ending.

There is, however, one short period of her life from which my mother remembers no songs. In the summer of 1929, when she was on the young side of four, her parents began the move from Berlin to Amsterdam that they had decided on during the previous winter. Walter thought that he could establish his own women's wear factory in Amsterdam and do better there than in Germany, where economic conditions had never recovered from the punishing hyperinflation after World War I. That year also saw the onset of the global depression of the 1930s. For over fifteen years, he had spent half his working time in Belgium and the Netherlands, and he had long-established contacts in both countries. He knew the buyers for all the big Dutch department stores and for shops in the outlying districts. Setting up his own firm in Amsterdam seemed like a reasonable risk.

It was going to be a busy and confusing period. Walter and Betty thought it would be easier on everyone if the children spent a few weeks in a *Kinderheim*, a sort of summer camp, at Bad Harzburg in the Harz Mountains, about a hundred miles south of Berlin. Hilde was much the youngest child there, and she cried continually, much to the annoyance of her older brother, who was having a good time. When her parents came for a visit, she remembers thinking: "If I cry loudly enough, they will take me with them"; but they didn't, though she ran after their car. When the three weeks were up, the children were taken straight to Amsterdam. They never saw the familiar apartment in Berlin again. It was almost a decade before Hilde consented to spending a single night away from home. But until she told me the story of the *Kinderheim*, she hadn't connected her homesickness with that event.

You are not allowed rage when you survive, whatever it is you survive: abandonment, abuse, death itself. You must adapt your own history to the guilt of being alive. You must always see the other person's point of view, as my mother has done until recently, when the wounds of her early childhood have started to bleed into her old age in ways surprising to us, her daughters. Her parents did the best they could at the time, she says. But now she's sometimes jealous of the attention her husband gets, a little resentful of the love we bestow on our own children and grandchildren, as if she were competing with them for a limited resource. I imagine her at four, her parents letting her cry in the wake of their departing car, her older brother self-sufficient and teasing her, her familiar home gone without even a goodbye, and wonder what the girl who came to Holland was really like. Perhaps she had never got quite enough attention from her parents, who were distracted and busy, despite her memory of them as perfect.

Autumnal Amsterdam, cold, rainy, and grey, must have come

as a surprise. Still, little Hilde adjusted faster than the rest of the family to the noisy street life and the Dutch language. The children of the neighborhood taught her the slang she needed in their raucous games. Jo made a slower adjustment and required nearly a year at a school for children of Germans living in the Netherlands before he joined the Dutch public system.

Until Hilde turned five and could enter the Dutch full-day preschool program, her mother Betty took her along to work at the modest factory Walter had established in the center of town in one of the old buildings lining the Herengracht. There (according to her) she acted as an interpreter when her mother talked to the employees.

Though she was the quickest to adapt of the Jacobsthals, Hilde still felt different from the Dutch people around her. On her first day of school, the teacher asked her to say something in German to the rest of the class. (The same thing happened to me on my first day of school in Brookline, Massachusetts, twenty-five years later.) The teacher no doubt intended to be kind. But as soon as my unwilling mother opened her mouth, the children howled with laughter; she sounded to them as if she were speaking Dutch in a perverse way.

The world has shrunk since then. The Netherlands, after all, shares a border with Germany, and nowadays its multilingual inhabitants live in a cosmopolitan society. But Hilde came to a world of towheaded, apple-cheeked children who had never been further from home than the seaside, or heard a language other than their own. Her dark skin and curls stood out. Her classmates sometimes included a child or two from the Dutch East Indies, and all the darker children were teased by the rest; not necessarily in a malicious way, but because they were conspicuous.

Hilde had another outward badge of difference. Her father designed her clothes for her, or brought them back from other European cities, and they were always stylish. It was his profession, after all, to recognize current fashions. The little girls in her class wore charmless, serviceable clothes. When Hilde was invited to a birthday party, the mother of the birthday girl invariably took her aside to get a good look at the flowing dress she wore. Soon five or six imitations appeared in the neighborhood. "They weren't nearly as nice, of course," my mother says, pride still detectable in her voice. She was the first girl among her playmates to wear trousers, a sort of Marlene Dietrich sailor outfit that delighted my tomboy mother but scandalized the neighbors. Class, invisible to a child but at least as conspicuous as foreignness, distinguished Hilde from her friends in the modest, rather tough neighborhoods where she lived during her first years in Amsterdam. My mother confirms this guess when she describes the children's fathers as postmen, policemen and lower-rank bank employees.

The Sloestraat, where they ended up after several moves, was more middle-class. But religion wasn't a particular source of difference in most Dutch neighborhoods; Dutch society was highly secular. Religious choices were considered as private as sexual ones, and belief in God was never discussed. Nonetheless, Dutch Jews didn't welcome these early immigrants from Germany especially warmly. Their ancestors had lived in the Netherlands for hundreds of years. Many families had arrived as refugees from the Inquisition in Portugal, in the 17th century, or had fled Germany for Holland in the 18th. If Dutch Jews were religious at all, they tended to belong to orthodox congregations. Otherwise, like the German Jews, they were highly assimilated. They sometimes thought that the new immigrants were rich and arrogant, though in reality most German-Jewish arrivals in the Netherlands had very little money, especially after the Nazis hardened their practice of appropriating all their property as the 1930s wore on.

My grandparents encountered some of these barriers when

they tried to join a synagogue in Amsterdam. They were told that
their marriage in a Reform temple, even by a rabbi as
distinguished as Leo Baeck, could not be recognized. Their union
was a fraud, and their children would have to be considered
illegitimate. It was this reception that prompted Walter to help
establish a Reform/Liberal synagogue in Amsterdam, after
emigration from Germany increased from a trickle to a flood. He
was part of a founding group that by 1933 included Otto Frank.

My mother says that there were no toys at home in that first year
– surprising, considering that the Jacobsthals had brought much
of their heavy German furniture with them – so Hilde amused
herself with the buttons and spools she found around the sewing
machines. She enjoyed visiting the caretaker's family, who lived in
the basement apartment of the building. They were called the
Mosterds, the Mustards. Their place was snug and shipshape,
including built-in cupboards made of shiny wood and porthole-
shaped windows with red checked curtains. They had two pigeons
in a cage, and sometimes they let them fly freely about.
    But the Depression had set in, and on top of that the
Jacobsthals were new arrivals. They first rented a damp apartment
on the ground floor of a building on the Noorder Amstellaan in
South Amsterdam – a neighborhood that became, a few years
later, the epicenter of the German-Jewish community in flight
from Hitler. There was no central heating, and my mother
remembers being cold all the time. Her bedroom wall adjoined a
wide gate that led to the gardens and the street behind, and it ran
with moisture in winter. Their furniture dwarfed the small rooms,
and hot water was a rare commodity. The children took their
underwear to bed with them at night so that they could stay under
the covers in the morning as long as possible. The adults
complained of rheumatism, and someone always had sniffles or a
cough.

The Mosterds' overheated apartment, with its coal-fired stove and its constant supply of hot chocolate, seemed a haven to the little girl. It didn't matter to them that Betty had to cut the toes off Hilde's shoes when they got too small, creating sandals, because she couldn't afford a new pair. Hilde wasn't yet in school, where her shoes would have been a social misery. Best of all was the Mosterds' son, Evert, who at ten seemed practically grown up to the little girl. When she learned to ride a two-wheeler at the age of five or six, a badge of independence in bicycle-riding Holland, he took her on a ride through heavy traffic from her house to the factory, much to the horror of her parents. It took some tact to applaud Evert and at the same time to forbid any further adventures.

The children's ups and downs might have been a welcome distraction during this difficult period. Betty, uncharacteristically, dissolved in tears sometimes. In Berlin, they had had a centrally heated apartment directly on the river across from the great public park of the Tiergarten, and could enjoy many little luxuries in the company of family and friends. Here, Betty couldn't even speak to the strangers around her, and they had too little money to buy shoes for the children. But they adapted quickly. They celebrated their first St Nicholas Day, like their Dutch neighbors, in December 1929. There were no real presents, but Hilde managed to buy a toothbrush for Jo, and was proud of her purchase.

The family lived in the damp, ground-floor apartment for nearly two years. In 1931, they moved to the first of two apartments in the Zoomstraat, still in South Amsterdam and still within walking distance of their school; in 1934, when a bigger place became available, they moved across the street and lived there until 1938. This was an area of three-story buildings, and the Jacobsthals by now could afford a second-floor apartment at a higher rent. In the seven years they lived in the Zoomstraat, Hilde became a well-established member of a group of neighborhood children. From the first apartment, she particularly remembers a stone balcony off the dining room that overlooked the street.

"It was nice," she tells me, "because you could stand there and spit on people's heads." She remembers dropping a purse on a string down to the pavement to make people stoop to pick it up, having learned such mischief from the gang of children she played with in the street. In all the pictures from that time, my mother Hilde looks energetic and a little disheveled, with perpetual scabs on her knees. Her brother Jo, four years older, was handsome and indolent, not one for active sports. As far as his sister could tell, he looked down his nose at these doings. The truth was probably that he wasn't included in them, and suffered. Conflicts between them became sharper and longer-lasting.

The continuing battle against the cold dominates Hilde's memories. Once the Jacobsthals could afford to keep a maid again while Betty worked full-time (unusual in that time and place), most of the domestic chores involved starting the stoves in the morning, and providing hot-water bottles for the beds at night. When they moved to the second apartment on the Zoomstraat, Hilde was given a large upstairs room with floor-to-ceiling windows, and a gravel roof outside where the family could sit in the summer. Her father designed the furniture himself in a modern, Bauhaus style – light wood, tubular metal legs, and a built-in sink and sofa. Everything was beige and green, fashionable colors then. When Hilde woke on winter mornings, the water on her nightstand had frequently frozen during the night. The maid brought her oatmeal, to warm her before she left the haven of her bed. In the winter, people sometimes became desperately ill with what they call *angina* in the Low Countries and English speakers know as strep throat, or with bronchitis and infections accompanied by high fever that took weeks to cure. Everyone was afflicted with the minor pestilences, chilblains and backs that bent too early in life, deformed by years of overwork in damp places.

Because Betty worked in the business, my grandparents needed household help, and they garnered their slender resources to get it. Their maids came from Germany or Austria equipped with variable skills. One woman, who was Viennese, made wonderful pastry; another had a short temper with children. Hilde didn't much like being put in their charge, but she accepted that the babysitting was necessary. Later on, Walter bought a car for his business trips. Because his war injury had left him deaf in the left ear, he was not allowed to drive and had to have a chauffeur. One icy night in 1937, on the way home from such a trip, the driver skidded off the road between The Hague and Amsterdam and straight into a canal. The car was not completely immersed and the driver managed to open his window and crawl out. Despite the lateness of the hour, he was able to get help almost immediately from some men passing by, and together they unfolded my long-legged grandfather out of his seat. Walter had hurt his back and possibly bruised a few ribs. He had to spend two or three weeks in bed once he was delivered to his wife, who was by then frantic with anxiety.

But Hilde remembers the convalescence fondly, because family life rotated around her father's bedside and for once he was home during the day. The car and the parental bed were, in any case, the places she associated most with the security of her parents' presence. Walter used his car at weekends, too, and the chauffeur apparently enjoyed taking the Jacobsthals on excursions. Because Hilde got carsick, she was allowed to sit in front, and she drifted off to sleep on the way home from the day's outing with her head cradled on the driver's knee. There were little rituals on the weekend – Saturday lunch bought from the delicatessen; Sunday breakfast, when the whole family lounged on my grandparents' bed, chatting, laughing and reading the papers.

I try to imagine the swings of emotion the family endured in the midst of these delightful routines. The catastrophic losses and consequences of World War I hung over the Jacobsthals, even as they enjoyed their hard-won pleasures. The shadows of the past – such a recent past! – lingered for them in their moments of play. On those Sunday mornings as they curled on his bed, Walter looked at his family with a smile of ineffable content. "Well, here we are again, the four comrades," he said most weeks. "All for one, and one for all. Here's to us, four comrades forever!" And he clinked his coffee cup all around.

Hilde's father was as much fun as ever, despite many years of austerity. With his great height and dimpled smile, he cut a glamorous figure at the seaside resorts they drove off to on summer Sundays. Like both his children, he knew how to play at life, even when he was working long hours. Several pictures show him staging mock fistfights with his little daughter, or lounging, one knee elegantly crossed over the other and a cigarette in its long holder extended from his tapered fingers, at a café among friends. He was younger by nearly a decade than FDR, but he had something of the same style.

Walter was a hard worker, industrious and creative, and his women's wear business, *Damesconfectie Jacobsthal*, grew steadily. But Betty never felt confident about their security in the world, and my grandparents continued to argue about money. Walter liked to come home with extravagant presents for her and the children: a diamond ring, a necklace, a vacation. My mother remembers how my grandmother exclaimed on such occasions: *Aber Walterchen, Du hast wieder so viel Gelt ausgegeben!* ("Walter darling, you've spent so much again!") "Gold and jewelry are good investments," Walter protested; but Betty inevitably took the presents back, to his bitter disappointment.

Not until they made their last move to the Sloestraat, in 1938, did the family achieve a level of prosperity that allowed Betty, now forty-six, to stop working full-time. Their German maids had ceased coming long before, to be replaced at first by local women and then by a weekly cleaning service. Their laundry was sent out, they had central heating, and life started becoming comfortable at last. They had lived in Amsterdam for nine years.

Chapter 3

My Mother Comes of Age

BY THE TIME Hilde turned twelve in February 1937, a coherent process of observation, now tinged with the perspectives of adolescence and young adulthood, replaced the scattered snapshots of her earlier years. Hilde came of age as Nazi Germany reached the zenith of its power. It was as if the inner intensity of her growth were matched by the demonic energy of the threatening world. The emigrants began arriving until they reached flood stage after 1933. As my mother tells her story, I imagine the flood pushing out more and more moments of peaceful private life, until the tidal wave catches up and drowns everyone.

The wave rolled along slowly, though full of horrors, like lava from some relentless volcano. There were seven years between Hitler's rise to power in Germany and the Nazi invasion of Holland; another three years before the full destructive fury of the Occupation was visited upon the Jews then living there. Yet every month brought more indignities, persecutions, restrictions and violence: then two more years before the war ended – twelve years in all.

The first sign of Hitler's ascendancy that my mother can remember came when their maid was summoned back to Germany to vote. All Germans living outside the country had to return for the Reichstag elections of March 1933, after Hindenburg had declared Hitler Chancellor. My mother says that these returnees were pressured into voting for the Nazi Party. She had only just turned eight, but she remembers how frightened the maid was when she returned to Amsterdam and told the family about her experiences. A Nazi network had been built up in Germany in just a few months. Every neighborhood had a block organization and a leader. Residents were threatened, and were afraid to vote against the Party.

The Jacobsthals knew that Hitler had won by the time they saw their maid again. In tears, she told them about the anti-Semitic slogans painted on walls and shouted on the streets. She was intimidated into leaving the family, and soon after her departure, the Nuremberg Laws of 1935 deprived German Jews of the rights of citizenship and of many other things besides. They also made it a crime for Gentiles to work for Jews, but at that point the laws applied, of course, only to Jews still in Germany.

My grandfather's mentor, Max Liebermann, now eighty-six, was one of the first artists attacked by the Nazis. He was President of the Berlin Academy of Art when Hitler came to power on January 30, 1933. By May 7, he had been forced to resign. At the time, he was the most conspicuous Jewish painter in Germany, but not a single protest came from a non-Jewish member of the art world, and when he died two years later, his paintings no longer displayed and his existence forgotten, only three "Aryan" artists attended his funeral. The Gestapo came with a stretcher to deport his bedridden widow in 1943, but she outwitted them by taking an overdose of sleeping pills. Dachau was established within days of that March election of 1933; on April 1 came the first boycott of Jewish businesses and professions, and in May, the first book-burnings.

Jews began to arrive in Amsterdam, first from Germany, later from Austria too. A new community began to develop among the refugees. My grandparents could be helpful, because they were so much better established than the new arrivals. Now it became possible to found a Reform temple like the ones their compatriots had left behind. Among the newcomers in 1933 were Otto Frank and his family. The Franks and the Jacobsthals met, initially, in the project of founding the congregation, which was duly named the *Vereenigte Liberale Synagoge van Amsterdam*: the United Liberal Synagogue of Amsterdam.

The synagogue became a cooperative effort between Dutch Jews who were dissatisfied with the limited religious choices available to them, and the new arrivals from Germany. The van Pelses (the van Daans in Anne's Diary) belonged to the congregation too, but the families weren't more than nodding acquaintances, except for Peter, who was one of the few boys in Hilde's Hebrew class. The class met on Wednesday afternoons almost from the inception of the congregation. Hilde was never an enthusiast, because Wednesdays were half-days at school in Amsterdam, and when all her other friends went off to play, she had to pedal off to yet another lesson. Margot, Anne's older sister, was in the same Hebrew class as Hilde: that was how they got to know each other much better after 1937.

The founding of the temple looms large in my mother's memory. During its brief existence, it formed a natural community. It offered strength of purpose and affirmation of identity at a threatening time. Hilde's friendship with the Frank family was nurtured in the energy of this common project. My grandfather, who for a while was president of the congregation, was an active and beloved figure in those circles. Some of my mother's sweetest memories from the waning days of her childhood focus on those oases of talk and warmth as the Nazis closed in.

Otto Frank came from Frankfurt. He had become a partner in an import-export firm, Travies & Co., which dealt mainly in spices. Otto's specialty was pectin, the naturally occurring food additive that puts the jel in jelly. In the beginning, Otto's own company, Opekta, was separate from Travies & Co., though the firms worked cooperatively and occupied the same building on the Prinsengracht. Most of Otto's colleagues appear in Anne Frank's Diary under pseudonyms: Hermann van Pels, a partner at Travies & Co, became Mr van Daan, a partner in hiding as well. During the war the two firms merged to become Pectacon B.V. The Gentile managers took over with the intention of handing the concern back after the war was over. Henk Gies (Jan in the Diary) became one of its managing directors, along with Johannes Kleimann and Victor Kugler (Mr Koophuis and Mr Kraler in the Diary).

Several times later in the 1930s, when the two families had become better friends, Otto took my mother and her family on a tour of the premises. Opekta was only a block or two away from my grandfather's ladies' wear factory. My mother still remembers how she looked forward to going there, because she enjoyed the overpowering scent of cinnamon and cloves and the company of the exceptionally friendly people in the office: Miep Gies and Ellie (Bep in the Diary); Henk, Miep's husband; and the two co-partners, Kleimann and Kugler.

In the early 1930s, the Jacobsthals and their relatives, like other immigrants from Germany, traveled freely between Berlin and Amsterdam. But after Hitler's accession, visits to Germany stopped. The flow was mostly into Holland, and mostly by people who either planned to stay, or were using the Netherlands as a way station on their flight from Germany.

his prominence as a leader of the new synagogue,
himself at the center of this movement of Jews from
through Holland. First in the Zoomstraat, then in
t, refugees came to stay for a day or a week on their
ewhere else. The early arrivals were Jews and anti-
Nazis had been arrested and eventually released. They were artists, writers, political activists. The first person Hilde saw who had suffered physical violence under the new regime was a family friend whose fingernails had been torn off during his torture at the Oranienburg prison in a Berlin suburb. Even with such terrible evidence, the Jacobsthals found it hard to believe that things could get much worse. They were eager to help those fleeing the persecution in Germany, but they couldn't take seriously any prospect that Germany would eventually overstep its borders.

As the years went on, Walter began to keep a file known as *4711*, after the famous cologne, in honor of the stinking situation in Germany. It got thicker and thicker as the "cases" came pouring in. Strangers were forever sharing Hilde's bedroom. As the numbers increased and the German authorities stepped up their systematic robbery of Jewish immigrants, people arrived in more and more desperate condition, so the Jacobsthals provided them with clothes and food; the synagogue by then had set up clothes banks, and organized supplies and advice for the travelers. My mother remembers putting up children from the transports out of Germany to Britain in the late 1930s, and going to the station to hand out lunches for the trip.

The children's transports increased in number at that time, though the biggest rush, again, was after Kristallnacht, November 9, 1938, when there was a brief shock response from the other countries of the world after years of cynical indifference. Britain, especially, took in ten thousand German Jewish children in the months before war was officially declared. Many of the children went to homes associated with Anna Freud, Sigmund Freud's daughter and psychoanalytic disciple, who had only just arrived in England from Vienna herself after an international outcry over the initial impoundment by the invading Nazis of the Freuds' passports. She did much more work with young survivors of the camps after the war. A number of the transports were organized and sponsored by Quakers. The remaining leaders of the German Jewish community, people like Leo Baeck and Wilfrid Israel, who had open invitations to settle in Britain or America, declined escape in order to escort the children across the Channel.

Still, as late as the summer of 1939, Hilde went to England for a few weeks on an exchange program, as most middle-class European children still do, to learn the language. The Jacobsthals had had an English girl to stay for a couple of weeks at Easter under the auspices of an agency called World Friendship Tours, and Hilde took off in August to stay with a family called the Starks, in Shooters Hill in southeast London, now part of the London Borough of Greenwich.

The Starks had a daughter, Jean, who was fourteen like Hilde. In London that year, they were already preparing for war. Sandbag barriers had been put up around important buildings. Dirigibles floated above the city, and the children were drilled in air-raid readiness and given gas masks. Hilde took the train home filled with a new awareness of the future, a future that might include actual battle. During the trip, she heard the news that Germany had invaded Poland.

As the situation in Germany grew worse, more German-Jewish congregants joined the small Liberal community in Amsterdam, and the circle of acquaintance enlarged and deepened. Hilde became close friends with Margot Frank, Anne's older sister, in 1937, at that turning-point age of twelve. The Frank family lived on the Merwedeplein in the same part of South Amsterdam as the

Jacobsthals. Although Margot went to a different school, the girls cycled to and from the dreaded Wednesday religious class together, talking all the way. Sometimes Anne tagged along, making a nuisance of herself. Margot and Hilde regarded her as an annoying kid sister, always barging in just as they were getting to the most serious part of their conversations. She was a baby, only eight. What could she know of the important issues in life? Anne wasn't regarded as a particularly good student, either. She got into the Jewish Lyceum, a competitive exam school, because the directors gave her the benefit of the doubt (she describes this herself in the opening pages of the Diary). By then – it was 1941, the year before the Franks went into hiding – Jewish teachers wanted to educate as many Jewish students as they could, and they knew her brilliant older sister by reputation; Anne's grades alone would not have qualified her.

Margot Frank must have had a lot of charm. My mother remembers admiring her, and speaks of her in language very like Anne's in the Diary: "I thought she was extremely beautiful," she says. "She had olive skin and shiny black hair and beautiful brown eyes and I always wished that I could look like her." She says too that Margot was much better-behaved than she was; Hilde was the mischievous one. But Hilde apparently had more in common with Margot than she imagined. Both were slender and dark-eyed, and they were often taken for each other. Although Margot went to the Meisjes Lyceum, a classical high school for girls, and Hilde went to the more practically oriented high school for girls, the Meisjes HBS (for by this point in the 1930s, she and her parents had decided that she would do better to learn modern languages and practical skills, if the universities were to close their doors to Jews), the teachers at these two schools rotated duties, and they constantly called the girls by each other's names. Margot and Hilde were the same age almost to the day: Margot's birthday was February 16, and Hilde's, February 18. "Because of that, Otto never forgot my birthday after the war," my mother tells me. The girls' fathers resembled each other a little, too. They were both tall. They were slim, elegant, gentle men who, like their daughters, became closer friends through their work at the synagogue.

There was not much visiting between the families, however, and this, my mother thinks, was largely because of Mrs Frank. Recent revelations about the difficult relationship between Anne and her mother were not entirely surprising to her, given the impression Mrs Frank made on the Jacobsthals. She was reserved and a bit cold in her manner: it was Otto and the girls who were popular. Edith Frank took life seriously. My mother says that she admires the extra determination that such a personality must have required to have endured the rigors of living in hiding.

The dentist Dussel, with whom Anne Frank had to share a room when he arrived at their hiding place in the Prinsengracht, came in for the lion's share of her disgust. "I always felt badly about how he was portrayed in the Diary because he was a sweet man," my mother says (my mother, however, calls many men "sweet"). "I suppose if I had shared a room with him I might not have thought so. At that time he came to our house almost every evening."

Fritz Pfeffer, as Dussel was really called, must have seemed ancient to the girls. He was in his late forties and early fifties during that period, exactly my grandfather's age. They were old friends, having been in the same rowing team in their youth in Berlin. "He was really quite good-looking," my mother says in the special voice she reserves for men she pities. I suspect that voice has nothing to do with Fritz Pfeffer's ultimate fate, but rather with a certain dimness she must have detected in him.

Fritz Pfeffer was a dentist – "Dr Pepper," my mother says, laughing. "I still have a couple of his fillings in my mouth. He was a bit heavy-handed, I have to say." Walter had helped to find him a job as a dental assistant in an office until he could get a Dutch license to practice, in the same way as Russian émigré dentists take such jobs in America while they wait to re-qualify. One of the comic scenes in the Diary involves Pfeffer's dental clumsiness. Anne describes a moment when Dussel examines an hysterical Mrs Van Daan and gets his dental pick caught in one of her teeth. She screams and capers about, as he stands calmly by. Anne could be devastating, and these were the two people who irritated her most in their cramped quarters.

But my mother remembers him fondly. "He came for his after-dinner coffee to our house," she says. "He always rang the bell. When the door opened and he climbed the flight of stairs to our apartment, he always said, '*Hallo! Und – was gibt's Neues?*' 'Hello, well – what's new?' When we heard the bell at a certain time of the evening, everybody in the family said, 'Hello, well – what's new?' We knew that Fritz Pfeffer had arrived." A less predictable moment occurred as well. One night Hilde accompanied him downstairs to see him to the door, and he stroked her face. "Your cheeks are like peaches," he told her. "You're lovely." My mother remembers her discomfort: "I had a strange feeling about it. It was the way he said it. But I liked it, too. It was one of the first times I felt like a woman."

Pfeffer and his non-Jewish companion, Lotte, had had to leave Germany in a hurry when the Nuremberg laws criminalized their relationship: they were guilty of *Rassenschande*, and their household was no longer recognized as legitimate by the German state. Hilde liked Lotte Pfeffer. She had a standing invitation to drop by Lotte's house for tea and cookies after school – a pleasant Dutch ritual of decompression that my mother adapted to our New Jersey suburb when we girls were growing up – because Lotte had a sympathetic way of listening, and was good company. She could be genuinely kind and helpful in an emergency, too.

In her early adolescence, Hilde developed a disconcerting habit of fainting. She told us often about one incident when she was about fourteen. She keeled over in the bicycle garage near her house as she was preparing to cycle to school. One of the men who looked after the facility found her, and Hilde woke up to find herself on a cot by the stove in the custodian's room. The man was chafing her hands anxiously. She can still recall the look of relief on his face when she started to come round.

It was thought that the faint had been caused by the touch of the cold metal handlebars, which had done something to Hilde's circulation. As an adult, she had to be careful to keep her hands warm. I saw her go giddy once on a sunny winter's day in Rhode Island, when she had forgotten her gloves in her eagerness to help us build a snowman. Probably there was a hormonal factor as well, because she fainted sometimes during the first day of her period, when her cramps were severe.

On one such occasion when Hilde was fifteen (it must have been in early spring, just before the German invasion), Lotte sent a cab to pick her up from school, brought her to her own house and pampered her until Betty, at the factory that day, could get home from work. My mother says that she and Lotte became quite close. After the war, she adds, Lotte had hoped at first that Otto might marry her. But, as I knew from early on, her friendship with Otto and my mother ended tragically after Otto published the Diary.

Memories of the Pfeffers seem, for my mother, to be entwined with the first hints of her own growth as a sexual being. When such moments surface from the general public emergency of those years, they are rare, like volcanic islands in a vast sea. In February 1938, for example, Hilde turned thirteen. In March, Austria was annexed by Germany. Then there were eight months between the Austrian invasion and Kristallnacht, on November 9, 1938, which brought German Jews to a new level of horrified understanding. The clear moments between crises must be measured in days sometimes, and dates become important. I find that many of the questions I put to her are framed in terms of particular, sometimes tiny, pieces of time. Was this before, or after? Would there have been time to...? What week, what day, what hour? Can you remember?

Many of the refugees in my grandparents' living room must have been arriving from Austria as well as from Germany. My mother tells me mostly about the people passing through, and what happened to them, but then there is another little volcanic island, a memory from the late summer of 1938. On Queen Wilhelmina's birthday on August 31, 1938, Hilde took part in a parade for children who had decorated their bicycles in honor of the occasion. Hilde had won a prize, and a local photographer had enlarged the picture he had taken of her and put it on display in his window. As she was standing in front of the shop looking at the photo, a young sailor approached her. She pointed at it proudly. "That's my picture!" she told him, and he invited her to go for a walk. They ended up on an isolated path along a canal, where he tried to put his arm around her. Filled with panic, she took to her heels. A nonevent, perhaps, but exactly the kind of thing a woman remembers with lightbulb sharpness when something she hasn't thought about before suddenly becomes clear, almost too clear. For my mother, I think, the personal panic associated with such small enlightenments merged too readily with the public terrors around her.

Her third memory of this type comes from the few spring months during which she was still in school after the Nazi invasion, but before June 1941, when Jewish children were expelled. The girls of the Meisjes HBS had been transferred to their brother school, the Jongens HBS, and put on half session, because the Gestapo had taken over the building in which Hilde, until then, had spent so many happy hours. For a week or two at a time, the boys went in the morning to be followed by the girls in the afternoon, and then the schedule was reversed, with the girls attending in the morning. It didn't take long for the teenagers to realize that they could leave notes for each other in the inkwells of the desks they shared. Hilde communicated for a while with a boy called Ben, who eventually told her his address. She daydreamed romantically about him and cycled by his house, in a neighborhood more modest than her own.

Soon they agreed to meet to ride bikes after school – bicycles in Holland gave children great independence, especially in cities. But Hilde was disappointed. Ben wasn't the boy of her dreams, and decidedly ordinary. Still, they met two or three times, and the last time she told him she was Jewish. The notes and meetings stopped immediately. My mother says that even as late as 1941, Ben's was the first Dutch anti-Semitism she had experienced personally. She still remembers it, despite everything that followed.

Just before the invasion, a group of Zionist teenagers not much older than Hilde arrived from Germany on their way to Palestine. First they planned to set up a practice kibbutz in the Wieringermeer, a dredged and reclaimed part of the former Zuider Zee, where they could farm. Some of them stayed with the Jacobsthals for a few days when they first arrived in Holland. My mother says that she began to realize what it meant for young people to leave their homes without their parents in a situation of such peril. She adds that the German teenagers were arrested later by the Nazis, and none of them survived.

Watching them, and the children on the transports on their way to England, the Jacobsthals began talking with each other about their own future. Recently they had put up Hilde's cousin Marion, the daughter of Walter's older sister whom my grandmother had helped in World War I, when she arrived on one of the children's transports from Berlin. She stayed with the Jacobsthals for a while before she went to England. Her parents, my great-aunt and uncle, were later deported to the East and never heard from again.

Hilde had hoped to study medicine and become a pediatrician, because she loved children. But circumstances had already dictated that she needed to learn as many skills as possible, in order to survive the next few years. Betty taught her as much as she could at home, and encouraged her in the study of languages and whatever was practical. She told her that she had to be able to turn her hand to anything, in case things got worse. Indeed, the refugees who got out of Europe in those years scattered around the world and took up whatever trade they could find. The highly educated Jews of Germany and Austria ended up as handbag-makers, seamstresses, confectioners, factory workers, and artisans of every kind, and often prospered.

Hilde was always a hard and willing worker, and though she was disappointed about not getting the classical education she needed for college, she adapted readily. What she couldn't imagine was being separated from her parents. She remembers going on a walk with them in 1939, when she was fourteen, down to the very words of the conversation. "I hope I'm never separated from you. You two are my rock of Gibraltar," she said to her mother. "I couldn't survive without you."

"Don't worry," her mother said with a smile, pulling her daughter close. "You won't have to. We'll always be together, no matter what." Every bedtime Betty came to kiss Hilde goodnight, and to listen to her recite the Sh'ma, the simple prayer which all Jews know: "Hear, O Israel, the Lord our God, the Lord is One." When the English translation of the complete *Diary of Anne Frank* came out in 1995, my mother was particularly struck by the entry of April 2, 1943, when Anne rejects *her* mother's offer to listen to her prayer because Otto can't come to her bedside. Edith Frank bursts into tears and leaves, and Anne, though she feels sorry, never wavers thereafter in saying that she cannot love her mother. Most of this section didn't appear in the original versions of the Diary.

"I said the Sh'ma either with my father or my mother, but I never went to sleep without it and obviously it was the same in Anne's household. At that time it seemed the absolute protection against evil. It was like a mantra," my mother says. "Anne's feelings about her mother were so strong, and so different from the way I felt about my own mother. That part reinforced my own intuition from that period that Edith Frank was rather a cold person. Even the way she reacted to Anne – she could have been lighter, warmer, more humorous. But then they were in hiding, and who can imagine the stresses they were all under?"

Meanwhile, the Jacobsthals carried on as before, helping the Germans and Austrians who had to be smuggled out of the Reich. Among the most important was Walter's younger brother Hans, who arrived with his wife Lou and his son Charlie in 1938 en route to Chile. Hans is a revelation to me, as I talk with my mother; I had never known of his existence before. He was a bit of a black sheep, a philanderer, and a gambler, too, according to family gossip: Walter got him out of Germany by paying all his debts. My mother and I peer at a snapshot taken just before they got on the boat. We agree that it's hard to tell from the picture what women saw in him. He wasn't at all handsome: short, balding, bespectacled, and no longer young. But perhaps he had some of his glamorous older brother's charm just the same. Charles Jacobsthal died in Chile in 2009, and his numerous descendants are still there.

Hilde's Aunt Jenny, her husband Paul, and their daughter Vera arrived last of all, in the spring of 1940. Their belongings had already been placed on board a ship waiting in the Port of Rotterdam to depart for the United States. But they had lingered too long. The ship was bombed during the German invasion of the Netherlands, and the Cassells had to stay where they were. My grandparents, as always, came through with an apartment and a means of subsistence; they were superb organizers.

Tante Jenny's escape route to the United States had been arranged by her beneficent but as yet unseen cousin Belle. She was the Nashville relative to whom the sisters had once before sent greetings in their eccentric English, on the back of a postcard featuring my infant mother. Working frantically, I surmise, to overcome US immigration quotas, Belle managed to get four of the required affidavits into Germany: three for Jenny's family, and one for a male relative whom my mother, again, mentions for the first time as we go over the details of these months. She has no idea what kin he was to anyone, nor where he came from, though she guesses he may have lived in my grandmother's hometown of Polajewo. At any rate, he arrived in Tennessee shortly before Jenny and her family were due, and promptly became mentally ill. We'll never know his name or the story of his disintegration, because it was never mentioned again, according to my mother. The awful part was that Belle and her husband were responsible for him for the rest of his life. This put a stop to affidavits for unknown relatives, and who can blame them? Jenny, Paul and Vera would have been the last beneficiaries of their cousin's generosity, though indeed Hilde later came to know Belle at last and to experience it herself.

If the nameless man from Polajewo had been stable, perhaps Belle might have tried again. The dates suggest that the affidavits came through late, after much struggle, and that she wouldn't have been able to do much even if she had wanted to. But when that source of immigration dried up, any remaining relatives had to recognize that they were trapped inside the Reich. The Littauer women had always been clearheaded. Shortly after the departure of Paul and Jenny, when it had become obvious that the only frontiers open to them were those to the east, Herta and Paula made a decision.

They were the maiden sisters, the softest and kindest of the four. They were the ones who had preserved the essential gynocracy of the Littauer clan, and had lived peacefully together for many years. They had worked hard all their lives. Had *they* been the ones chosen to arrive in Nashville, they would have made themselves useful and popular. But they had been not been chosen, and there was no way out. One day they closed all the windows and doors of their apartment and turned on the gas. It was a more merciful gas, though they couldn't have known it, than the rat-poison Zyklon-B of Auschwitz or the carbon monoxide of Ravensbrück or Treblinka. They were in their own home, by themselves. They had the dignity of clothes, hair, names. The gas came from the stove on which they had prepared their meals for so many years, not from the industrial human-cooking ovens of the camps. My great-aunt Paula was fifty when she died, and my great-aunt Herta was forty-four.

Chapter 4

Invasion, Amsterdam 1940

ON MAY 4, 1940, A SATURDAY, my grandfather Walter celebrated his fiftieth birthday. The congregation of the synagogue made much of the occasion, since Walter was an important and popular figure there. My mother has a snapshot of him, not on his birthday but on the day the temple was dedicated, sitting on the dais in a line of men dressed in coats and ties. My grandfather is the only one wearing a coat with tails, but he carries it off, sitting relaxed with his long legs crossed. In the German Reform manner, the men don't wear hats, not even the rabbi, though most of the women do. My grandfather looks elegant and serene, and you can tell from the picture why he was probably so well-liked. There's a lack of pretension about him, a warm happiness which is neither excessive nor pompous; good humor, and a certain solidity, too. My mother remembers the pride she felt in her tall, handsome father as they walked home hand in hand through the spring sunshine. The whole community joined them for coffee and cake after the birthday service.

Early the following Friday, May 10, 1940, German troops invaded the Netherlands. Paratroops landed first, in the countryside and on the beaches. Strange rumors flew that the paratroopers were dressed as nuns, to avoid suspicion among the people. I imagine the sky full of nuns, their habits tolling like bells as they swing gently from side to side on their descent: killer nuns, butterflies in reverse, who shed their wings when they hit the ground and emerge in the chrysalis-grey uniform of the German army; nuns like a plague of locusts, darkening the night sky with thousands of darker clouds. I imagine empty fields suddenly thick with nuns taking a midnight stroll, nuns who, when they meet up, have a tendency to form squadrons and goose-step; nuns on the march on every country road, even in the mostly Protestant part of the country.

It is unlikely that there was truth in this panicky belief, though I've seen references to it in other invaded countries at the time, notably France. The rumor probably arose out of the German technique of tricking people into submission. The German air force first flew over the Netherlands during the night before the invasion, leading the Dutch military to think that they were on their way to England. But over the North Sea, the planes turned around and came back with their bombs and flying nuns at the ready, and people woke at 4:15 to the sound of guns. The Dutch air force was wiped out within two days; most of the Dutch navy was not even in port. On May 14, German airplanes firebombed Rotterdam, although the Dutch military had already surrendered; in addition to the 900 dead and wounded, 78,000 people were made homeless by the raid. By then, the royal family had already left for England, to the initial shock and demoralization of the population. An hour after the bombing of Rotterdam, the Germans announced that they planned the same treatment for Utrecht. General Winkelman, commander of the Dutch army, told his soldiers to lay down their arms. Five days after the invasion, the Netherlands capitulated.

Compared to the inhabitants of the rest of Europe, the Dutch were untried. Unlike Belgium, they had been neutral in World War I, and that neutrality had been respected. Their military services had become woefully out of date, and many in the government were pacifists who expected support from the League of Nations if things went wrong. Officials and citizens liked to refer to their country, especially the western part where the big cities were located, as "Fortress Holland," a land whose skilled engineers could organize a defense through the crafty use of flooding. My mother talks about the way people thought, and all the historians confirm what she says: "The Dutch had fought Spain and gained their independence in the sixteenth century. They had fought the French in the seventeenth century in the same way. They had been clever at tricking their enemy. They had used the canals, they had built towers and fortifications quickly and against all odds. They thought of themselves as heroic spirits, and they had a kind of myth that the decent little underdog will always win." As I read the accounts, I am struck repeatedly by that false sense of security, despite all obvious evidence to the contrary: the flat countryside of the Netherlands, so accessible to every soldier and tank; the fate of surrounding nations; the clear intentions and overwhelming preparations of the Nazis. Most poignantly, it had apparently never occurred to Dutch leaders that the Germans might not invade by land or sea, but by air.

Louis de Jong, the great Dutch-Jewish historian, never fails to applaud the many heroic acts of resistance the Dutch engaged in right from the beginning, but acknowledges, sadly, that the Dutch were almost too comfortable during the invasion to understand what was happening to them. What applied to the Dutch at large applied twice as much to the Dutch Jews. "...[F]aced with the Holocaust, which was as murderous as it was relentless," he writes, "the Jews of the Netherlands, having found shelter in a country that was rightly famous for its tolerance, were victims of their own past."

My grandparents labored under no such delusion. They knew perfectly well what was happening in Germany, though no one at the time could imagine Hitler's ultimate plan for the Jews. At the first sound of gunfire that morning, as German soldiers poured into the city, the Jacobsthals and neighbors Jewish and Gentile gathered in a ground-floor flat of their building. They thought they would be safer from bombardment there. "This is the end," they said to each other, and for the first time Hilde saw despair in her parents' faces. Thousands of Jews fled to the blocked and bombed-out port of Ijmuiden, but only a few hundred managed to leave the harbor; most people had to return home again, trapped on the suddenly hostile soil of their homeland. Many refugees from Germany and Austria committed suicide in the panic of those early days. They had already seen the face of evil.

I suspect that even my grandparents really hadn't understood the full story, because they had left Germany long before Hitler had taken over. Their years of relief work had given them more understanding of danger than most Jews in the Netherlands, but not as much as the recent arrivals from the Greater Reich. At that moment, they were caught briefly in a position rather like the one my sisters and I have been in all our lives. Their minds were loaded with facts and images, but they had very little direct experience of persecution.

And then – nothing, for the first few weeks at least. The Germans were visible everywhere, and German-language films replaced Dutch ones in the theaters, but outside of the new flowering of the Dutch Nazi party, the *National Socialistische Beweging* – the NSB – and the installation of *Reichskommissar* Arthur Seyss-Inquart, a veteran of the Austrian *Anschluss* who was responsible directly to Berlin, the first few weeks were quiet.

It is upsetting to learn how readily most government officials accepted the new rules and transferred their loyalty from Queen Wilhelmina to the Führer, and how quickly they obeyed their Nazi masters (in fact, General Winkelman's recent predecessor as commander of the army had become prominent in the Dutch SS). The NSB never had more than fifty thousand members out of a population of nine million, though many of these native thugs were quickly given positions of authority. It turned out that the NSB had been the source of the sudden increase in smuggled Dutch army uniforms across the German border in the weeks before the invasion. Benighted Dutch frontier policemen, still in the grip of the dream of invulnerability, found this odd, until they were fired upon by German soldiers disguised in Dutch uniforms during those early days in May. But what about all the people who simply went along with the new regime, and the informers later on who could get a cash reward for finding Jews and their helpers? There seemed to be hundreds of thousands of those about, a thousand for every brave person who spoke up.

Those who did protest often suffered for their courage. Citizens who took advantage of the long Dutch tradition of freedom of speech were, at first, unversed in subterfuge, and so they stood up at every stage in the early days of the Occupation and let themselves be seen. Some wrote letters or petitions, others spoke in public, or published articles or pamphlets. Sometimes they were horribly punished, and sometimes, puzzlingly, there was no reprisal. Quite a number of senior Dutch officials, union leaders, journalists and a single professor, Dr Cleveringa of Leiden University, protested the invasion in the early years, and all paid with long sentences in concentration camps and, in most cases, death. It was certainly not true, as has sometimes been alleged, that resistance would have been costless.

The Germans moved relatively slowly at first in their repressive measures, not because they had any respect for the autonomy of the Netherlands, and not because their intentions toward the Jews and their newly annexed Dutch vassals were any less brutal than in the rest of Europe, but because the nations of the West and North – Holland, Belgium, Scandinavia – had a reputation for tolerance which caused the Nazis to hesitate, though only slightly. In most areas their citizens were "Aryans" like the Germans, but this spurious racial connection didn't help them for long. Hitler thought of them as a "rubbish of small nations" whose wealth could be exploited without regard for their institutions, which he considered insignificant. Still, the Nazis didn't think that anti-Semitism would be as enthusiastically embraced in the Netherlands as in, say, Poland. Just after the invasion, in fact, the Burgomaster of Amsterdam summoned Jewish dignitaries to the Town Hall to reassure them that the German military command offered no threat to Dutch Jews. The Nazis had already learned in other countries that people were only too willing to be lulled out of their worst fears, and they used this disbelief as part of their arsenal of propaganda. Their true intentions were more accurately expressed in an article from July 19, 1940, published in a Nazi journal and unearthed by the historian Jacob Presser: "We are awaiting orders…then we shall pounce."

When the occupiers saw how docilely the vast majority of the population lay low and looked the other way, they moved ahead. The Germans intended to use the Netherlands as a base for an invasion planned against England. The most common song the jackbooted troops sang as they marched in the streets of the big cities was "*Wir fahren gegen Engeland,*" "We're sailing against England," and by the autumn of 1940, the North Sea coast was sealed, first against German Jews and then against the Dutch themselves. This meant that the RAF bombed the Netherlands incessantly. The Dutch could no longer pretend that the war would happen somewhere else.

*

The summer of 1940 has been described by survivors of the invasion as one long held breath. There was an unreality about the quiet weeks. Every now and then there would be a small change, but nothing that fundamentally altered the conditions of life. The Dutch press ceded control to the Nazis within days of the capitulation; that was an important change, but its effects were not yet obvious. Few soldiers were visible on the streets, the weather was beautiful, and no restrictions had yet been imposed on the Jews. For these reasons, my mother says, a false sense of security developed, and people began to think that the crisis would soon blow over.

The big events happened in other countries. There was talk that the war would end soon, even when all the evidence pointed the other way. The evacuation of Dunkirk had taken place in May, just after the German invasion of the Netherlands; the French capitulated in June; and the Battle of Britain began in August. A few anti-Jewish measures went into effect immediately: the expulsion of Jews from the Dutch Air-Raid Service on July 1, and the prohibition of ritual slaughter on July 31. But these did not affect large portions of the Jewish population, though refugees from the Reich reminded their friends that the abolition of kosher meat had been the first edict the Nazis had imposed in Germany itself. My grandparents must have wondered about the arrest of Simon de la Bella, the Vice-President of the Dutch Federation of Trade Unions, on July 20. He was a Socialist, and he had managed to get the Union funds out to England just before the Germans got to him. But there were plenty of other Socialist leaders in the unions who were not arrested. Could he have been singled out for being a Jew? The Secretary General of the Department of Social Affairs protested, and was removed from office within a few weeks; de la Bella was sent to Dachau, where he died on July 11, 1942.

My mother was fifteen in the summer of 1940, and what she remembers luminously is her membership in the girls' rowing team at her school. She had joined the year before, and although she didn't know it at the time, the spring of 1940 would be her last with the group. Throughout our childhoods, she described perfect days on the water in the company of her friends. She never took up the sport as an adult, because that was hardly possible for women in the 1950s and '60s. The short seasons of 1939 and 1940 still make her sigh when she thinks of them.

The family didn't dare take a summer vacation that year. Hilde was thrilled when one of her rowing teammates, a girl called Jane Hoek, invited her along in late July for a week or two on the Hilversumse Heide, an area of countryside about an hour's drive from Amsterdam. The Hoek family rented rooms in a small farmhouse. The parents slept in one room, the children in another, and they shared the kitchen with the farmer and his family. The Hoeks walked all day on the heath and came home about four to a supper of pea soup or rice in milk, followed by an evening of games. It was a wonderful holiday, in Hilde's opinion.

My mother realizes that she had suppressed this memory, one of the brightest of her childhood. Like others from this time, it has recently re-emerged under the pressure of our conversations. She says that the connection between the families was broken soon after, although it seems to have continued in some form through the summer of 1942. The Hoeks had no interest in politics: the father was a postman, the mother a housewife. "When things got bad, we lost touch," she says. "They must have thought it was dangerous. I'm sure we were the only Jews they knew."

At the end of the summer, and in early September, the Nazi bureaucracy moved relentlessly into motion. The first regulations applied to German Jews living in the Netherlands: they had to leave The Hague and coastal areas, and Jewish refugees from Germany were asked to report to the Aliens Department. The

Dutch Jews reacted, on the whole, with indifference to this news, because the people affected "were not even Dutch." The decree must have applied to my grandparents, who were not yet citizens. They had tried to speed things up, but citizenship was a slow process. Applicants had to live in the Netherlands for ten years. The Jacobsthals arrived in Amsterdam in the autumn of 1929. By the time they met the residence requirement it was the autumn of 1939, when the country was overrun with immigrants from Germany. I imagine that they applied for citizenship as early as they could, and that their applications were whirled along in the flooded gutters of those overworked offices until the German invasion put an end to the confusion. My grandparents were often unlucky in their encounters with history.

The more comprehensive anti-Jewish decrees began to appear in the autumn of 1940. The schools "were instructed not to appoint, elect or promote anyone of Jewish blood, that is, anyone having a Jewish grandfather." In the Netherlands, as in most of Europe, teachers are civil servants, and Dutch officials protested that this edict violated the Dutch constitution, which guaranteed full civil rights to all religions. But when the Germans informed them that race rather than religion defined groups in the population, the officials capitulated immediately and agreed to use the Nuremberg Laws of 1935 as their model.

On October 18, the Aryan Attestation Forms were announced for members of the civil service; Aryans were ordered to fill out form A, non-Aryans, form B. These, too were generally signed without protest, although entire staffs of some schools, including the Amsterdam Lyceum, refused to comply at first. The Dutch-Jewish historian A. J. Herzberg wrote of this measure that "each signed his own death warrant, though few appreciated it at the time." There were some outstanding individual examples of resistance, but not much organized protest. An academic lawyer, Professor Paul Scholten, sent a petition with 1700 signatures to

Seyss-Inquart in which he wrote that "there is no Jewish question in the Netherlands, and that it was a matter of indifference whether a scholar is Jewish or not." Lieutenant-Colonel Pierre Versteegh resigned from the army to avoid signing the Attestation Form; he was later shot as a member of the Resistance. N. H. de Graaf, leader of the Youth Service, resigned as well, and Dr J. Koopman, a young theologian, published a pamphlet in ten thousand copies, urging his countrymen to defend and protect the Jews.

When the next decree, on November 4, 1940, ordered the dismissal of Jewish officials – including university professors – there were student demonstrations and a strike at the University of Delft. These were led by a student leader, Frans van Hasselt, who was arrested in the summer of 1941 and died in Buchenwald in 1942. At Leiden, the professors themselves resisted. When Professor Cleveringa made a public speech against the measure, he was arrested and imprisoned for eight months, and the two universities, Delft and Leiden, were closed down for the duration of the Occupation. Fewer than 1 percent of a total of 200,000 civil servants in the Netherlands, including all schoolteachers, professors, and members of the armed services, were Jewish. One of these was Leo Polak, a professor of philosophy at the University of Groningen, in the northern part of the country. In a letter he sent to the Vice-Chancellor of the university, he announced his refusal to accept his dismissal. The Vice-Chancellor turned the letter over to the Germans. Professor Polak was arrested on February 15, 1941, during the infamous period of early violence against the Jews, and sent to Dachau on December 9, 1941, never to be heard from again.

In tandem with the destruction of "Jewish influence" in the civil service, the occupiers began to attack other sources of survival for Jews. In October, they demanded that all businesses owned entirely or in part by Jews, or having Jewish stockholders,

register with the authorities. In December, they announced that
Jewish employers could not employ non-Jews. In early 1941, they
demanded the registration of all Jews on forms filled out in
quintuple copies, in return for which the registrants received a
yellow identity card. Registration offices were kept open day and
night so that deadlines could be met, and the Germans declared
that they were highly pleased at the efficiency of the Dutch
administration in handling this challenge.

It was a Dutch idea to make the cards very detailed, so that
forgeries would be difficult. They included a black J stamped
twice on different parts of the document. I still have my mother's
photograph for this purpose; sitters were instructed to expose
their left ear, doubtless for the racial identification purposes of
which German eugenicists were so fond. By September 5, 1941,
figures submitted by the Census Office revealed a total of 160,820
registrations. Of these, 140,552 were Jews, who required the black
J on their cards; 14,549 were half-Jews, labeled B I, to indicate
two Jewish grandparents; and 5,719 were considered quarter-
Jews, labeled B II, to indicate one Jewish grandparent. The Nazis
expressed pleasure that there were so few "half-breeds" in the
Netherlands compared with Germany.

In January of 1941, Jews were barred from all cinemas in
Holland. The cinemas were required, at any rate, to show *Jud Süss*
and other German anti-Semitic films. Many non-Jews boycotted
cinemas for a time, but not for long. Dutch city councils
everywhere refused to label businesses as Jewish and to put up
segregationist signs, as the German authorities required that same
month, and in most places the Germans and Dutch Nazis had to
do the work themselves.

The violence began in February 1941. One evening, my
grandfather came home with a swollen face and collapsed just
inside the front door. He had been pulled off a tram and beaten

up by a group of Dutch Nazis and their sympathizers. The family couldn't know that this was just one incident in a calculated campaign of terror organized by H. A. Rauter, the head of the SS in the Netherlands. Gangs had been instructed to engage in just these kinds of random beatings and acts of vandalism, and the Dutch police were told not to intervene. Rauter hoped to provoke Jewish resistance, and he succeeded almost immediately. A Dutch Nazi, Hendrik Koot, was wounded in a street fight in a neighborhood where poor Jews lived, and he died soon after. Rauter himself wrote an article about Koot's death in the Dutch Nazi weekly, *Volk en Vaderland*, and suggested that "a Jew had ripped open the victim's artery with his teeth and sucked his blood out."

This was the pretext for sealing off the ancient and tiny Jewish quarter in the center of Amsterdam on February 12, 1941, to create the first ghetto in the history of the Netherlands. On the same day, the Nazi administration sent for the leaders of the Jewish community and instructed them to form a new entity, a Jewish Council, which would henceforth serve as the official negotiating body between Jews and Nazis. The leaders included the President of the Council of the Great Dutch Synagogue, A. Asscher, whom the Nazis routinely referred to as "merchant Asscher"; the rabbis of the various German-Jewish, Sephardic and Dutch Jewish synagogues in Amsterdam (two of whom refused to serve); and Professor David Cohen, who was not present at the first meeting but became co-president with Asscher. Professor Cohen had been President of the Committee for Jewish Refugees, which had been set up in 1933 but was soon raided and disbanded by the Nazis; and through that work, or through the Liberal Synagogue, he had come to know my grandfather quite well. The men who agreed to serve on that momentous February day probably thought that they could help make the best of an impossible situation, but they soon found themselves fatally compromised in the role they were to play over the next two and a half years. My mother thinks that my grandfather was approached about serving, but he turned down the offer. The Council, when it took its final shape, did not include a single German Jew, although later research by Bob Moore suggests that German Jews were better protected by the Council than was originally thought. No working-class Dutch Jews served, either. The refugees found themselves on the front line of Nazi terrorism once again.

They didn't have long to wait. A second incident occurred in South Amsterdam, the heavily Jewish area in which the Jacobsthals lived, on February 19, the day after Hilde's sixteenth birthday. Two ice-cream parlors (both called Koco) run by German-Jewish partners called Alfred Kohn and Ernst Cahn, had been vandalized several times by roving thugs. A group of customers had tried to help by arranging their own makeshift self-defense. When a German police patrol broke into one of the shops, the customers fought back. Two patrons were shot on the spot, the owners were arrested, and Cahn was tortured but wouldn't tell the Nazis who was responsible for organizing this small act of resistance. He was shot on March 3, 1941 – the first Jewish person to die at the hands of the Germans in the Netherlands.

The Nazis raided the Jewish quarter on Saturday, February 22 – the Sabbath – and again on Sunday, February 23. They rounded up 400 Jewish men, so-called hostages, aged between twenty and thirty-five, in Jonas Daniel Meyer Square, the central point of the Jewish quarter. The Dutch police, to their credit, were appalled, and even managed to smuggle a few men to safety, but they couldn't do much because the Germans filmed the raid. There were tourists around on Sunday, presumably from other parts of the city, who had come to gawk at the newly "picturesque" Jewish ghetto, and they too witnessed the extremely brutal arrests.

The group of Jewish prisoners was sent first to Buchenwald and then to Mauthausen, supposedly to engage in hard labor. Only three young men survived, one of these because he was held back in Buchenwald as a guinea pig for the SS "death doctor" Hans Eisele, rescued by other prisoners, and kept in hiding until 1945. The rest of the Dutch group died within a few months of deportation.

The arrests in Jonas Daniel Meyer Square finally aroused ordinary Dutch citizens to outraged action in a famous general strike on February 25 and 26. The movement began among the dockworkers in the Port of Amsterdam, and (with the exception of support shown in Denmark) it was the only mass protest by non-Jews on behalf of Jews in any country in the whole course of the war. But the Nazis had constituted the Jewish Council for just such emergencies. They cynically pretended that the strike was being instigated and led by Jews, and they informed the Council that if it did not stop the next day, they would arrest 300 Jews. If it went on for a day after that, they would shoot 500 Jews. Frantically, the leaders of the Jewish Council sought out the strikers and conveyed this message, and the strike came to an end. The Germans had learned that the Dutch could be threatened effectively, and the terror increased.

I have strayed a bit from the story of my own family, because it doesn't make sense without the larger story of the Nazi occupation. And there is another thing: while it is still possible, I want to name as many individuals as I can among those who resisted the inevitable march of events. History has swallowed up so many; I'm grateful when Jacob Presser, Louis de Jong, A.J. Herzberg, Walter Maass and Bob Moore, the historians upon whom I have relied so heavily for this general account of the Occupation, recall specific people and the acts which have kept them human and alive. In answer to the terrible idea of "Aryan attestation," the registering of degrees of Jewishness in

October 1940, these moments of daring are an attestation to courage, kindness and individuality, the only antidote to the demagogue's subversion of language and thought.

One of the most destructive legacies of Nazism has been the routine vandalizing of ordinary language, its recategorization of ordinary human experience. Because the Nazis always referred to "the Jews," Jews found themselves scrambling into a single anonymity, becoming "Jewish leaders," "the Jewish Council," "the Jewish community," instead of the lively, quarrelsome, sometimes loving, sometimes nasty collection of loosely affiliated neighbors they had been before, no different from their neighbors who happened not to be Jewish. Suddenly the world was redefined according to the bogus taxonomy of race, and it became a false world, false to its core, with a nightmare language so malignant in its effects that it destroyed the common decencies of speech. That is the language George Orwell understood so well, and which survivors of the camps have had to learn to speak no matter how unspeakable, and it has dirtied us forever. I wonder if the American and other governments would have learned to "pacify" Vietnamese villages by napalming them, or to "fight Communism" in El Salvador by killing Indian villagers, or more recently to torture prisoners by practicing "extraordinary rendition," if Hitler and Stalin had not shown the world how to separate word and deed.

By April 1941, the Germans had insisted that the Jewish Council put out a puppet newspaper, the *Joodse Weekblad* (Jewish Weekly), which replaced all local Jewish papers and served as the official bulletin board for all future edicts and announcements. The existence of such a paper isolated Jews even more from the surrounding population. It continued until the autumn of 1943, when the Council members themselves had been deported and there was no one left to publish it. In that month, April 1941, Jews had to turn in their radio sets. They were forbidden to move from one place to another, were barred from orchestras and the Stock Exchange, were separated at work; during the course of the next few months, the *Joodse Weekblad* informed them that Jewish professionals could no longer work for non-Jews, that Jews could not own farms, and that they were barred from swimming pools, public parks, hotels, and horse races. During the summer the appropriation of Jewish property and businesses began. On June 4, 1941, a raid in response to a Jewish resistance bomb attack resulted in the arrest of the 300 German-Jewish boys from the Wieringermeer, the ones the Jacobsthals had helped when they first arrived. They were sent to Mauthausen, and there were no survivors.

On August 29, 1941, Jewish children were required to attend separate schools from Gentiles. By September 25, 1941, Jews could no longer go to zoos, cafés, or restaurants, or use sleeping or buffet cars on trains, or visit nightclubs, theatres, cinemas (forbidden in January), sports grounds, beaches, art exhibits, concerts, libraries, museums, or auctions. When another hundred young Jews from the eastern town of Enschede were sent to Mauthausen on September 13, 1941, Asscher and Cohen of the Jewish Council protested, and the Nazis promised to "look into the matter," since words were cheap. A Dutch Reformed minister, the Reverend Nanne Zwiep, visited the relevant Nazi commander, General Christiansen, with a protest letter representing all the churches in the area. Christiansen behaved in a way that seemed "extremely kind-hearted" to Zwiep, who must have been surprised when not a single Jew was released and he himself was sent to Dachau six months later. He died before the end of 1942.

During the autumn of 1941, the Nazis continued their assault on German Jews living in the Netherlands. On November 25, German Jews living abroad were deprived of their nationality, and their goods were considered the property of the Reich. The idea was that the revenue from these expropriated possessions would be used "to solve the Jewish problem." On December 5, all German Jews were required to report to the *Zentralstelle fur jüdische Auswanderung*, the Central Office for Jewish Emigration. In January 1942, the first deportations began, first of supposedly unemployed Jews to work camps in the countryside. These men had been made unemployed by the myriad regulations of that autumn, which were aimed toward the eventual dismissal of all Jews from gainful employment. By the late spring of 1941, mass killing in eastern Europe had begun; the Nazi occupiers knew that the Reich was no longer interested in the emigration of Jews, but in their elimination. Reinhard Heydrich and Adolf Eichmann were already using "evacuation" as a euphemism for murder in the summer of 1941, before the Final Solution gave it a name.

Meanwhile, my grandparents and their friends carried on as well as they could. On April 22, 1942, when the regulations came in that forced Jews to turn their businesses wholly over to "Aryans," my grandfather was assigned a German caretaker, or *Treuhänder*, as the term was, named Wilhelm Grimm. Curiously, this name does not appear on the official documents of the time, for reasons that may always remain unclear.

Much has come to light about my grandparents during the German occupation as a result of the work of historians at the NIOD Institute for War, Holocaust and Genocide Studies and at Dutch public television during the preparations for a program about my mother. Their findings, especially those by R.C.C. Pottkamp and Gerard Nijssen, are particularly relevant for the latter part of the war and its aftermath, but Herr Grimm remains a mystery. Grimm purportedly lived in a hotel in Amsterdam during the week, and went back to visit his family in Germany on weekends. Walter became an employee in the firm he had founded and lost, and somehow managed to go to work every day as before. It was because his car had been requisitioned almost immediately after the German invasion that he was on a tram the day the thugs attacked him.

In the autumn of 1940 Hilde returned to the Meisjes HBS, which she had been attending since the age of twelve. She had always loved the beautiful old building on the Euterpestraat and the benevolent atmosphere that prevailed there. She sang in the choir at a performance at a local YMCA on November 30, from which she has kept the program. Boys and girls from neighboring schools teamed up to put on a variety show of considerable ambition. The choir sang a number of selections, including patriotic Dutch songs and folk songs, interspersed with the fourth act of *Adam in Exile*, by the great 17th-century Dutch dramatist Jost van den Vondel; a scene from Molière's *Misanthrope*; and Shakespeare's *All's Well that Ends Well*, Act IV, scene 2. Shortly after this performance, the Germans requisitioned the school. At this point the girls moved to double shifts at the Boys' High School. The girls' school became Gestapo headquarters, the scene of such incalculable suffering that the Euterpestraat, named for the muse of flute-players, became a symbol of horror. After the war, the Dutch renamed the street after a Resistance hero, Gerrit van der Veen, who was carried to his execution on a stretcher after having been paralyzed during a raid on German installations, but insisted on being held upright to face the firing squad.

In the spring of 1941 Hilde was banished from the girls' rowing team. She loved rowing so much that she had already begged her father to buy her a little boat for her birthday that February. Walter could not make such a promise at such a time, and suggested that she try to earn the money herself. Hilde knew that *de Telegraaf*, the leading Dutch newspaper, published stories on its children's page, and paid for them too. To her amazement, the paper accepted her first story and several more. She remembers using her own name without difficulty, perhaps because names didn't appear on the printed page. They were fairy stories, mostly, rather like the ones Anne Frank tried her hand at in the Diary.

With the money, Hilde bought a secondhand canoe. It required quite a bit of fixing up, in which she was helped by her brother and a few friends. The canoe had to be registered with the harbormaster's office so that it could be anchored in the waterways of the city, and by then Jews could neither own nor register a boat; so Hilde's friend Jane Hoek came to the rescue (it seems that Jane was still in touch with Hilde, as late as a year after their vacation together). I have the certificate in a folder of oddments. A *cano* called *Daydream* – an English name – is registered on June 30, 1941, for a harbor tax of 75 guilders. *Auf dem Wasser bin ich glücklich*, my mother wrote some years after the war next to a snapshot in which she wears her characteristic wide grin on an obviously lovely day in her canoe (which seems to be a kayak, in fact) – *On the water I'm happy.*

In September, Jews were forbidden all access to the water, but Hilde managed somehow just the same, because there a group is in the sunshine the year after, now wearing the Jewish star (mandated on May 3, 1942). Young Jo has a girlfriend now, and a guitar. Sometimes he serenades her with mock ardor, sometimes he pretends to hit his sister over the head with it, and everyone has collapsed in giggles. Jo at twenty-one looks astoundingly like his father. My mother has always said that Jo refused to wear the star. In the photo his jacket is elegantly draped over his shoulders, Italian-style, with no star in sight. The young people are casually breaking many German rules, for which they know the penalties. They cannot so easily give up sunshine and laughter, even under threat. In another month, Jo will have disappeared into the Underground. Hilde will not see him for over a year.

*

The family had endless discussions about what to do. My grandparents had volunteered in the Jewish relief organizations in the late 1930s, but they had not asked for help in emigrating to the United States or Britain when that had still been a possibility. Now they were trapped in the Netherlands. At Passover, they modified the traditional ending wish of the Seder: *L'shanah habah b'Yerushalayim* – "next year in Jerusalem," to "next year in New York," but they didn't expect either wish to come true. The question of going into hiding came up but was never seriously considered. Walter's great height made him so conspicuous that he thought he would be a dangerous person for someone to shelter (or so my mother was told; this story doesn't make sense to me in a nation whose men are among the tallest on earth), and neither of my grandparents could bear the idea of confinement.

They made some attempts to look out for a hiding place, and one came up in the spring of 1943 in the industrial area called the IJ, across the Port of Amsterdam – the site of Fokker airplane factories and the shipyards of North Amsterdam – but it was destroyed in an Allied bombing raid. I suspect that there is more to this story than my mother knew; perhaps an empty promise of protection from some quarter. In the end there weren't many choices left. My grandparents' anxiety focused on the children, for whose future there could be some hope, or so it seemed to them then, and the children grew restive. It was depressing to hear every new twist and turn of events discussed so obsessively. After the Germans instituted a dusk-to-dawn curfew for Jews at the end of June 1942, the domestic anxiety had become even more oppressive, and there seemed to be no escape from it.

By the summer of 1941, when the family guessed that it was only a matter of time before Jewish children would be expelled from the schools, Hilde had begun looking into day-care nursing as a possible alternative to her dream of becoming a pediatrician. She had already volunteered at a day-care center in the

Vondelstraat, not far from where she lived, during her last year at the Meisjes HBS in the Euterpestraat. She had told her parents then, with a fifteen-year-old's confidence, that she wanted to be a doctor who also owned an orphanage "where all the little girls could wear shorts and pants." She could be happy if she were working with young children and doing something active. Besides, she was so close to completing the first level of her secondary education that she thought she could manage the exams with a little tutoring at home. When, in fact, the decree came on October 1, 1941 (for Amsterdam) that Jews must attend Jewish schools, several of her Gentile teachers broke Nazi rules by coming to her house to help her study for her finals. This was a characteristic gesture of support for many Jewish students.

In the autumn of 1941, after a rigorous circuit of interviews and tests, Hilde was officially taken into training. She was sixteen, not eighteen, but the current emergency led to some relaxation of the rules; still, few girls as young as Hilde enrolled. In the wake of their expulsion from the public schools, most Jewish students chose instead to go to the newly founded or expanded Jewish schools, as the Frank sisters did. The nursing course had always been tough, but now that both students and professors were segregated by race, classes were taught with new intensity by Jewish doctors and nurses who had been thrown out of the medical schools. The training amounted to about the equivalent of a full nursing degree, though it was compressed into just two years, with an additional concentration on what would be called early childhood education in the United States. The first year consisted mostly of classes, lectures and labs now run by professors of medicine instead of by nursing instructors. The second year was an apprenticeship at a day care center, or crèche.

At first the center had been open to children of all backgrounds. It was in a working-class area, and provided support for working mothers. The children often required medical care as well as education. The young staff checked daily for head lice (not then an affliction of the well-to-do, as it has since become), and for serious diseases, diphtheria and tuberculosis as well as the more innocuous illnesses of childhood. But as Nazi segregationist regulations went into effect, the Gentile children dropped out and only Jewish children remained. The courses and Hilde's practice work with children kept her very busy and out of the house all day, a good thing given life at home.

In the first half of 1942, Jews were subjected to new regulations affecting food and transportation. Jews could buy vegetables, fish and meat only from Jewish shopkeepers, who were themselves denied access to the general wholesale markets. Jews could shop in Jewish and non-Jewish stores only between the hours of three and five in the afternoon, that is, at the end of the day when the best goods had been picked over and rush-hour crowds packed the shops. Jews could not use public transportation; soon enough, Jews had to turn in their bicycles. Not long after Hilde began work at the day care center, which was located on the edge of the Jewish Quarter, she commuted on foot from her home in South Amsterdam, forty-five minutes to an hour each way.

As the Jacobsthals struggled with the endless restrictions and insults that, my mother says, "were just a kind of appetizer for the violence later," they were kept from despair by the kindness of friends, and sometimes of strangers, too. Neighbors offered to shop for food, looked for hiding places for the family and stored valuables for Jews being forced to turn everything they had over to the Nazis. The head of the Kroeze family, for example, was a banker who had helped my grandfather set up his business upon his arrival from Berlin and had also helped him avoid arrest by the Germans on several occasions. The furniture and silver that the Jacobsthals entrusted to this family were kept throughout the war and returned to Jo afterward. The kindness of Gentile friends mattered enormously, of course, and some became as close as family. But the Jews of Amsterdam found themselves increasingly isolated and dependent upon each other for practical support and solace. As long as they could, they frequented the few establishments run by and still open to Jews: the Oasis and Delphi ice cream parlors, which Anne Frank mentions in the first pages of the Diary, and the Delicia restaurant, run by members of the Jacobsthals' congregation. The restaurant was on the Beethovenstraat, in an area of South Amsterdam with musical street-names just around the corner from Hilde's school, now Gestapo headquarters. For the largely German Jews of the Rivierenbuurt quarter of South Amsterdam, where the Jacobsthal and Frank families lived, the Liberal synagogue was another meeting-place. My mother still has her ticket for High Holy Day services in the autumn of 1941. No one could know that they would be the last held in that building, for soon after the Gestapo ejected all congregations from their synagogues. By July 1942, the deportations had begun in earnest, not to end until September 1943, when the Netherlands was considered *Judenrein*, Jew-free.

Despite the increasing terror, Jewish life, incredibly, went on. I find a mimeographed program in the folder of scraps for the Chanukah services of December 6, 1942. By then, I assume, the congregation had been meeting for some time in rented rooms or in people's homes. Nonetheless the service contained one song after another sung by the choir and by soloists. I try to imagine the thinned ranks as they sang of joy and thanksgiving and deliverance from persecution, accompanied by a trio of musicians on flute, cello and piano. The young rabbi, L.J. Mehler, who eventually died at Bergen-Belsen, gave a sermon on *Heldendom*, heroism. I wish my mother could remember what he said. The theme is, in fact, traditional for Chanukah, a liberation holiday which celebrates the rebellion in 165 BCE of the Maccabees against the Hellenized Syrians who then occupied Israel. The circumstances under which this particular sermon was delivered must have been overpowering, like living through the first Chanukah before the Maccabees knew they would be victorious.

Rabbi Mehler was popular among the young people of the congregation. When formal Hebrew school became impossible, he conducted Sunday morning discussion groups for them at his home where they could air their anxieties and concerns. It was at the meetings of this group that my mother and Margot Frank became closer, and it was there, later, that my mother first heard the news that the Franks had apparently emigrated safely to Switzerland. In fact they had gone into hiding in the Secret Annex, but not before a carefully planted rumor about their escape had made the rounds of the Jewish community. People were becoming used to the fact that friends and neighbors suddenly disappeared, mostly into the maw of the German bureaucracy of death, but sometimes into safer routes out of Holland. When Margot didn't turn up on Sunday, July 12, her classmates and the rabbi rejoiced at the thought that she was on her way to her cousins in Basel.

In June of 1941, just about a year before the Franks' disappearance, Miep, their protector during that period, had married Jan Gies. A book called *Anne Frank: Beyond the Diary* contains a picture of Otto and his daughters walking happily to the wedding. Miep herself was glad, my mother says, not only because she was marrying a man she loved, but because she could at last exchange the Austrian nationality she hated for Dutch citizenship. In all my years of intimacy with the Diary and its characters, I had always thought that Miep was Dutch. My mother tells me that she had been sent from Austria as a small child just after World War I by impoverished parents who couldn't afford to keep her. There had been an arrangement that allowed Dutch foster-parents to adopt underprivileged or orphaned children from the defeated countries of Europe.

I reflect on this. Miep herself was a refugee with a painful history. She could have kept out of all this and hidden in the safety of the new identity she so ardently craved. But something in her kept her by the side of these new refugees, her friends and employers, and she became a living example of Rabbi Mehler's *Heldendom*. I met her briefly in 1995, at the launching of the newest American translation of the Diary, and was struck by her forthrightness and modesty.

Open fraternization between Gentiles and Jews ended in 1942, and the Jewish population had begun to shrink. At the time of the Chanukah service of December 1942 a number of congregants would already have been sent to eastern Europe, and the Franks had been off the scene for six months. They had rushed into hiding, Anne explains in the Diary, earlier than planned when Margot received a call-up notice from the Gestapo on July 8, 1942; the first notices had gone out on July 4. She would have been in one of the first groups scheduled for deportation to the East. These first deportations consisted almost entirely of German Jews hand-selected by the Jewish Council on the principle familiar in the unemployment offices of peacetime: last in, first out. (There is some evidence, however, that German-Jewish workers on the Jewish Council may have helped to protect other German Jews to a degree.) These notices didn't speak of deportation, but of forced labor service in Germany. The non-Jewish population received them as well, and Dutch youths were frequently collected off the streets and sent straight to the train station.

In the case of the German Jews, the Nazis focused particularly on girls over fifteen. Hilde received a notice, too, but she was given a deferral because she was a nurse; one didn't question these irrational distinctions. Jacob Presser, one of the important chroniclers of this period, describes the graduation exercises at his Amsterdam Lyceum, at which sixteen-year-olds received their diplomas in the knowledge that they had to report to the Central

Station the next day for transport to Westerbork, the Dutch camp where deportees were held before they were sent on in cattle cars. A seventeen-year-old stood before her parents at the ceremony and asked them what she should do. "Don't go!" people shouted, but some parents did let their children go, fearing worse fates for them if they did not. After all, they had already heard about the hundreds of young men and boys who had died at Mauthausen.

The Gestapo soon abandoned the method of informing transportees by mail, because so many became "divers" (*onderduikers*) and disappeared Underground, or otherwise didn't turn up. Instead, they began conducting raids on neighborhoods late at night. The Nazis used a special word for the raid: *Razzia*, a word that even sounds terrifying. Hilde, who by the late summer of 1942 was working at the day care center, became adept at avoiding a *Razzia* as she walked to and from home during the rare periods when she got off work. Sympathetic passersby would glance at her star and whisper warnings and suggestions for ways around the raid. Sometimes she found herself slipping into doorways or alleys, just to stay clear of the sounds of the arrests. She was never stopped on the street herself, perhaps because of her nurse's uniform, the white dress and shoes, and the white cap on her head. The Germans always respected a uniform, she says. When the canals froze over during the harsh winter of 1941–2, she and her friends skated to and from work in a group, like a flurry of young swans; they were allowed a respite of exercise, speed and fresh air, and they were never questioned. That is one the few bright spots in her memory, like the pond in a Breughel landscape where older children skate while the slaughter of newborns goes on at the edge of the ice.

Hilde's work was physically demanding. The young women worked for two weeks on day duty, from eight in the morning to six at night, followed by a week of night duty; then two days' break at home. They began staying overnight later on, when the deportations started in earnest and they became involved in the rescue work for which the crèche became known. Remarkably, the crèche was still handing out diplomas of certification as late as the spring of 1943, when Hilde received hers. The director was Henriette Pimentel, a woman aged about sixty from a distinguished Sephardic family. The Sephardic Jews were the last to be deported, because the heads of their community had managed to get the Nazis to buy the bizarre argument that they were citizens of Portugal, a neutral country. Nonetheless Miss Pimentel was deported to Auschwitz on September 17, 1943. The crèche remained open for one more month to process the last of the deportees, and then closed for good in October 1943. Her assistant at first, until Jews and non-Jews could no longer work together, was *juffrouw* (Miss) Burghout, a non-Jewish woman in her forties.

The crèche was run by the *Vereniging Zuigelingen-Inrichting en Kinderdagverblijf,* the United Organization for Infant and Child Care. Though its title didn't show it, it was Jewish in origin and had been non-denominational in its intake and outlook. The head of the organization was a controversial figure called Walter Süskind, a member of the Jewish Council. Hilde and her co-workers had mixed feelings about him. He had managed to establish a certain freedom in the way the crèche was run, and this had enormous implications from July 1942 until late summer, 1943. But the young nurses at the Center, and many others throughout his life, came to regard him as a traitor, a fraternizer, even as they used the crèche as a base for Resistance activities.

"I was so involved with working with the children. He leered at young girls in an unpleasant way, and he seemed one of those powerful men who consorted with the enemy," my mother says. In fact, he was a victim of the Nazis, who held his wife and daughter at Westerbork to keep him in line when he became the

Jewish Committee member "in charge" of deportations. His apparently cozy chats with German officers distracted them while rescues took place. In the end, he and his family perished at Auschwitz, Süskind himself possibly at the hands of other inmates, who regarded him as a collaborator.

Because his negotiations with the Nazis saved lives, he has been recently rehabilitated as a hero. From 1982, Maurice and Netty Vanderpol, a Dutch-Jewish refugee couple from the Boston area, began drawing attention to Süskind's achievements. The Vanderpols enlisted Tim and Karen Morse in the making of a film, *Secret Courage: the Walter Süskind Story*, which premiered in 2005 and included interviews with my mother. Hilde was at first surprised by the celebration of Süskind. She hadn't been aware of the role he had played at the time.

"We were young and impatient," she says now. "We didn't understand compromise." The picture of the crèche carried in the *Boston Globe* in 1990 shows my mother's apron and legs in the background; everyone is smiling at a little boy who has fallen asleep on the potty, shorts draped around his ankles. My mother has the same photograph.

The Center was on a street called the Plantage Middenlaan, across from the Joodse Schouwburg, a theater that in the early days of the Occupation was re-classified as exclusively Jewish and then, when performances stopped, as the deportation center for Westerbork. Its address became notorious. All the Jews collected during the *Razzias* were brought to this point on the Plantage Middenlaan, whole families, my mother says, where they waited sometimes for days, sleeping in the theater seats and wandering in the crowded courtyard.

Although they didn't know it, the nursery nurses had free access to the Schouwburg because of Walter Süskind's arrangements behind the scenes. They could come and go as they pleased, taking people in and out as they glided past the guards, sometimes using a passing tram as cover. In their laundry baskets they often carried infants, handed to them by desperate mothers who whispered pleas for their children's safety before turning away to hide their tears. Many mothers couldn't bear to give up their children when the chance was offered, and these children were universally deported.

The young women brought messages and money between the Schouwburg and the world beyond its walls. They even managed to get adults out by taking people firmly by the arm and walking them across the street. Nursing mothers, for example, were allowed to leave the Schouwburg with their infants to stay with them at the crèche, and then the real anguish began: should these mothers relinquish their babies to the staff, or should they take them along to whatever fate awaited them in the knowledge that they were at least together? The guards rarely questioned the nurses' behavior, and the petty clerks of the place assumed that the young women had been given permission for what they did. Strange exceptions and playing favorites were part of the rules, after all.

These activities changed the nature of the work that went on at the crèche. When the terrorism and then the deportations started, the young women found themselves looking after children from the Schouwburg day and night. "Sometimes they lived with us for a week or two," my mother says. "We had children from the tiniest infants up to twelve. And sometimes children were put on our doorstep. Parents had somehow known that they would be deported and wanted their children saved." There was, according to the historian and television director Matthijs Cats, a sharp increase in foundlings during these years, and all were assumed to be Jewish.

One of the foundlings was named Remi van Duinwijck by the staff. His last name came from the place where he had been discovered, a little town near Haarlem; his first, from a popular children's book in Holland at the time, about a little boy who is abandoned and alone in the world. My mother has a picture of him. He was six or seven months old when he was found, and perhaps ten months old when he was deported in the last raid on the day care center in the summer of 1943, after Hilde had left herself. He had a particularly charming way of smiling around the thumb tucked in the corner of his mouth. But there was no chance of saving him, because he became the special pet of Ferdinand aus der Fünten, the SS officer in charge of the Schouwburg, who visited him at least once a day, my mother says, and asked for him every night by name. Such favoritism meant that the SS, for a time, was more tolerant of freedom of movement among the nurses, but it did nothing to save the children. In fact, the officer's affection only made the death sentence more inevitable, and Remi joined the other parentless babies on the boxcars.

By then, during the winter of 1942–3, Hilde lived mostly at the crèche. The work was too urgent and challenging for the usual schedule and, if anything, became more demanding at night, when the SS came through to check that all the children were present. They did a head count but didn't have individual names, and the young women soon found a way to save some of their charges with the help of the newly formed Dutch Underground. When Underground members came to the back door of the crèche, also at night, the young women handed them children to be taken to safety, mostly with Dutch farmers, and stuffed the empty cots with teddy bears and blankets to make it look as though they were still occupied. The Germans raided orphanages and brought the children to the Jewish theater. The young women took care of them for a few days, and then they disappeared. Homes for emotionally and intellectually disabled children – the Children's Home for the Mentally Ill, for example, whose inmates arrived in the early spring of 1943 – were emptied out. None of these children returned.

Hilde never had a moment's doubt about what she was doing. She knew that she had no control over the SS. Every child rescued, every nursing mother escorted out the door was a little victory, however temporary. Even now, when she speaks of those children, her voice grows warm with affection and sorrow. She considers that it was better for them to have had some loving care than to have had none. I look at the half-dozen pictures that she has kept from that time, and I see a beautifully set up and organized crèche, the kind every working parent nowadays would delight in, with lots of staff and toys, modern child-sized wooden furniture, and big windows streaming with sunlight and plants, in the Dutch fashion. The children, with their roly-poly limbs and their wide unblinking eyes, look as if they had just been released from one pair of arms or another. I want to hear about their schooldays, their lovers and their grandchildren, but every one of them died before they reached kindergarten age, every one except for those who were successfully spirited away by the Dutch Resistance and were neither betrayed by spiteful neighbors nor lost in the confusion of war. Five to six thousand children passed through the crèche during the war years, and between five and seven hundred of them were successfully hidden.

By then, the Jacobsthals' natural gaiety had disappeared, but not their steadiness of purpose. Life became a daily obstacle course between close calls and sleepless nights. With Jo gone and their own chance of a hiding place in the IJ vaporized in that direct bombing hit, Walter and Betty centered their efforts on keeping their daughter safe. Just recently, a man in his mid-thirties who rented a room from their downstairs neighbors, the Cohens, had been executed suddenly by the Gestapo. Apparently he had had a secret life in the Resistance. My grandparents must have been heartsick about their son Jo.

Before he died in 2005, my Uncle Jo reminded us that he had been arrested with the family the first time, probably in the spring of 1942, when they were rescued from the Schouwburg by Wilhelm Grimm, the *Treuhänder*. Herr Grimm had not been chosen by their father, but had been assigned to the firm by the Occupation government (confusingly, records from Amsterdam have yielded a different name, someone called J. Tijssen, but these records have proved highly inaccurate in many places, say the historians at NIOD, perhaps because a recording clerk confused two people, or miscopied). He was not a Nazi, and he saved the family on a number of occasions. As Jo and my mother remembered it, he simply went to the Schouwburg and told the guards that Walter Jacobsthal was an essential employee and that Hilde Jacobsthal was a nurse who was needed at the Schouwburg itself. This strategy worked on a number of occasions.

After that attempted arrest Jo decided that it was time to disappear, and he joined the Belgian Underground. He had made contact through a small clothing business where he had been apprenticed. Once the Jewish owner had been forced out, the business was run largely by Tinus and Dirk Bolt, non-Jewish partners there. The Bolts and their associates had a workshop in the Albert Cuypstraat, the site of a market then and now, where they bought up men's secondhand hats and other felt material, and remade them into ladies' hats. These were smuggled across the border into Belgium, where, apparently, they sold very well. The Belgian smuggler was Flemish, and in addition to his dangerous occupation, he was a member of the Belgian Underground. Through him, Jo got into Belgium and became part of the network there.

In Amsterdam the arrests accelerated. In 1942 and early 1943, Hilde had marched her parents out when they arrived at the Schouwburg, in the way she had helped so many others. She took them across the street to the day care center, where *juffrouw* Pimentel gave them a cup of tea in quiet celebration, and they melted into the crowds on the street.

In the spring of 1943 Hilde had the good fortune to come down with diphtheria, often a killer disease. This gave the family six weeks' quarantine. Dr Lopez-Cardozo, their physician of Portuguese-Jewish origin, took cultures from her and used them to create false lab tests for as many of his patients as he dared. Infectious diseases had become an asset in this topsy-turvy world. When I talk with her again about the arrests, she reminds me of the power of her nurse's uniform, which had protected her so often before. Every time the Gestapo knocked on the door and Hilde happened to be there, she put on her uniform before answering. The men tended to be young, sometimes German, sometimes Dutch. They quailed visibly when she hectored them about the quarantine. She told them that diphtheria made no distinction between Jews and Germans, civilians and SS men.

"You really *said* that?" I find myself asking again. "Several times," she adds. "Once I got there when my parents were already on the truck, and I just pulled them off." I imagine Hilde standing there in her uniform in the middle of the night, the white wings of her cap flying off her dark curls, eyes blazing, like Nike, the goddess of victory, or like the goddess Hygieia herself. She was a nurse who carried infection, a diseased person dressed as a giver of health. She was Jewish, a walking source of contagion according to Nazi ideologues, and a young, exotic-looking woman. She overflowed with meaning at those moments, and she gummed up the vicious machinery that was trying to crush her family. I cannot know if these events happened in the way she says they did. Hilde in her mid-teens possessed an almost comic self-confidence. She shared this quality with many survivors, the vast majority of whom were teenagers or young adults during the war. When my sister Dorothy, then a journalist, asked my mother about the Jacobsthals' eight rescues in a first taped interview long ago, the disbelief in her voice was audible: "Nobody else got away with that," my sister says; but my mother insists. Her memory has been remarkably accurate in all our discussions, and no historian has ever disputed it. The more one learns about the war, the more surprising it gets.

"I know I've told you lots of times about the Dutch Nazi who came once, haven't I?" my mother says to me, as if reading my thoughts. I've never heard the story she tells me, and I can't tell if it's a dream she might have had, or reality. One night, she says, the Gestapo knocked at the door, accompanied by a young Dutch Nazi who was not quite as hardened as his companions. My grandfather, astoundingly, invited them to sit down in the living room. And then the young Dutchman announced that he wanted to take Hilde out on a date. He told Walter that Hilde wouldn't have to wear her star. He could take her dancing and maybe for coffee, and he would be sure to bring her safe home. Hilde trembled at this proposal, and Walter, trying to keep his voice steady, told the young man that his daughter was too young to be dating anybody yet, and he couldn't allow it. But perhaps they could work something out. Then he managed to slip some cash into the young man's hand with the suavity he had used in happier times for headwaiters. Somehow the group was mollified, and left.

By then, the Jacobsthals had decided that it was becoming too dangerous for Hilde to remain at home at all. The six weeks' diphtheria quarantine ended in June, and they had run out of means of protection. People were being arrested on the street as well as in *Razzias* at night. It was unsafe for Hilde to return to her work at the crèche, and she went into a sort of informal hiding, spending her days and sometimes her nights at Dr Lopez-Cardozo's, where she helped out in his practice. But she became uncomfortable with him, though he had saved her more than once, after he made a pass at her, and she sought refuge in other people's houses.

One family in particular had become close friends of the Jacobsthals. Jo Scholte was originally from Rotterdam, where his wife Zus ran a tobacco shop. He had taken a job in Amsterdam at the beginning of the war, in the hope that he could eventually move there with his wife and three children, Tini, Kiki and Kees, to escape the constant bombing raids on the port city. He took work first with Mr Cohen, the neighbor whose boarder had been executed. Mr Cohen was Jewish, but his wife was not. Eventually Mr Cohen had to give up his business and leave. His wife stayed in their comfortable apartment; she and their daughter, Marion, survived the war.

Jo Scholte lost his job when Mr Cohen's firm went under. At around the same time (March 1943), Zus's shop in Rotterdam, together with the family's flat above it, took a direct hit in an Allied raid. Kiki, who was seven at the time, remembers the trauma of the bombing, which left them homeless. "The British wanted to bomb the harbor, and they hit the center of town instead," she tells me on the telephone from her home near Bergen, in Holland. Kiki remembers being so frightened that she ran through the streets until Zus tracked her down. The Scholtes took shelter with Zus's sister, a farmer's wife, in the same area where Kiki lives now, while Jo looked for housing in Amsterdam and continued his dangerous commute under the threatening, bomb-filled sky.

My grandparents found the Scholtes an apartment in the Hunzestraat, where they still lived when I met them as a child. The firm devoted an entire working day to the production of linens, curtains, and clothes for the family. How my grandfather could have managed this in a business he no longer owned, or found property when he had no right to rent, I cannot say, but it was done somehow, and everyone agrees on this version. The events of 1942 suggest that Herr Grimm, who bore the same name as the brothers who collected fairy tales, was a kind of fairy godfather himself. He had no desire to rob my grandfather of his rights or his dignity. Perhaps Walter did have some authority left under those unusual circumstances, and used it to help the

Scholtes. He charmed other people to a degree rarely seen, and he was clearly skilled at managing his affairs, even under the Nazis. Research by René Kok, a historian at NIOD, yielded still more evidence of Walter's ability to confound the Nazis, but the paper trail still can't explain exactly how he did it. After his arrest, there was nothing for the Nazis to plunder. No assets remained from his business or from any bank account. This was most unusual. Most probably, Walter had arranged his affairs so that nothing would fall into the hands of the SS.

Under these emergency conditions, the warm response of the Jacobsthals cemented the bond that had already been developing between the two families. The Jacobsthals entrusted some of their goods to the Scholtes, and Hilde sometimes spent her days at the Scholtes' apartment in the early summer of 1943, when it was too dangerous for her to be out on the street or at home. Jo and Zus Scholte were the sort of people who simply didn't consider danger or suffer from moral uncertainty. They had no reason to put themselves into jeopardy over the fate of a Jewish family, but they never spent much time mulling over the rights and wrongs of the situation. They had not formally joined any Underground association (though I'm sure that Jo Scholte was deeply involved, without mentioning the fact to Hilde). Still, they knew how to get in touch with the right people and how to get extra ration books when they were required, and they never hesitated to help a fugitive. Most likely they had helped her brother before her, and now they hid Hilde gladly as the circle closed around her.

The search for a hiding place for her had become more desperate as arrests accelerated during the spring and early summer of 1943. In April, Hilde found Vera Cassel, her cousin, at the Schouwburg. After the Cassels – Hilde's Aunt Jenny, her husband Paul and daughter Vera – found themselves trapped in the Netherlands in 1940, Vera had looked for work. She had recently become a nanny for a family called Luft, and was twenty years old at the time of her arrest. She and her employers were taken together. Hilde tried to march her out of the Schouwburg as she had done with so many others, so that Vera could dive Underground and take a chance at saving herself. Indeed, an escape would have been easy, since Vera had a nurse's uniform like Hilde's, but she refused. For once in her life, she put her foot down and became positively willful. My mother has wondered ever since whether the downtrodden Vera secretly longed to lay down the burden of existence; whether her childhood had been even unhappier than Hilde had guessed. Among her papers, my mother still has the postcard Vera sent her parents from Westerbork. It was scrawled in pencil and either smuggled out of the camp by a softhearted guard, or tossed from the train, as often happened, and been picked up after a few days of lying along the tracks. The length of time between the date of composition, April 26, 1943, and the date of the postmark, May 1, 1943, suggests the latter. Vera disappeared after that, followed shortly by her parents, who were arrested a few months later. On her postcard, Vera writes:

Geliebte Eltern!

Heute werde ich nun wohl weggehen. Ich kann Euch nur ein Ding sagen: ich bin ruhig und gefasst, ich bin jung und kann das Leben meistern. Ihr braucht keine Angst um mich zu haben. Ihr braucht auch nicht zu weinen, denn wo ich auch bin Entfernungen können nicht trennen. Mut halten ausserdem bin ich nicht allein. Nun noch etwas Lufts ihr wisst wohl wer das ist, waren goldig zu mir, ebenso Frau Bannas, wenn Ihr es möglich machen konnt beiden immer zu schreiben u. wenn es geht ersteren Pakete zuschicken wäre ich Euch sehr sehr dankbar. Noch einmal alles alles Gute viele, viele 1000 Küsse fur immer. Grüsst und küsst alle von mir, Eure Vera.

In another hand at the bottom:

Liebe Cassels, Trotz viele Bemühungen ist uns leider nicht... (illegible) Gruss, Margot

This is how the postcard might be translated:

Dear Parents,

Today I am really going away. I can tell you one thing for sure, I am calm and collected, I am young and can handle life. You shouldn't worry about me. You shouldn't cry either, since wherever I am distance cannot separate us. Keep your chin up, besides I am not alone. Now something about the Lufts you know who I mean, they were sweet to me, also Frau Bannas, if you possibly can both write to me always & if it can be done send a few parcels I would be very very grateful to you. Once more all, all the best many many 1000s of kisses forever. Hug and kiss everyone for me, your Vera.

In another hand:

Dear Cassels, Unfortunately despite many efforts we were not... Best, Margot

In July, a couple who had recently moved into the Jacobsthals' building told them that they had found a possible hiding place for Hilde. A doctor's family out in the country, where there were fewer German soldiers, needed a young woman to help with the children. They seemed to be willing to take on someone fleeing Amsterdam, no questions asked. Hilde didn't want to go, and argued with her parents about the impending separation. But they insisted. They reminded her that they had neither the money nor the other resources needed to hide themselves, but that they couldn't bear the idea that she, who was young and flexible, should pass up such an opportunity. So on July 23, 1943, she went uneasily, accompanied by the young couple. The fact that she hardly knew her companions increased her doubts about the situation. "I was reluctant to look at these hiding places," my mother says. "I didn't have a good feeling about this one, either. I always asked my parents, couldn't we all hide together somewhere?" In the full expectation that this possibility would not amount to anything, my mother remembers telling her parents that she would be back the next day to tell them about the trip. That was the last time she ever saw them.

After her harsh encounter with the doctor's family who were supposed to hide her, Hilde made her clandestine return to Amsterdam early on the morning of July 24 to find her parents gone. In shock and despair she made her way to the Scholtes' apartment on the Hunzestraat, less than a mile from her parents' home in the same general area of South Amsterdam. It was still early, but Zus answered the door right away. "As soon as she saw me, she started to cry," my mother says, telling the story in dialogue, as if she remembers every word. "She said, 'Did you go to your parents' house?' When Hilde said yes, Zus told her that "last night was the biggest raid of all. Everybody seems to have been picked up. There are practically no Jews left in the city." Hilde cried too. "This time I wasn't home," she said. "Every other time I was able to help them and get them out, and this time I wasn't home. I must go after them."

But Zus reminded her that the Germans no longer brought prisoners to the Schouwburg; they were shipping them directly to Westerbork. When Hilde continued to protest, the Scholtes locked the door of the apartment to keep her from leaving. My grandparents had asked them long before to look after Hilde if they should be arrested, and Jo and Zus knew that Hilde, on her own, would walk straight into the arms of the SS. Zus sympathized deeply with Hilde's desperation, but insisted that her parents would not have wanted her to follow them.

The Scholtes' apartment had no hiding places in its four rooms. The two girls, Tini and Kiki, had folding beds in a bedroom too small to contain any other furniture; Kees, the five-year-old boy, slept on the sofa in the living room. Guests were offered a folding bed in the dining room, which was about eight foot square. There was no space to spare, no privacy, and not much food, either. For the time being, Hilde would have to share the Scholtes' limited rations. The heating and fuel no longer functioned. The Scholtes had learned to bake makeshift bread on top of the small wood-burning stove they had installed in the living room. Then there was the danger of sheltering her at all. Private conversations had to be carefully arranged in the tiny, many-windowed apartment. Despite these obstacles, the Scholtes infused the few weeks Hilde spent there with a warmth that has lasted into the next generation. They did their best to comfort her, and even managed to make her laugh once or twice; and she found the strength to keep going. Jo and Zus remained the closest thing she had to parents until they died too young, Jo in the 1950s and Zus in the 1960s. My mother speaks often of her gratitude and their courage. "They could have been found out at any time," she says, "and they would have been sent to prison or to a concentration camp, or shot. They knew the risks, but they took me in without hesitation."

The children were too small to be entrusted with the truth about Hilde's identity. The Scholtes decided that the safest way would be to turn her into a country niece who had come for a while to help Zus with the housework. This ruse would explain why she never went out, and the children could mention her, the

Scholtes hoped, without arousing suspicion among their ever-curious neighbors. Hilde's face was not entirely new in the street, since she had often visited often before, but it was not an "Aryan" face. Making her a blood relative seemed the best idea. Kiki remembers the moment vividly. "It had to be just ordinary that she was living with us…it didn't have to be kept secret." She recalls that the children addressed Hilde, who was all of eighteen at the time, as Auntie Ina.

In addition to the great risk the Scholtes took in hiding Hilde, they had to contend, at first, with her tears and pleading. She was wild with grief and guilt that she had been away when the Gestapo came, and she was convinced that she could save her parents as she had saved them before. She says that she found a way (mysteriously, to me) to sneak out of the Scholtes' apartment the next day and return home in the hope of rescuing a few items. This venture, too, was risky, because the Germans generally sent around a moving van, courtesy of a Dutch firm called Puls, to confiscate all the loot the arrested families had left behind. Hilde went the back way, by persuading her sympathetic next-door neighbors to let her in and using the communal balcony to gain access to her parents' apartment. She grabbed everything she could carry inconspicuously on the street: a couple of albums and framed photographs and some documents. "I don't know why I didn't take my father's sketchbooks," she says, "but I had to rush. It was so dangerous." These items were left with the Scholtes. Along with a few bits of silver and jewelry, the painted glasses Hilde had helped her father select for her mother, and a Rosenthal vase that had been entrusted to the Scholtes earlier, they were scrupulously preserved until they were returned to Hilde after the war.

A couple of days after the arrest, a postcard arrived from her mother. It had been tossed from a deportation train, or perhaps mailed by a sympathetic guard, in the same way that Vera's card had been two months before. It was addressed to the Scholtes and contained a simple message: "Please tell H. that we are on our way and that whatever she does, she must not try to join us." Hilde saw that her parents knew more than they were saying, and took these last words seriously. She stopped trying to resist the Scholtes' advice to stay put until a safe haven could be found for her.

By early August, Jo Scholte had managed to make contact with the other Jo, Hilde's brother, and had told him the news about the arrest. It was arranged that my Uncle Jo would sneak Hilde into Belgium. She and Jo Scholte set out by train for Maastricht, a town that has since become famous as the site of the founding of the European Union. It lies in an appendix-like southern loop of the border where the River Maas, or Meuse to French speakers, separates the Netherlands from Belgium. Once more Hilde traveled without her star, and Jo Scholte risked being sent to a camp or shot for accompanying her. He was determined not to leave Hilde until he was sure that she had been delivered into the care of her brother.

As if that were not enough danger, the train was buzzed by British bombers. Jo and Hilde dove out of their carriage into a ditch, thinking that they might be hit. But they got to Maastricht safely and met up with Jo Jacobsthal in a hotel lobby, as had been previously agreed. Jo Scholte took the train back to Amsterdam, leaving the two Jacobsthals to make their escape. It was August 4, 1943, the day before my uncle's twenty-second birthday.

After a few hours of careful wandering around Maastricht, Hilde and her brother strolled down to a deserted stretch of riverbank, where they were to meet the smuggler's rowboat at midnight. Jo's outfit had done this sort of thing many times before when they helped Allied airmen out of Holland. But Jo wasn't exactly sure of the spot. He didn't deal with the actual smuggling end – more often he guided people toward France and Spain with his organization, Dutch-Paris – but he knew that this stretch of the river was somewhat less populated by the SS guards and dogs who normally patrolled its banks. Jo always had an abysmal sense of direction. He got lost in places where he lived for decades, and he was hopeless when the terrain grew unfamiliar. I was skeptical when my mother told me that he had helped people out through such long and complicated routes. I didn't see how he could have reached the Pyrenees, since I knew that he couldn't find his way from one end of his own town to the other.

This navigational flaw probably explains why midnight came and went and no boat appeared, though Jo had himself been delivered to the appointed spot earlier the same day, when he had crossed from Belgium to meet his sister. "We walked several miles in one direction and then in the other, but no boat showed up," my mother says. It was amazing luck that the SS with their bloodhounds and searchlights hadn't appeared yet, either, but surely it was only a matter of time until they did. Jo made a decision: they would have to swim across.

So they hid the little suitcase she had brought and bundled their clothes into her raincoat. Fortunately she had a bathing suit with her – it was summer, after all, "and Dutch people always pack one in the summer, just in case," she says. Jo stripped down to his underpants, and they set off. The Maas varies in width and depth at Maastricht, with strong currents. Hilde intended to swim across on her back, carrying the bundle of clothes as high above the water as she could. Things went smoothly at first, but then, about halfway over, Jo developed a cramp in his foot. For a while Hilde had to haul him with her right hand while struggling to keep her clothes dry with her left. She managed to keep her brother afloat and not drop her bundle until the cramp passed. They soon realized that the current, which they had had to battle midstream, was helping them now; they could let it carry them to the Belgian side.

And then, miraculously, they were in Belgium, frightened and tired, but for the moment safe. They had not been spotted, despite all their splashing. They rested a little in the long grass on the riverbank and let the warm summer breeze dry them off; then they changed into the clothes Hilde had somehow kept out of the water. Hilde discovered later that her light-colored raincoat had a large footprint on the back where she had stepped on it in the dark, but fortunately she didn't have to wear it those first fine summer nights.

They walked until they came to a farmhouse where a light was still on. It was three in the morning, but Jo insisted on asking for directions. The farmer told them what village they were in and how to get where they were headed. They were in Limburg, where the inhabitants spoke Flemish, and neither the farmer nor his wife seemed much daunted at sheltering two bedraggled strangers in the middle of the night. The farmer's wife gave them beds for a few hours and breakfast when they awoke, and refused to take any money. Hilde and Jo heard later that she told the whole village that a couple of English paratroopers, one dressed as a woman, had come to her door. That was Jo's trademark way of doing things: a mixture of daring and derring-do, real heroism and flamboyant bungling made him conspicuous and popular, not always in convenient order.

The village to which they asked directions was called Lanaken, and it turned out to be only five kilometers, or about three miles, from where they were. The boat, which had indeed turned up at the correct meeting-point, would have brought them directly to the spot. Once he had been put on the right path, however, Jo made no more errors. My mother's spirits soared at the unaccustomed freedom, despite her sadness and the danger. "It was a beautiful morning and we set out very early. The sun was shining and the birds were singing. We walked on and on," she says in the little girl's voice she assumes when her story seems like a fairy tale even to her, so many decades after the events she recounts.

It turned out that the people who had taken them in had called ahead. Jo's contacts in Lanaken (by 2013 a town of about 24,000), had already heard the rumor that English parachutists had landed and were on their way to the farm there: houses in the country were on party lines, and the tale had probably been passed on by the telephone operator. Jo's colleagues were furious that he had created such an obvious breach in security. He should never have mentioned names or addresses; he shouldn't have asked any questions at all.

Hilde was told to rest in the orchard while the people at the farm discussed their plans. She recalls the moment vividly: "In the orchard there were trees with ripe plums. I was told to pick as many as I wanted. I hadn't had fresh fruit in a while. All these little things become significant. They're the things that you don't forget – the smells of the orchard, and the plums, lying there."

I wonder whether that moment, the culmination of nearly two weeks of intense emotion and physical strain, became the foundation of a new personality in my mother. That personality may be the one I have known all my life, but perhaps she had been subtly different until then. She allowed herself the animal joy of being alive on a fine summer day when death had been snapping at her heels. She had not had a chance to give in to her grief at her parents' arrest, nor to examine her fears about their unknown fate. She didn't let herself feel or think. She was alive, she was eating a plum under a hot blue sky, and for the moment she was safe.

Chapter 5

In the Ardennes, 1943

BEFORE HILDE HAD time to devour many plums, she was on her way again. My Uncle Jo's carelessness about announcing the location of the safe house made it safe no longer. The idyll in the orchard ripened in intensity as my mother remembered it over the years, partly because it was so short, only a few hours. It set the tone for her stay in Belgium, a period of about eighteen months filled with adventure, danger and strong personalities. But when my mother tells of her life there, the summer mood dominates. There is a lushness, an abundance about her descriptions that reminds me of a Flemish still life, or of Beethoven's Pastoral Symphony. My mother must have felt a bit like an animal released into the wild, after all the years of strain and confinement, and such a burst of physical freedom in the warm countryside colored her perceptions from that moment.

Belgium was hardly a haven. It had been occupied in the same month as the Netherlands. Its legitimate government had fled to England, although King Leopold and the royal family remained in Belgium until they were arrested by the occupiers in the early summer of 1944. They were imprisoned in Austria during the few remaining months of the war and eventually liberated by American troops. Other nations, and many Belgians, regarded the behavior of the Belgian royal family with suspicion. After all, Belgium had a collaborationist government, and a group of Belgian Nazis served with German soldiers on the Eastern Front. Still, Belgium was in some sense uncontrollable, and that was what made life there possible for my mother and her brother.

A Resistance movement sprang up in Belgium as soon as Germany invaded. Its infrastructure and techniques had been developed in World War I and were easily revived. The linguistic divide between French and Flemish could be used to create confusion, and there was greater ethnic diversity than in Holland as well. The French-speaking Walloons of southern Belgium were often dark, and foreigners could be hidden more easily among them than among the mostly blond Dutch. The Belgians tended to pay less attention to such distinctions in general than did the Dutch. There were natural connections to the French Underground, so close at hand, and linguistically identical. It is amazing to me, for example, that my Uncle Jo, thinly disguised as Jerry Staal, an English-speaking Dutchman, really did nothing more to protect his identity as he escorted fallen Allied flyers across Belgium to the French border. His confidence saved him, but not his looks, which were thoroughly Semitic. Yet even the Gestapo when they arrested him never took him for a Jew. He was a bit of a flimflam man, and a good actor.

My mother says that the Belgians, who had been invaded once before, were much cleverer at resistance than the Dutch. She and others have told me about the Underground workers in the post office, for example, who opened official notices from the German occupiers and warned Jews and Resistance members of impending deportations; and about medical workers who faked X-rays in order to save children in orphanages and patients in hospitals. The forging of false documents for all kinds of purposes was a specialty. In all this, both the Dutch Reformed Church of the Flemish-speaking provinces and the Roman Catholic Church of the French-speaking areas did their share. Despite many arrests, executions and deportations, the Belgian Jews fared rather better than the Dutch Jews, who had one of the lowest survival rates, as a population, of any in Europe: about 34,000 out of 140,000.

Jo participated in the Resistance as a member of Dutch-Paris, as this branch of the Underground was known. Participants spent most of their time helping fallen Allied airmen to safety on a route that often began in Holland and ended in Portugal, where they could catch a boat to England. Jews and political refugees were helped in the same way, although their numbers were smaller and their passage more perilous than that of the airmen.

Jo, like Hilde and other Dutch Resistance workers, was particularly valued for his linguistic abilities. He could communicate with the mostly English-speaking airmen, as well as with everyone en route to Spain. Resistance workers generally knew few people beyond those in their immediate group, to make detection by the Nazis harder if they were arrested. They were arrested all too often. Sometimes someone was taken who knew a great deal about the general network, and if that person collapsed under torture, terrible consequences followed.

A book called *Flee the Captor,* by Herbert Ford, focuses mainly on one of Dutch-Paris's leaders, John Henry Weidner, a French Seventh-Day Adventist. It is short on specific details, but gives an idea of the work of the group and the dangers involved in it. My uncle knew Weidner quite well as a colleague. Many of the group's members were deeply religious. My mother thinks, in fact, that her first job in Belgium was wangled through connections between Dutch-Paris and the Dutch Reformed Church.

The transformation of my mother's identity from Jew to non-Jew still required urgent measures from the outside in, although it's the inner transformation I wonder about. When she left the plum orchard that afternoon in August, she was still eighteen-year-old Hilde Jacobsthal. She and her brother caught the long-distance *tram vicinel* to Brussels, where Jo brought her to a hideout that appeared to be, and indeed was, a boardinghouse. Boardinghouses made ideal hiding places in a metropolis, because the young people staying there looked like students or young workers, and a high turnover among residents didn't arouse suspicion in the neighborhood. So Hilde stayed a week with a woman who could do her bit against the Occupation and make some money too. Food had to be brought in by fellow residents, all young Dutch men fleeing forced labor under the Germans. They already had their false papers, and could move about freely. By the end of the week, my mother had become Hilde Staal, a Dutch nurse who didn't want to be forced to work in Germany. She had aged six years in that time, and had bleached her dark curls. She was officially a member of the Dutch Reformed Church. Her passport said that she was twenty-four, leading people to think that she had some experience of the world. She had to hide her actual innocence and let others make their assumptions. She remembers how she was called "*eelDAH,*" with a French accent.

Contacts in the Dutch Reformed church sent her to a children's home in the Ardennes, in a village called Lustin. Lustin proper is on a hill on a bend of the Meuse about halfway between the towns of Dinant, to the south, and Namur, to the north; Lustin-Gare, as its name suggests, contained the local railway station. The establishment had a somewhat English-sounding name, *Home pour enfants débiles.* It was a simple summer camp for poor children from Liège who were thought to be physically frail. The Germans had plundered the Belgian countryside for food after the invasion, and there had been widespread hunger, as in Holland, until the farmers found their own way of resisting the theft of their crops by harvesting a little on the sly and burning the rest. As always, the young, the old, and the poor had suffered most from the effects of the German pillage, and the Dutch Reformed Church of the area was doing what it could.

Hilde took the train out to Lustin-Gare by herself, and then had a long, hot walk up the hill where the children's home was located. The director, a Dutch woman thought to be trustworthy, was expecting her. Hilde, with her training, had been told to expect work as a *moniteur* or counselor, but was informed upon arrival that all those positions were filled. She was welcome to help out in the kitchen, if she wished.

It was lovely countryside, with hot cornfields all around, but the work was hard. Hilde shared an attic room with five other women, and a bed with the cook, who was a peasant woman of about seventy who spoke a *patois* difficult for my mother, with her good but correct high school French, to understand. There was no running water, and the women used a wooden bucket as a chamber pot. They woke at five every morning, when Hilde sat outside and peeled large quantities of potatoes and other vegetables for the lunchtime soup. One of her daily tasks was to clean the outhouses – containing old-style toilets, where you stand up over a hole – which she did from a distance with a hose, because, she says, you didn't go up close if you could avoid it. In the morning, before the children had their porridge, the community gathered for a prayer meeting and hymns, which Hilde thoroughly enjoyed because of the singing. There was grace before every meal, and prayers before bed for the staff as well. The work was so exhausting that she could hardly keep her eyes open by then.

Despite the endless household chores, the atmosphere was cheerful. With the exception of Hilde's bedfellow, the staff was young and friendly, and Hilde loved the children, who were aged mostly between eight and fourteen. Once in a while, if there wasn't too much work, the staff could join the children on hikes and in the singing, and there was, of course, decent food and fresh air – that was the point of the place. Hilde, who had been malnourished in Holland for a long time and had just left childhood herself, rejoiced in the food. Remembering those days, she mentions the oatmeal particularly, which was served with *sirop d'or*, golden syrup. The children retreated to their dormitories for an afternoon siesta, and then emerged at about four for a *goûter*, a meal consisting of milk and bread with jam or honey. That was a free period, when children and staff mingled briefly.

There was a piano in the day room and one afternoon, Hilde heard a familiar tune. It was the *Hatikvah*, the song that became the national anthem of Israel, and a pretty little girl called Miriam was picking it out on the keyboard. Hilde went over to her and said, "I know that tune." Miriam looked at her. "Are you Jewish too?" she asked. She told Hilde that her parents had put her in the home in the hope that she would be safe in case they were deported. She didn't know what to expect at the end of the summer. Hilde looked out for Miriam during the scant month she spent at the home, and warned her never to play such a tune again; the wrong person might recognize it next time.

The warning turned out to be more necessary than Hilde had thought. All was going smoothly until her brother paid a surprise visit, accompanied by a friend, about two weeks after her arrival. He announced that he was a messenger for the Dutch Reformed minister who had put in a good word for Hilde at the home, and had come to check on his sister. Because Jo was so hard to miss, the director noticed him just as everyone else did, and her suspicions were aroused. She began to question Hilde about this visitor. Who was he? Why wouldn't Hilde admit that he was connected to the Underground? She denied any knowledge of such a thing. Jerry had a job in Brussels, that was all. He had come to see her because they were family. But Hilde was the only foreigner at the Hôme, and the director didn't buy her protestations.

Hilde didn't fully understand the reasons for the director's aggressive questions, although they worried her. It wasn't until she talked to some of the farmers during her chores that she learned more. One of Hilde's tasks was to pull a wooden cart around the surrounding farms to collect milk for the children. This involved a five a.m. start, and after a while, as Hilde's French improved, she got to chatting with the farmers. They were under constant pressure from the German occupiers to turn over their grain, and, again, they often burned their fields rather than comply. There were terrible reprisals, and it was hardly surprising that, almost universally, they were members of the Resistance. They asked her often who she was and where she was from, since her French was still imperfect, but she avoided replying too specifically until she knew which farmers she could trust. Then she told them the false truth – that is, that she was a Dutch nurse fleeing the Germans, and they reacted with astonishment.

"You're hiding in that place? Don't you know that the director's husband works with the Gestapo in Brussels?" Hilde admitted that the woman had been asking her some tough questions, and that she was worried. The farmer who had warned her promised to look around right away for a better place. "You'd better try to get away as soon as you can," he told her. "You're not safe at all."

The next night, the director called Hilde into her room again. She was a tough-looking woman in her forties, stocky but not fat, with reddish-blond hair in a pageboy. Her husband was a relatively low-ranking officer in the Gestapo, perhaps a captain. My mother thinks that the director spotted Jo as a Jew, and then saw through Hilde's disguise as well. As the wife of a Nazi officer, she knew that the Germans weren't really rounding up nurses in

Holland, and she must have detected a Jewish bend in Hilde's prominent nose.

This time the director made no attempt to mince words. "I want you to tell me about your brother's activities," she said. "I know that he's in the Underground. And if you don't tell me now, my husband is coming from Brussels in two days. He works for the Gestapo. And he will find ways to make you talk." My mother has told us this part of the story often, and it has made us laugh every time. The woman sounds like a character from a bad comedy. Could she really have said that? There are many elements of the Belgian story that even my mother finds comic, almost as if the entire country were merely the stage set for an operetta. But this was a frightening and dramatic moment. Hilde was by now an experienced escape artist, and she made up her mind to run away.

She decided to confide in a young woman of her own (real) age, who came from Liège. Hilde planned her escape for the next night and they agreed that the young woman from Liège would deny knowing anything about Hilde's departure. On her morning rounds after her questioning by the director, Hilde told the farmer what had happened. He had talked with a Monsieur Dupuis, the regional head of the Underground, who had said that he would take Hilde in. The farmer instructed Hilde to come to his farm that night, if she could. With the help of the young woman from Liège, Hilde waited until the others were asleep – this was not difficult, because everyone slept very deeply there – and left through a window. Fortunately the roofs of the building were angled so that she could scramble from one to another, and so to the ground. It was September 3, 1943. Hilde had been in Belgium just under a month. This time her only possessions were the clothes she was wearing as she walked through the night to the farmer's back door.

In the morning, the farmer took Hilde to Lustin-Rivière (now known simply as Rivière), not more than a couple of miles away. This was a village located directly on the Maas, called the Meuse in this part of its watershed. They had to cross the river on a small ferry. Near the ferry landing, my mother noticed a beautiful vegetable garden, an orchard and flowers in abundance. These belonged to Monsieur Dupuis, who met them at the gate. He told Hilde that his dangerous work in the Underground had made it difficult to keep household help. He had a wife, Madame Dupuis, and two daughters who were fourteen and sixteen years old. If Hilde became their housekeeper, she could be helpful in the movement as well, because she knew several languages. Hilde gratefully agreed, thanked the farmer who had helped her, and followed M. Dupuis into her new refuge.

I phone my mother about a few details. I can feel the narrative tugging at me with its insistent undertow. By now my mother, the heroine of this story, has entered the mainstream of her life's adventure, as if she had waded again into the Maas. That river, with its changes of name and its swift currents, carried her along in those days as she changed identities and languages. This is the part of the story that everyone has always wanted to hear. In my childhood, I could guarantee myself an audience of slack-jawed listeners just by telling the tale. I let the plot carry my telling along, just as the currents of the river carried my mother.

But I resist the forward pull of narration for a moment, because the Dupuis's garden is as good a place to rest as any, and because I can't help noticing that my mother herself loves the gardens of Belgium, and the buzzing countryside rich in flowers. It was typical for her to notice the good days, and to let the warmth of summer, as I have said before, overspread the memory of the two bleak winters she spent in Belgium. But she remembers one beautiful day later in that same month of September 1943 in particular, because it was the first moment when she could allow herself to acknowledge the truth. "What has happened to me?" she thought. "I'm completely alone in the world."

It wasn't only that she was alone and in constant danger, though that's part of what makes her story so compelling. She had become a different person once again. M. Dupuis arranged shortly after her arrival for new identity papers for her. She was still a twenty-four-year-old Dutch nurse with bleached blond hair, but now her name had become Colette van den Bergh, and she was a Catholic. That change of religion explains the completeness of her disappearance from under the suspicious nose of the Nazi captain's wife. She had moved only two miles away, after all, and technically she hadn't left the village. But she was hidden in plain sight among the French-speaking Catholic majority, in a good family, at that, and no member of the Dutch Reformed community could penetrate those layers of privilege and tradition. So my mother was secure amid the candles and incense and the worship of saints, and to this day she has an ecumenical knowledge of both religions. During my childhood she could recite the Lord's Prayer in French (Catholic version), knew the saints' days, and could sing a number of Protestant hymns.

Hilde had passed through three metamorphoses in six weeks. She had become a fugitive; she had changed her name and her religion twice. Even her language had been taken from her. She couldn't speak Dutch in that environment, and she was just developing some fluency in French. It was another piece of luck that she and her brother picked up languages almost effortlessly. They both spoke good English, from their time in the exchange program. Before long Hilde was taken for Belgian, although French was her fourth language. That is not what I mean by her change of identity, either. All these quick changes required rapid adaptation, and they made her feel her loneliness, no doubt; but despite their profound effects they were changes from outside. I wonder if, inside, she still felt herself to be Hilde Jacobsthal, a young Jewish girl in search of her lost parents.

I think not. I think that the moment in the orchard and the subsequent events that developed from it changed Hilde. The woman who gave birth to my sisters and me was different from the woman who would have emerged from a relatively normal upbringing in Holland. I don't mean just because of the obvious changes that all of us know are serendipity as much as choice: whom we marry, where we go. I mean that my mother's habit of *building a wall*, which she learned during her days in the Jewish day-care center and perfected in her flight from Amsterdam, became a dominant feature of her personality. It sits oddly with her wide grin and her capacity for joy – these show up, even in darkest times, in her memory for songs, sunshine, play and food – but it has affected, especially, her relations with other people. She seems tolerant of people and indulgent of their faults, up to a point, but sometimes I think it's because she is simply disengaged, even from her children, even from her husband, in some part of her being deeper than love. She is loving, none of her children would doubt that, but under her love is a place that cannot be reached.

We think that people recover from sudden blows because they live to tell about them afterward, and because the telling is first a kind of emollient and then a kind of scar tissue, a plastic surgery smoothed over the suffering place. But that metaphor contains a truth about the often-told tale of past pain; it's another disguise, a counterfeit identity. It's as if even I, my mother's daughter, can't get past Colette van den Bergh any more. Hilde Jacobsthal is buried too deep for me. Perhaps she has been dead all these years. Perhaps she died of shock when she saw the Nazi seal on her parents' door.

My mother has always hated the way her history has dominated our lives. She didn't want to be pitied, or to be the source of bad feelings in other people. Perhaps there is a subtle something else in that reluctance. This is the story that, all her life, has defined her, has defined *us*. Now I can draw a liberating power from the telling which I never had when it was told by her. Then it seemed like a crushing burden. Now its terrible weight is helping me, helping *us,* move on, like a car or locomotive gathering steam.

I have never known what to do with this history. It makes a better tale than anything that has happened in my own life, and it has to some extent paralyzed me. My mother may have become more dependent on that state of affairs than I have realized. Her history has what Joseph Conrad called *glamour,* a hypnotic magic that has transfixed succeeding generations, as well as her own. Now it could seem to her that her story is being expropriated, taken from her, its evil enchantment finally confronted and dissipated after several lifetimes of bondage. She cannot bring herself to recognize, either, that any skill or art of mine is involved in the retelling. She prefers to think of me as transparent, like a glass jug that contains her story and distributes it to the world. I cannot expect her to feel unconditional joy at the prospect of this narrative. For both of us, it is a matter of identity, impressed into our deepest selves. Perhaps all children demand of parents exactly the responses parents are incapable of giving. Like the brood of sparrows outside my skylight window, we all stick our greedy mouths in a parent's face, no matter how old we grow. My mother never had the chance to be angry or greedy with her parents; perhaps that's why there is that remoteness at her core.

And so I return to the Dupuis's garden, where my young mother has been waiting in freeze-frame for me to release her into her new existence. There are few places as pleasant or as interesting to take shelter in, despite the risks. Once more, my mother's memories begin with food, after the hunger of the last year in

Holland. Even at the children's home, the food was limited in quantity, and filling rather than wholesome.

One measure of the Dupuis's generosity was the readiness with which they invited Hilde to their table. They had just had their midday meal when she arrived, but they were expecting her and had saved a portion even before they had looked her over to decide whether or not they would risk hiding her. Hilde didn't know that there was any uncertainty at the time. She had simply assumed that this was her next safe house.

The meal was Belgian hare, the national dish in those parts, which my mother has always prosaically referred to as rabbit, gloriously cooked in cream and wine with applesauce and vegetables on the side. I know, because that dish became the ritual meal of welcome whenever we visited the family after the war. It was borne triumphantly to the table amid a flurry of laughter and reminiscences: "*Tu te souviens, 'Eeldah, ton premier repas chez nous?*" ("Remember your first meal with us, Hilde?")

In 1967, when I was eighteen myself, I visited the Dupuis with my parents and sisters. They lived in Ghent then. They were a French-speaking family in the middle of a hostile Flemish city. I don't know quite how they ended up in that isolated spot; they seemed fish out of water. The ritual meal was sinfully delicious, beyond anything I had ever experienced, and it was just the beginning of a period of polite overeating that nearly killed us. There must have been a pint of cream in every dish. There were many courses, and it was impossible not to eat; these dear friends would have been mortally offended.

The Dupuis told Hilde later that their hearts went out to her as soon as they saw her that first day in their garden on the Meuse. They let the farmer know that she could stay, and invited her to join them at the table. Once she had phoned the special number in Brussels that she had been given if she needed to contact her brother, known to the Dupuis, as to everyone in the Underground, as Jerry Staal, she was considered trustworthy and was accepted into the household.

M. Dupuis was an important figure in the neighborhood. He owned the cement factory that was the main source of income in the village, and his wife was higher-class than he, from gentry stock, or minor Belgian nobility. "But practically everybody you met in Belgium seemed to be minor nobility," I say. My mother admits that they seemed to be thick on the ground in the Ardennes, though most were poor.

The Dupuis family, however, was prosperous, and M. Dupuis had taken on additional status as head of the local Underground. He was a small man, stocky from all that Belgian cooking. His wife worked hard in the house, despite their affluence. Running a mansion on three floors where three sophisticated meals a day were turned out required all female hands, and Mme Dupuis worked alongside the servants, as ruthlessly enslaved by routine as they. When she went out, a car and driver waited for her, even if it was just to have her hair done. It was a 19th-century life in many ways. My father has always said that the Dupuis household reminded him of something out of Stendhal. The furniture was dark and heavy and portraits of Napoleon hung everywhere. The golden bee, an emblem of the house of Bonaparte, was even enameled on the Regency demitasse cups.

The Dupuis had married for love. When my mother arrived Mme Dupuis was not yet forty. She was pretty, with prematurely white hair and an unlined face. She was quite seriously overweight, which can surprise no one who has spent any time in that household. The two daughters, Tity and Alice, were educated at home, because the Dupuis were afraid of what might happen to them at the local school in the presence of boys. The atmosphere was swollen with sexual and general bodily anxieties that went unexpressed, on the whole, muffled in the swaddling of routine.

Hilde was taken into the confidence of all members of the family. After all, they thought, she was a nurse who had seen the world. She soothed, advised, and recommended remedies for every twinge. To Tity and Alice, she was like a big sister. When she brought them up their breakfast in bed in the mornings – *brioches* freshly made in the kitchen downstairs, and hot chocolate – they would talk with her about anything that entered their minds. My mother's gratitude to the Dupuis knows no bounds. They were courageous and kind in every possible way. But Alice and Tity have told us that she contributed something new to the household herself. Hilde's arrival was a breath of fresh air in a claustrophobic provincial life.

The Dupuis were well off, and well-respected because they didn't take their privileges for granted. It was because of Mme Dupuis' status as the daughter of landed gentry that the family could continue to live comfortably during the brutality of the German occupation. Her relatives had a number of tenant farmers who, in this emergency, paid the rent in kind rather than in cash, and the grain, meat, goats and pigs of their payments frequently appeared in the Dupuis's kitchen. The Dupuis kept their own chickens and grew all their own vegetables and fruit. It was harvest season when Hilde arrived. In the warm weather, she made apple butter in a copper kettle outdoors, saw animals being slaughtered for the first time in her life, and helped in the sausage-making. She was a city girl, and these mysteries were new to her.

As the Dupuis's housekeeper, Hilde worked as hard as she had in the children's home. There were important differences, however: the women of the family labored alongside her in conditions of complete equality. Her description of the work there is a piece of social anthropology from a vanished world. Once a month, Mondays were devoted to laundry. The women started work at 4 a.m. by getting the vats boiling in the cellar. Doing the laundry involved the hard labor of boiling, stirring, bluing, starching, drying, and carrying clothes, tablecloths, sheets and towels from the basement to dry outside, or up to the attics in inclement weather. Every Tuesday was devoted to ironing, Wednesday to mending; but these chores were fitted in around the constant cleaning of the house, and the cooking. On Saturdays *on faisait le samedi.* The stairs, attics and cellars of the three-storey mansion were cleaned on hands and knees from top to bottom. The household had a vacuum cleaner, but most tasks were done by hand. Dusting took forever. Generally there was no free time.

During a regular week, Hilde got up at 5:30. All the shoes of the family were lined up on the basement steps. First she lit the wood stove in the kitchen and then she shined the shoes. On Fridays, the Dupuis baked. There was a full bake oven in the cellar, and the family made enough loaves and pies for the week as well as rolls for the women's lunch that day. As a treat, they were allowed an egg, which they could prepare any way they liked.

Hilde became an excellent cook, learning how to bake and to prepare the midday soup and other dishes. The recipe for one soup, a French *marmite* of chicken, beef, vegetables and herbs, was passed on to me and has become one of my sons' favorite meals. While she was stirring the big pots, making dinner or preserving whatever was in season, Hilde heard all the family superstitions and prohibitions, which revolved mostly around the fatal power of women. Menstruating women were told to stay away from the bread, for example, because the dough wouldn't rise if they touched it. If for one reason or another they came in contact with it, they had to make the sign of the cross on the loaf before it went into the oven.

Other social aspects of life in this self-sufficient little universe were even more interesting. Hilde went to Mass every Sunday and said her rosary with the other women. One day, when Mme Dupuis had lost a diamond ring peeling potatoes and everyone had turned the household upside down searching for it, she invited Hilde to come along to a monastery in Namur. There she consulted Père le Perce, a clairvoyant priest who had helped her on other occasions. A guest a few years before had lost a gold mechanical pencil during a visit to the Dupuis. It was winter when they had gone to Père le Perce. He told them to wait until the snow had melted, and then to look through the leaves on the tennis court, where they had indeed found the missing object. This time, Hilde watched the priest holding a little gold cross on a chain. He asked Mme Dupuis to say prayers he suggested and to concentrate on the ring as hard as she could; then he closed his eyes and furrowed his brow. He told her go look among the potatoes stored in the cellar. As payment, Mme Dupuis made a donation to the church. Then she and Hilde went home, and, sure enough, the ring was among the potatoes, as he had said.

Mme Dupuis confided in Hilde as much as her daughters did, thinking, like everyone else, that Hilde was far more mature and experienced than she actually was. M. Dupuis, Hilde was told, could be lordly in more ways than one. He considered all the young women who worked around the establishment fair game, and his attempts at seducing them had caused much heartache. My mother tells me that I am not to put that down, nor any of the subsequent story; she doesn't want anything to tarnish the memory of her benefactors. I feel a twinge of betrayal in writing her secret, but somehow I doubt that the Dupuis would really mind. Their frailties cannot diminish their heroism or their kindness. They just seem human instead of superhuman, and anyway, such disclosures are hardly shocking. They are the stuff of the tragicomic maneuvers between the sexes in such closed societies, all the more eccentric because of the war raging outside.

Hilde appreciated Mme Dupuis's frankness after M. Dupuis turned up at the door of her little attic room. He had taken it upon himself to wake her in the mornings, ostensibly to spare her the use of an alarm clock. He had even installed a cold-water sink for her, so that she wouldn't have to climb downstairs to use the common bathroom. That was an unprecedented step, the rest of the household told her, a token of his respect for her. This respect, tinged respectfully with lust, characterized his treatment of her. He gave Hilde her own water supply partly out of self-interest, and partly because he really admired and trusted her. She was his partner in the work they did for the Underground, which went on unabated during this period. He was used to a feudal setup in which servant girls were uneducated and could be intimidated, even flattered, by the attentions of the head of the household. Hilde was middle-class, and had led what he thought was a sexually adventurous life.

They argued, she sleepily from her bed, he standing in the doorway asking if he couldn't warm up a bit under the covers, until at last she used the ultimate weapon and threatened to tell Madame. She never worried that he might betray her out of resentment. He was an honorable man who never went beyond verbal persuasion. He simply didn't believe that a woman of her age and experience, as he thought, could be a virgin, or might object to his attentions. Monsieur was persistent, nevertheless. In the end, my mother found a diplomatic solution by asking Madame Dupuis to wake her. She was sure that the reason for the change was clear to Madame, and life resumed its normal course.

Normality, in those days, was all a matter of perspective. Often Hilde's nights were busier than her full days. During the day, Monsieur Dupuis was *Monsieur le directeur,* the owner and CEO of his cement plant. He went to work from nine to five, like any other businessman. At night, he helped transport fallen Allied pilots to safety, and looked after other refugees as well. He helped Jews and political fugitives into hiding. People from the Underground came and went all the time, as Hilde had, through the garden at the back, and left after dark.

Hilde was often given assignments at night. She was a courier, like so many young women across the border in the French Underground. Her task was to transport false papers to the fallen pilots and other fugitives hidden in the hilly countryside of the Ardennes. These were usually hidden in her clothes, on the assumption that even if she were stopped, she was unlikely to be strip-searched. Young women supposedly aroused less suspicion than men if they came across a German patrol, though the number of women tortured and killed on such missions suggests that this notion was theoretical at best. In the Ardennes, however, German soldiers were scarcer than elsewhere in the country, unless they were on specific missions of which the Underground usually had ample foreknowledge. Hilde was often used as an interpreter, as well, because almost no one spoke English in that area. Sometimes she translated documents from French to English or vice versa, but mostly she helped the fugitives and their helpers to speak with one another.

I have often asked my mother how she felt about engaging in such perilous work, alone at night in the middle of unfamiliar countryside. "I felt that my life was worth very little," she says. "I had no one, I had no idea what had happened to my parents, and I had to pretend to be someone else all the time. I didn't care whether I lived or died. I could afford to be reckless."

On the surface, there was no sign of all this turmoil. Life was physically demanding, down to the foreignness of the language, and emotionally exhilarating. Every day lived in the sunshine or in the severe frost of winter was a day torn from the hands of the enemy. But underneath it all was a sadness, not exactly depression because Hilde infected others with her energy and exuberance, but a sadness that surrounded the crater formed by the shock of separation from her parents. At least she was useful, she told herself. At least she could help the Dupuis and the English-speaking aviators she met at night. Thousands of airmen were shot down in the occupied Netherlands and in Belgium and were brought through the Ardennes into France. Louis de Jong suggests that from Holland alone, 3000 Allied officers, escaped prisoners of war and aviators were passed on to Spain; all of these would have come through Belgium, in addition to those whose trek began in the Belgian battle zone, or who had escaped into Belgium from Germany.

This was the work in which Hilde's brother had been engaged since his first escape into Belgium, and it was extremely perilous. Jo came to visit once in a while with his usual flamboyance, often with a friend. My mother remembers one occasion when he came late at night from across the Meuse. He could have crossed over the lock upriver, as Resistance fighters generally did to avoid notice, but instead he woke the ferryman. He was wearing some sort of uniform, and upon arrival knocked on the Dupuis's front door, terrifying everyone inside with thoughts of the Gestapo, and causing more commotion in the village. The next day it was the talk of the town that a tall stranger had come to M. Dupuis's house. This was attention the family didn't need.

In February 1944, Hilde celebrated her nineteenth birthday at the Dupuis's house – I suppose she sang "Happy Birthday" to herself, since no one else knew either her real birthday or her real age – and shortly after, she received a message through her Underground connection that her brother and other members of his group had been arrested in Brussels. Jo had a photograph and a letter from her in his pocket at the time, against the most basic rules of Underground work. Hilde was lucky to have been warned. Even at the prison camps, anti-German guards leaked information, and word got to her before the Germans did.

Monsieur Dupuis arranged for Hilde to go to a farm owned by an aunt of Madame Dupuis, one of the landowning gentry who had been so helpful in the past. This lady was also Madame's godmother, and Hilde had met her when she and the girls had gone to visit over Christmas. They had attended Midnight Mass and had enjoyed themselves very much there. My mother remembers that the aunt had put out flannel nightgowns on all the beds, to be sure that everyone was warm enough.

M. Dupuis decided that Hilde ought to take off for the farm even before the Underground had issued instructions for her next safe house: the danger was too great for any hesitation. She was put into a truck designed for hiding people. It had a small niche in the back covered over with the hay and vegetables that made up the load. There were German guards on the road and the truck was stopped, but they didn't discover her. She made it to the farm safely that night, stayed for a single day, and was told to take the train to Gembloux, a town about ten miles north of Namur. In the meantime – Hilde learned later – the Gestapo came to the Dupuis' house and demanded to see her. The family professed ignorance so skillfully that the Gestapo left them in peace, never guessing that Hilde had spent over five months there until her departure the day before.

This time she was received as a guest by a family called Carton de Tournai, at a mansion much grander than that of the Dupuis. "Let me guess," I say. "They belonged to the Belgian nobility."

Of course, my mother says. They were anti-German; the head of the household had died fighting Germany in World War I. Mme Carton de Tournai was now a widow, and she lived with her two daughters, Germaine and Bérangère, in grand style despite the war. Sumptuous meals were served by uniformed maids in a manor house surrounded by magnificent gardens on a main street of the village. The family had kennels for breeding dogs. Hilde, who had been riding in a truck under a load of cabbages barely thirty-six hours before, was received as if she were a guest for a country weekend. She felt uncomfortable in this setting, especially after she told the women, as the Underground had instructed her, that she was Jerry's sister. They looked at her strangely, she couldn't think why, but said nothing until they sat down by the fire with their coffee after dinner that evening.

Under their continued cross-examination, she told them about the escape she and Jo had made, and a good deal about their background, though never, of course, the truth about their Jewishness – not even the Dupuis knew that. Puzzled by the doubt in their faces, she finally confronted them. "What's wrong? You don't trust me. You don't think that I am his sister. Do you think that I'm a spy?" she said.

The very thought made Hilde smile, despite her anxiety. She knew that she was not destined for a career as a double agent. As soon as she smiled, the women saw her resemblance to her brother, who had the same wide grin. They told her then that Jerry had told them that they should expect his girlfriend, not his sister, but that otherwise their stories had matched up in every detail. They thought, of course, that Hilde had heard pieces of the story but not the critical portion about her relationship to Jerry, and concluded from these inconsistencies that she was an impostor. Her brother had simply embellished the tale, because telling things straight was not in his nature. But because my Uncle Jo inspired such confidence in the people around him, they concluded that Jerry must have had his reasons, and they left it at that.

Hilde spent about ten days as a house guest with Mme Carton de Tournai and her daughters. They were kind and distant; they received her as a matter of duty and left her to herself. She was grateful but restless, with nothing to do. The uncertainty about the fate of every member of her own family clouded her hours. During those few days, my mother got to know the brother of Germaine and Bérangère, who was the heir to the family fortune. My mother has told me that M. Carton de Tournai lived in the castle at Gembloux, which had a tower and a moat. He was married and had two little girls, and his cousin, François-Xavier

Gérard, lived with them. M. Carton de Tournai asked Hilde to teach them all English, because she was eager for something to do during the limbo of her stay.

But the family was concerned about her safety, and doubtless about their own. The town of Gembloux had been the scene of a major battle in the German invasion of Belgium and France in 1940. It was situated directly on the railroad that the occupiers used to transport armaments, supplies and soldiers to and from Germany. The sympathy of the Cartons de Tournai for the Resistance was an open secret and they were regarded with some suspicion in the town by local Gestapo and Nazi collaborators. February turned into March. The spring of 1944 was on the way, and François-Xavier, who was a member of the Underground like the rest of the family, had an idea. Hilde could go to help his sister, who lived in Couvin, near the French border south of Charleroi. François-Xavier's brother-in-law worked as an engineer in the little town, and the family was overwhelmed with difficulties. Mme Carton had three small children, two boys and a girl. The girl had just died at the age of two of scarlet fever, and now the mother, who was pregnant again, had fallen into a deep depression. They were in desperate need of help. This was just the kind of situation in which Hilde's skills could be of some use, and she was glad for the opportunity.

François-Xavier took her to Couvin on the train. On the way down he confessed that he had fallen in love with her, and he wondered if she could love him in return. He recited appropriate poems by Verlaine, and sang her songs. François-Xavier was about ten years older than Hilde, nearly thirty, and she found the idea of his affection comforting, though she didn't or couldn't share his feelings. For the moment she turned her attention to the new world she was about to enter. Adaptation took energy, and she had become used to suppressing her internal voices under conditions of perpetual crisis.

The Cartons de Tournai of Couvin were in a far worse state than Hilde expected. The wife had not gotten out of bed for several weeks, the husband had no idea how to perform the simplest household task, and the young farm girl who acted as maidservant was too unskilled to cook or clean.

A little searching on the Internet suggests that there was an oldest boy, Benoît, who would have been six, but though my mother remembers his name, she has either forgotten his presence, or he was not in the household at the time. She tells me that the surviving boys, Pierre, aged four, and François-Xavier (presumably named after his uncle), aged a little over one, were kept in high chairs all day. They were underdeveloped and unwashed. The four-year-old was still in diapers. My mother says that she had a clear mission, and she worked sixteen-hour days cleaning the house, doing the laundry and caring for the children. Hilde must have been a dynamo at nineteen. The Dupuis, for example, remember that she introduced them to the idea of decorating a Christmas tree – my Jewish mother, who had learned about Christmas trees in Berlin – and that they cut stars out of the tops of cans to hang on its branches. In Couvin, her energy began to show results quite rapidly. She got Mme Carton de Tournai out of bed, and began to invite the neighbors in. She became friends with the local priest, who was a young man. By June, when the news of D-Day was filling everyone with fantastic hopes, the little boys had become used to clean clothes and play outdoors, and had begun to walk and talk at levels appropriate for their age. Hilde took them on picnics, and organized excursions.

She had become particularly close to the local doctor, whose son and daughters were her real age. Once a week, on her afternoons off, she would meet up with the doctor's daughters and their friends and go on a picnic, if the weather was good, or plan some other outing together. The girls were unusually tender-hearted, and had nicknames for each other. They dubbed Hilde *la biche douce*, the gentle doe, because of her soft, dark eyes. Those eyes had seen more, of course, than anyone in that neighborhood knew. The young women were Girl Guides, members of the European Girl Scouts, an organization that, even in wartime, encouraged an active idealism. Hilde enjoyed the inclusion in their meetings and campfires during the early spring and summer, but she was restless, and desperate to find out what had happened to her parents.

I imagine my mother taking on all that responsibility for a household, and isolated from young people of her own age in an identity she had not chosen. She must have been glad indeed that the doctor had such friendly children. Hilde admired him because he worked for the Underground at night as well as ministering to his regular patients during the day. His task was to go into the mountains and woods of the Ardennes and treat wounded members of the *maquis,* the underground army that constituted the armed wing of the Resistance movement. She began to work as his assistant, and learned a great deal from him. My mother's life begins to sound like a novel in which no one takes time off for rest or refreshment. I wonder when, if ever, she slept, between tending to the needs of the family, going to campfires, and healing the fighters of the *maquis.*

During the summer, the doctor delivered Mme Carton de Tournai of a daughter. This must have been Brigitte, born August 5, 1944. Because the hospital was not considered up to standard, the doctor came to the house, and Hilde assisted at the birth. The mood of the family continued to brighten, especially as news of Allied victories began to filter through to the village; everyone hoped that this time the war would finally be over.

Mme Carton de Tournai did not have enough milk to nurse her baby, and Hilde had to look for wet nurses. An ad was placed in the local paper, and new mothers who had ample milk responded. Because there was no refrigeration, Hilde bought an old bicycle from the doctor's family and took five trips a day into the countryside, making the rounds of nursing mothers in the farmhouses. She knew many of them through the doctor's family, because she had driven with one of the daughters once a week to collect milk and butter, eggs and flour, and fresh vegetables. The doctor was popular, and the farmers insisted on giving him such gifts. She carried a breast pump with her and, at the height of summer, brought the milk straight back to feed Brigitte. "We worked it out, we managed it," she says, sounding surprised anew after all these years that the milk didn't spoil and that she didn't collapse. Hilde continued to run the rest of the household as well. When she could get hold of flour, she took it to the baker to be made into special white bread for Mme Carton de Tournai, because she needed the extra nourishment.

When the time came for Brigitte to be baptized, the family asked if Colette, as they referred to Hilde, would like to be godmother. Hilde escaped this close call by telling the family that she was Dutch Reformed and couldn't take on the ritual responsibilities demanded by the Catholic Church, leading her suitor, François-Xavier, to take her for Protestant as well. The incident caused her to reflect with more care on his role in her life. I'm amused by the way she talks about him. It's so obvious that she was never in the least in love. He would not have seemed demanding if she had felt anything for him.

She describes François-Xavier as annoyingly attentive. He visited her all the time and wrote poems in her honor. When he proposed, Hilde was tempted. She was quite sure that she didn't love him, but then she didn't know what love was. Perhaps love would come eventually, especially if her fate was to be otherwise alone in the world. But François-Xavier didn't know her background or even her real name, and Hilde thought that this might be a stumbling point.

François-Xavier wanted Hilde to enter the Catholic Church.

Otherwise he couldn't marry her, since he wanted to raise their children as Catholics. My mother was pleased enough to talk with the local priest, as François-Xavier wished, because the priest was already a friend of hers and involved in the Underground. She met him formally a number of times to discuss the possibility of her conversion, and finally she told him that she could never become a Catholic. She could not accept the act of faith – the basic belief that Jesus was the result of an Immaculate Conception, that he was born of Mary, a virgin, and was the son of God. She could not be dishonest about this matter with her friend the priest, even though she continued to go to services every Sunday and tried in other ways to comply with François-Xavier's wishes.

Early on, before they had even set out to cross the Maas together, her brother Jo had warned her that she must never under any circumstances reveal that she was Jewish. She could tell her benefactors anything but that, because the danger to them of sheltering a Jew was far greater than that incurred by any other clandestine activity. People sometimes survived imprisonment for protecting fallen fliers or for working in the Underground, but for sheltering Jews, almost never. Inevitably they were tortured and sent to concentration camps. And now Jo himself had been arrested. Hilde was sure that, despite his obviously Semitic appearance, he had not admitted to being a Jew. She didn't know whether he was alive or dead, but she hoped that he had successfully suppressed the fact of his true identity. In her relationship with all the Belgians she had met, she had used her false identity to cloak her true one; and now she found herself in the peculiar position of having to pretend scruples about Catholicism which, in the face of the reality of being Jewish, were absurd.

Her handling of the relationship with François-Xavier showed how young she really was. She didn't know what to do. She was starved for affection, but not from him. He was not in love with the woman she knew herself to be, and she couldn't imagine when she could tell him the truth.

Meanwhile the armies of liberation were approaching. As before, personal dilemmas melted before the massive realities of war. News of the death camps had been filtering slowly back from the East. Hilde first heard something about them while she was still at the Dupuis's, late in the autumn of 1943 or early in the winter of 1944. M. Dupuis came into the kitchen one day where Hilde was working alongside Madame. He said that he had heard about Jews being killed when the Germans introduced poison gas into railway cars. Neither of her hosts knew that my mother was Jewish, so she had both to express her horror and to keep it under control. She couldn't bear to think that this might be the fate of her parents, so she simply "built a wall," as she has always said, around the news and tried to entomb it in some part of her being where she could forget that she had heard it. More rumors reached her in Couvin as the Allied armies approached from the south during the summer of 1944. As they got closer, my mother told François-Xavier that she couldn't promise marriage. First, she had to go back to the Netherlands to find out what had happened to her own family.

The days grew stranger. During the latter part of August and the beginning of September, German soldiers came through Couvin on their retreat. If they were members of the SS and not regular soldiers, they engaged in every sort of viciousness on their way toward the German border. They shot pedestrians in the streets, blew up bridges and mined streets and fields. This was the enactment of Hitler's scorched-earth policy: Hitler ordered his soldiers to destroy everything as they returned to Germany. He had plans, apparently, to destroy Germany itself before the Allies could get there. He expressed his views in an editorial written on his orders for the *Völkischer Beobachter*, the Nazi Party newspaper: "Not a German stalk of wheat is to feed the enemy, not a German mouth to give him information, not a German hand to give him help. He is to find every footbridge destroyed, every road blocked – nothing but death, annihilation and hatred will meet him."

To her dismay, Hilde had to share the house with German soldiers for a few days, not SS but infantry. Everyone knew that some of the worst casualties of the war were occurring just then, in these last apocalyptic days of the retreat. Bombers flew overhead, and the world seemed to be exploding. Civilians were caught in the crossfire and spent most of their time hiding in the cellars of their houses. "I've survived all these years," Hilde thought, "and I'm going to die getting liberated."

Despite everything they had already endured and the cruelties they witnessed every day, Hilde and the other villagers found themselves pitying some of the retreating soldiers. They came through on foot and in horse carts; they looked disheveled and exhausted. Most were infantry who had been on the march for weeks. When they spent a night at the Cartons de Tournai, the family ignored them as much as possible, and Hilde hid, fearful of what they might do if they discovered her true identity. Still, the Cartons couldn't help noticing how longingly many of them looked at the small boys and the new baby. Sometimes they spoke, though no one answered them, of their own children and how they missed them. "They were scared, they were tired and hungry and wanted to be back with their families," my mother says. "Many of them were old because, by that time, they mobilized old men and boys. It was odd, because we hated them and we pitied them. They were not all murderers. They were mostly just ordinary people."

They began to hear tanks advancing in the distance, the first sign that the US First Army was on the way. They kept abreast of events by listening to the BBC broadcasts from London. Hilde warned the Carton de Tournai family that she was going to leave as soon as the village was liberated. They knew that her brother was in jail, and that she wanted to track him down. In the days before the Allies were expected, she made pastries – the classic French swans to be filled with whipped cream – so the family would have something special to offer when the troops arrived.

On September 3, 1944 – a year to the day since Hilde had arrived at the Dupuis's garden on the Meuse – people stood on the outskirts of town and watched the American tanks come in across the ridges near Couvin. First they heard the familiar roar of the last few days growing louder and louder. Then they saw the Americans come over the hill. The guns and turrets of the tanks appeared, with five-pointed stars on their flanks. Then, raising their bodies out of the tanks, draped on the sides, smiling and waving, dust-covered, helmeted, came the first GIs. Perhaps these were the soldiers of the Ninth Infantry and the Third Armored Brigade, who certainly passed through this region. There were other people marching, too; more GIs, and the young fighters of the *maquis*, out of their hiding places for the first time in four years. They wore belted jumpsuits made of hopsacking, their uniform, and now and then one of them raised a rifle in a gesture of jubilation. When they entered the village, the townspeople cheered, walked beside them, and invited them home for a glass of wine.

Hilde's contacts in the *maquis* told her to meet them the next day if she wanted to come along with them. Through the doctor, they knew that she was looking for her imprisoned brother. Their plan was to travel to Brussels behind the American troops and flush out collaborators. Hilde was given a uniform and, for the first time, a gun, but she couldn't see herself using it. The group requisitioned cars and trucks, not that any struggle was involved, because people gave up their vehicles joyfully to the Resistance fighters, or so my mother says. On September 4, Hilde said goodbye to the family that she had restored in the six months she had spent with them, and moved into the next phase of her life when she climbed on a truck with the young partisans of the *maquis*.

I notice that she has not spoken about the Cartons de Tournai as warmly as she did about the Dupuis, despite her pity for the mother and fondness for the children. She doesn't remember all their names. I wonder what the family made of her. Was she as instrumental in their recovery as she thought? Were they fully (and if so, heroically) aware of the risks they took in keeping her with them? Béatrice and Etienne went on to have five more children, nine in total, but two more girls died in infancy after the war.

I ask my mother what it was like to have lived with Béatrice's paralyzing grief when she herself had lost every member of her family, as far as she knew, and couldn't express her feelings. Losing a baby, my mother says, seemed so outrageously awful that she had only sympathy for Béatrice. The work was satisfying and exhausting: she had found chaos and made order. She was the one who took care of everyone, and she didn't expect that the family would be much interested in her. The youthful intensity of her friendship with the Girl Guides sustained her during those months. She couldn't wait to start looking for her family, and to be free and active again.

On the road, the young people saw all the destruction of the recent battle: fallen houses, dead horses, burned-out tanks, and the retreating Germans in their horse-carts. Columns of prisoners of war passed by. In the towns, women who had consorted with the enemy were publicly tortured. They were stripped and had their heads shaved. Some had been professional prostitutes, some, in the eyes of their fellow-citizens, had prostituted themselves by socializing with German soldiers. "And there were a lot of them," my mother says. "There were terrible scenes." The *maquis* group was the first to enter Namur, where they were greeted with the same rapture they had encountered along the road; the troops must have been sweeping north from France into Belgium and then east into Germany. The young people stayed in the château that dominates the town.

When she and her comrades reached Brussels, which had been liberated by British troops on September 3, 1944, the same day as American troops had freed Couvin, she met Jacques Grenez, a man of about forty. It turned out that he had been imprisoned with Jo, although he had been released earlier. I call my Uncle Jo in Switzerland, and he explains that he had been in prison in Brussels before the Allies arrived on September 3. Jacques Grenez, his cellmate for a time, had been liberated after having been arrested for a minor offense. He had provided shelter to an Allied pilot who parachuted into his garden, and the Germans had caught both men.

Hilde wasn't hopeful about the chances of Jo's survival. She knew about the technique such Underground cells used when all members were arrested, as had happened in Jo's case. One person volunteered to commit suicide, and the others, when questioned, could say that only the dead person knew the information and had never taken the others into his confidence. (*Flee the Captor* describes the example of David Verloop, who threw himself down a flight of stairs to avoid endangering his comrades.)

But Jacques Grenez told her the good news that Jo had been alive a few weeks before. He offered to help get her settled in Brussels so that she could try to find her brother. She had no money, having worked for nothing in exchange for the protection the Belgian families gave her, and Jacques Grenez offered her enough to tide her over, telling her that she could pay him back whenever she found it convenient. She says that people often helped each other financially in those confusing days. Hilde repaid him immediately after the war.

Jacques Grenez gave her the name of the boardinghouse where Jo had been staying when he was picked up by the police. According to Jo, all the inmates were arrested. At the time, they included several Allied pilots who were being sheltered there and some members of Jo's immediate group. The two middle-aged sisters who ran the place were sent to Ravensbrück concentration camp and never returned. Jo, seventy-six when I talk with him, describes them as "old ladies of forty-five or fifty," with an artlessness that tells me that they have remained in his memory as they seemed to him when he was only twenty-three himself.

My mother adds that the group was among the 150 or so unfortunates who turned up in the address book of Suzy Kraay, a young woman who worked in Dutch-Paris and was picked up by the French police and tortured by the Gestapo in Paris just before Jo's arrest. Herbert Ford describes the event in a chapter devoted to her in *Flee the Captor*. Suzy Kraay knew that she should not have been carrying such a document, and tried to get rid of it in the street on her way to the police station. She was stymied by malice or by French good manners: "Mademoiselle seems to have dropped something," a passerby said to her, and handed the offending notebook right back. Forty people died in camps as a result.

But at the time, Hilde could not know that her brother had been swept up in that major disaster. She knew only that she had to find him. She went first to the Red Cross to enlist their help, and then to the Dutch Consulate, where she met a group of Dutch young people who had gone Underground as she had. Many were medical students and nurses. Eventually, this became the core of a unit that worked for a while with the British St John's Ambulance Unit and the British Red Cross.

To her indescribable relief, her inquiries bore fruit. She learned from the Red Cross that her brother was being held at Bourg Léopold, or Leopoldsburg in Flemish, a prison about forty miles east of Antwerp and not all that far from the point at which they had first entered the country. The prison was being run as a concentration camp for political prisoners. She knew at once that Jo had not been arrested as a Jew or been subsequently treated as one. That was probably why he was still alive. She had not heard a word from him since the day she had learned of his arrest seven months before, though her hopes had been raised by Jacques Grenez's account of having recently seen him.

After a while, she was told that the prisoners at Bourg Léopold had been freed, and that Jo knew she was in Brussels. But when he didn't turn up for several days, she began, again, to assume that he had died; so few prisoners of the Gestapo ever returned. Then he arrived in Brussels, weak and emaciated. He told her that he had been in the British sector during Liberation, and that the British had taken the camp a week before Jo was scheduled for execution.

In the course of several long telephone conversations in the late 1990s, my uncle fills in some of the circumstances of his arrest and imprisonment. He sounds soldierly and nonchalant. I can imagine him talking with the RAF pilots he helped across the Belgian border. He certainly learned their lingo: bits of 1940s military slang pop up in his excellent English; like my mother, he moves effortlessly between languages. He talks about his postwar life after "all that palaver." He used to hurry us along in childhood by saying "chop chop!," and sent us into gales of laughter when he asked us to "give him a tinkle" on the telephone.

"During that part of the war," he tells me, "my hiding place was a German jail. I was arrested under the name of Jean-Paul Lambert. Of course I had excellent false Belgian papers, and they never tortured me. We were imprisoned in Gestapo headquarters in the avenue Louise in Brussels. They had made cells in the cellars for people under interrogation. We saw people come back who had been beaten and tortured. First I thought I'd pretend I didn't understand German. Then I pretended that I was a Dutchman who had been born and raised in Paramaribo, the capital of Surinam, in the Dutch West Indies. I knew they couldn't check up on the truth of that story.

"My 'confession' consisted of telling the Germans that I was a Dutchman using false Belgian papers. After the avenue Louise, I was jailed in St-Gilles prison in Brussels. Then I was transferred to Bourg Léopold, which had been a training camp for the Belgian military and was now a German concentration camp. It was not a health spa but we were not ill-treated. We were forty people in a barrack. We cut meat in very thin, almost transparent slices with a hidden razor blade we had, so that everyone could have something to chew on during the day. We were ill fed but not starved. I still have the cookery book of the camp. It had recipes for a horse's head cooked in forty liters of water – I found it when we were walking around after the liberation.

"In the military camp, we were treated as soldiers and 'protected' by the Geneva convention of 1929. We had a theatre company, with a bit of transvestism for the women's parts, and extra food from the Red Cross – we particularly looked forward to the spaghetti or macaroni we got from them once a week – and some of the older prisoners had pets. When the food got really bad towards the end, the pets started disappearing, and you would see notices on the camp bulletin board: 'TO THE PERSON WHO ATE MY RABBIT BUGSY: I HOPE HE POISONS YOU AND ROTS YOUR GUTS.'"

Despite Jo's later claim that Bourg Léopold was not as severe a camp as some others, Hilde was shocked by her brother's appearance. Still, he recovered quickly and regained some strength. Like Hilde, he was eager to become active again, and to get into the Netherlands. He and Hilde joined the young people from the Dutch consulate and formed a Dutch-speaking Red

Cross unit that would perform rescue work under the supervision of British forces in Antwerp and, eventually, in the parts of the Netherlands that were beginning to come under Allied control. By an irony of fate, the Netherlands was the last country in Europe to be released from the Nazi yoke. In about the third week of September 1944, the dozen young people of the Dutch medical unit began their work in Flanders, moving west of Brussels to start with and then steadily eastward toward southern Holland.

Hilde, liberated in early September of 1944, didn't know that most of the Dutch still had the terrible Hunger Winter of that year ahead of them, and that the big cities of northern and western Holland, including Amsterdam, would be affected worst of all. The failure of Operation Market-Garden, a massive Allied air and paratroop assault on the Rhine bridges launched on September 17, slowed the Allied advance into Germany. The most disastrous part of the operation occurred at Arnhem, where British troops held one end of a bridge for nine days and nights in a vain wait for supplies that never came. Of the ten thousand paratroopers and glider pilots who landed there, 6000 became prisoners of war, 1400 died, and only 2398 escaped.

As a result of this miscalculation, attributed by some historians to Field Marshal Montgomery and his subordinates, the Dutch were more than ever cut off by the Germans on all sides while the victorious Allies moved through the rest of Western Europe. Holland finally got help when airdrops of food were ordered directly by Churchill. But these supplies didn't arrive until April 29, 1945, just one day before Hitler shot himself in his bunker and Allied troops poured into Germany, and only a week before the German surrender. Sixteen thousand people in the Netherlands died of starvation during those months, while most of the rest of Western Europe was already rejoicing.

Before my mother and her brother could embark on this new aspect of the rescue work they were so eager to do in the few areas of Holland where the Allies had access, François-Xavier arrived in Brussels. He had bought a ring, three rooms' worth of furniture, and a life insurance policy of which Hilde was sole beneficiary, all without consulting her. Hilde balked. She told him that the future was still too uncertain to make plans. She would not, as he wished, return with him to Gembloux.

Then François-Xavier brought in his own heavy artillery, his brother Pierre Gérard, the Dominican priest, whom Hilde had not yet met. He had just arrived from England with the Belgian government in exile, and had joined the Belgian Army of Liberation with the rank of corporal. "He was a fantastic man," my mother says. "If he had not been a priest, and if the situation hadn't been totally ridiculous in the first place, he would have been my choice."

There was some emotional kinship between them that gave their long conversations warmth as well as candor. Now that she was no longer in hiding, she was able to tell the priest the whole truth: not merely that she had scruples about Catholicism, and not only that she intended to do rescue work with her colleagues, but also that she was a Jew. She told François-Xavier too. He insisted that her Jewishness made no difference to him, but the priest had different advice. Although he sympathized with her and felt sorry for his brother, he counseled Hilde against the marriage. He confirmed her suspicion that, although the Cartons de Tournai were a family whose high ideals had led them into Resistance work, they harbored anti-Semitic prejudices as entrenched as their Catholic nationalism. There was a chance that she might be accepted among them if she became a devout Catholic, but no one would ever forget that she had first been a Jew.

I suspect that the priest, a cooler head than his brother, saw immediately that Hilde wasn't in love and understood how young she really was. He could not in justice counsel her to take steps that would lead her and his brother to a life of great unhappiness.

He had an idea of what she had been through already. Things were left ambiguous for the moment, and she went off as planned with the special Dutch unit.

Their goal was to help treat civilians in newly liberated areas of Belgium and southern Holland. They worked together with the British Friends Field Service, the British Red Cross and the order of St John, just behind the front lines. Many of their British comrades were Quakers who would take any risk as long as it didn't involve killing.

The work was certainly dangerous enough. In Flanders, local people had been bombed out of their homes and were otherwise casualties of the vicious fighting in that part of the country. Belgium and Holland had been bombarded by both sides during the Allied offensive, and eastern and southern areas would come under fire again a few months later, during the Battle of the Bulge. But the medical people attended to other problems as they came up in the disorder of war. Hilde helped a doctor in the unit when a farmer's wife gave birth, washing and tending the newborn. The group was quartered in civilian homes in the villages they passed through. They stayed for days or weeks at a time, depending on need. In one village, the women were given two rooms above a baker's. They slept on the floor on straw mattresses provided by the British Army, and had the luxury of hot water to wash in every morning when the baker got his ovens started.

When they arrived in Limburg, a name that applies both to an eastern province of Belgium and to a southern province of the Netherlands, the true devastation of the war became obvious. The SS, again following Hitler's directive to leave scorched earth behind as they fled, had mined large areas, fields and roads. They had kidnapped any civilians they could find and hauled them back into Germany for forced labor. By now so many of their own people were either dead or conscripted that there had been shortages of workers throughout the war, and slavery had been used to make up the difference. As a result, the local population had hidden for months – in basements and cellars, and sometimes in holes in the ground. They were starving and filthy, and now they were caught between the lines.

With the German army in desperate and vengeful retreat, villagers tried to escape by running toward the British lines across mined fields. Many people were seriously injured as they tried to come across, but they had few alternatives. If they stayed where they were, there was a good chance that the Germans would capture the men and take them back to Germany. They were stuck, my mother says, "between the devil and the deep blue sea." The medical unit picked people up in their ambulances when they saw them racing through the minefields, though the drivers were not sure of safe passage, either: some of the minefields had been cleared and some had not. Fortunately, no one in the unit was blown up.

My mother has pictures of this period. The group eventually penetrated Holland as far north as Eindhoven, and set up tents in a sort of base camp near the Dutch town of Weert. Before they could feed the people, they had to delouse them and treat them for scabies and other conditions. Malnutrition, dirt and darkness had taken a terrible toll. But my mother remembers how they cheered and clapped when people made it safely across the fields. Every life saved was a victory in that time of random death. The children were amazed at the food the members of the medical unit handed out when they reached the Dutch towns. The younger ones had never seen white bread or chocolate, or oranges or bananas.

They were quick to celebrate their liberation nonetheless. It was thrilling to be back in Holland. The young people were greeted with jubilation. Children paraded in the streets waving flags and streamers and wearing orange-colored paper hats in honor of what was hoped to be the early return of the House of

Orange. The joy and relief are palpable in the pictures, where children wear droll knitted hats with pointed ears and wave little flags, squinting into the cold late-autumn sunlight. The exuberance jumps out at you. A young member of the rescue group, labeled "Shifty" in the photograph album, is chronicled as he washes his laundry. He looks jauntily at the camera, a cigarette drooping from his lip. He must have been a favorite with the young women, because he is disproportionately represented in the snapshots.

Young Hilde waves at the photographer and flashes her broad grin as she sits on what looks like a log, perhaps writing a letter to François-Xavier. How far away he must have seemed at such moments! My Uncle Jo, who became a leader in the little group, gives instructions in one picture, in which civilians are being transported to safer territory. In another, he sits over a meal with a couple of other men in front of a large Nazi banner in what must have been, until very recently, German officers' quarters. Jo and his friends must have enjoyed the pose of blithe oblivion to the backdrop.

On December 16, the Battle of the Bulge began, and once more the members of the group began to fear for their safety. The battle lasted for exactly a month, until January 16, 1945, with terrible casualties on the Allied side. This period, during which German forces made a ferocious attempt to defend the German border from the inevitable Allied invasion, was one of the most desperately confused of the whole war, not least because the Allied generals continued to squabble with each other and to contend for the honor of being first across the Rhine.

The Bulge refers to a loop of territory the Germans re-conquered around the town of Bastogne, in the Ardennes, but the line stretched north of there as well, through the narrow area of the Dutch/Belgian border already so familiar to my mother and uncle from their initial escape. They were just on that wavering frontier, and the German army was very close. Even after the battle had officially ended, the front line in this border area didn't move much. The groups that went out scouting for needy civilians now had to be even more concerned about German patrols. It was not clear whether the Germans were advancing again, or were still in retreat. They were dangerous either way.

The group at this point had been pulled back just to the Belgian side of the border, and were quartered at a Trappist monastery in the village of Achel. They were so close to the German lines that one day Jo and his colleagues from the British Field Service didn't return from one of their missions. Their co-workers assumed that they had either driven over a mine or been taken prisoner; Hilde didn't know it then, but Jo had been arrested by the Germans. She was alone once more, but this time, at least, she was surrounded by friends – quite literally Friends, Quakers, in many cases – who supported and encouraged her, and with whom she was no longer in disguise. One young man, Gordon West, a British Quaker, kept her spirits up when Jo disappeared, and remained with her unit for months afterward when they went into Germany.

Something strange happens to Jo's part of the narrative. Uncle Jo, my semi-reliable narrator, has no recollection of my mother's presence in this Dutch medical group, and even more strikingly, no memory of his arrest and second imprisonment. I push him. I remind him that there are photographs in which brother and sister appear together, and that people like Gordon West and others remember them both in that context. I ask how he can possibly forget being arrested for the second time – how he can forget that Hilde heard a message from him on her birthday the following February on a Red Cross–sponsored BBC broadcast; how she tracked him down in the spring with the help of other workers, and can name the camp where he was held.

Even without such a spectacular case of amnesia, Jo has consistently cut her out of his memory of places and events. He's like Khrushchev, snipping Stalin from snapshots. "Your mother never did any Underground work," he tells me. "She wouldn't have understood – she was so much younger." When I tell him that she was a courier and translator and helped with the medical work during her hiding, I can almost hear him shrug over the phone.

On the face of it, there's an explanation for all this forgetting. In the course of the writing of this book, my Uncle Jo, who died at eighty-four in 2005, was diagnosed with Alzheimer's disease after I first questioned him about the events in Belgium. On top of the bad and selective memory he has always had, he should have become more unreliable than ever; but when he was sharp, he was clear in all details.

Jo supported my mother's memory of the Trappist monastery in Achel. The group was quartered there, and most of the original monks had been evacuated. The Trappists had to waive their usual rules in order to allow the group to stay, because it included women. They were eager to help the Allies in any way they could. The young people slept in cells in separate wings of the building for men and for women. Jo remembered Shifty, the darling of the women's camera; he even knew that he became a doctor and retired in Amsterdam.

My mother provides the human touch. She laughs as she describes their stay. The Trappists were delighted by the presence of women and by the disruption of their routine of restraint and silence. There was much mutual admiration, because the Trappists had helped refugees throughout the war.

One monk, who was in his thirties and worked in the fields, was called Brother Michael. Against the rules, he enjoyed chatting with his guests, and offered them fruit and vegetables. He loved smoking, and the young people obliged him with cigarettes.

One day, the abbot appeared while Brother Michael was with the group. He tried to hide his cigarette under his habit. But smoke came out of his sleeves, and the abbot caught him and forbade further contact. It was decided that the young women caused too much of a sensation, so they were billeted in a private home.

My mother phones me a few days after the conversations about Jo and his memory lapses. She tells me with much excitement that she has found a battered little notebook from that period. Her notes were scribbled in pencil and set down in snatched intervals during the first few months of 1945. They don't always correspond to the correct dates, because they are stuck in every which way among hastily scrawled addresses and along cramped margins. They are faded, and the original Dutch is hard to read. But they shed a clear if fitful light on the events of that period. They confirm Jo's arrest and his subsequent message. They also give a picture of what it was like to work in that harried unit before and during the Battle of the Bulge, and they vividly depict the uncertainty and even hysteria of life for a person without nationality or identity at the end of the war.

My mother tells me that an officer in the British army gave her the notebook on New Year's Day 1945. Like all the young women with nursing or medical training, Hilde had been given the rank of lieutenant with the Dutch and British forces, and later she held the same rank when she worked with the American army. She says that there was always an officers' club near where she was stationed, and social events associated with it: a New Year's dinner, an officer's ball, a movie or concert. My mother reads out the first entry over the phone about a champagne supper in Brussels with two British officers. She has begun to worry that I will think that she spent all her time hanging around with British officers and having a good time. I tease her: even as a grandmother, she has a freshness or naïveté that has always attracted men just because she is almost absurdly wholesome. "It was all very innocent," she says. "We were ships in the night."

By the end of January, Hilde and her colleagues were traveling back and forth to Brussels in a state of high anxiety during their odd days of leave. They had heard that the unit was about to be disbanded, because the Dutch government had decided that they did not have official status. They had been taken on by the British because all of them had skills and had been working in the Resistance or hiding underground in Belgium. The Dutch army, on the other hand, showed no interest in helping them to restore their original identities. They seemed intent on impeding their movement in any direction, and the young people were getting worried. Once the war had ended, the bureaucracies of peacetime attacked, creating endless impediments to the basic business of survival. The arrival of Dutch women officers who had spent the war in England didn't help. Unskilled themselves, they treated the survivors of the Underground as interlopers, whose lack of identity papers made them non-persons. (The historian Bob Moore confirms that Hilde's difficulties weren't unique.) Hilde had begun applying to various organizations for a position, including UNRRA, the United Nations Relief and Rehabilitation Administration.

The notebook records the fact that Jo was arrested on February 3, 1945, while on "recky," as the slang was for the group's reconnaissance missions. The commanding officers of the group knew about the arrest from the Germans, who were obliged to notify the Red Cross about the capture of ambulances. Then there is a gap until February 24, when Hilde catches up with several previous events. About her twentieth birthday on February 18, she writes that she was in Achel with the Trappists: "singalong and presents, party. In the evening, the Friends gave talks. Gordon and Godfrey brought us home. It was a day full of warm friendship and understanding. News from Jo. UNRRA General Tschihatchev."

My mother remembers her relief when a message came through the Red Cross on the nightly BBC broadcast that Jo knew was a fixture in the group's routine. With characteristic rakishness, Jo wished her a happy birthday and coincidentally mentioned that he was alive and well. The last name in Hilde's diary entry was also significant. Several members of her group were supposed to have forty-eight hours' leave to Brussels to try to clarify their increasingly uncertain situation, and the Russian general had been mentioned as a resource.

On March 18, according to the little notebook, Hilde had an extraordinary encounter. The group was stationed in a small Dutch town called Schaik and quartered with a Dutch farming family. The farmers had been looking after a little boy of four or five who turned out to be one of the children Hilde and her colleagues had smuggled out of the day care center in Amsterdam. The family planned to find his parents so that he could be reunited with them. The prospect of success was grim, but none of the group in Schaik had yet realized that. My mother says that children who made it to the care of farmers in the south of Holland had a high survival rate, despite the proximity of the front.

On March 21, Hilde was summoned to Brussels by UNRRA, presumably in response to her application, but all was confusion when she got there. Then she met General Tschihatschef (Hilde spelled his name differently each time it appeared), and he resolved her difficulties with a flick of his hand by getting her a post with the British Red Cross. My mother says that he was from the Soviet Union and looked like Yul Brynner, slim and elegant. He cut through the red tape without giving it another thought.

François-Xavier is not mentioned in these hasty notes from the first half of 1945. The relationship had come to an end. Once she was surrounded by people who had suffered losses like hers, who also spoke Dutch and had the same background, she felt an enormous sense of freedom and relief. In her desire to be completely honest, she wrote to François-Xavier explaining that she was going back to her own life. Though she was grateful for his love and kindness, she could never marry him. Their relationship had been a dreamlike interlude in the midst of persecution, despair and fear, but now it was no longer possible.

She got a terrible letter back from his mother, who said that Hilde had taken advantage of François-Xavier. Hilde was a scheming Jewess who wanted his fortune, but now that she had gone back to her own people, she had betrayed him in the way typical of people of her faith. His mother concluded by saying that François-Xavier had had a nervous breakdown upon the receipt of her letter and was in a sanitorium. And it was all her fault.

What a narrow escape, I think. I try to imagine what such a woman would have thought of Hilde if she *had* married François-Xavier. The fact that Hilde had turned down all his wealth had done nothing to soften the woman's bigotry. In her grief at her son's unhappiness, she just found a different hypothesis to drape her prejudices upon. I wonder what became of François-Xavier, and whether he had ever really entered a mental hospital. I haven't been able to find a trace of him, though many of his nephews and nieces have apparently flourished. Did he marry? Did he live out his days in some draughty Belgian castle, surrounded by grandchildren and portraits of his ancestors? I hope he found consolation soon after his breakdown, and also escape from the harshness of his kinfolk. I should like to imagine that it wasn't Hilde's Jewishness that caused his collapse, but rather the rejection itself. It would be a pity to think of him as an anti-Semite.

Hilde's new life with the British Red Cross began on April 11. Some members of her former unit, Gordon West, for instance, had been placed with her in this new one. The Germans had started bombarding Antwerp with V-2 missiles on October 13 and terribly intensified their attacks during the Battle of the Bulge: 1610 V-2s fell on the single city of Antwerp, compared with the 1190 that struck England as a whole. They had been part of Hitler's campaign to recapture the great port city, which Montgomery had failed to secure properly during the liberation of Belgium in September. The Germans had mined the harbor, making it unusable for Allied shipping, and German troops had managed to escape behind the advancing Allied lines in the first days of the invasion. The V-2s were part of a general German campaign of demoralization that gained force with the missile attacks on England and, of course, with the Ardennes offensive during the Battle of the Bulge.

The little notebook closely reflects the confusion in the way events took sudden and unexpected turns. Hilde thought that the group would be aiding the victims of the missile attacks. She was hastily trained as an interpreter and sort of EMT at British Red Cross headquarters, a beautiful old country house on the outskirts of the city. She learned to drive a Jeep, an ambulance, a motorcycle, an army cycle, a small truck and a large truck.

She undertook one task on her own initiative. She could not believe that the British, with excellent food supplies, could turn out such execrable meals. After her own period of starvation in Holland, she couldn't bear the waste, and she asked for permission to do the cooking. With a couple of assistants, she took over the kitchen and began feeding her group of twenty people. According to her notebook, her efforts were well received.

Within a day or two, everything had changed. The American armies first crossed the Rhine during the second and third weeks of March, but headway into Germany was slow. It wasn't until April 14 that the first British troops arrived at Bergen-Belsen concentration camp. On the same day or very soon thereafter, a call arose for volunteers from her unit to go to the assistance of the British medical staff there. Hilde put herself forward right away. She was to go into the heart of Germany, to find out firsthand what had happened to her friends and neighbors. And at last she would have a chance to look for her parents. The group departed for Bergen-Belsen on April 18, 1945.

During this period, my mother says that extreme feelings of grief and horror contrasted sharply with the exuberance of being alive, young and free. She knew dozens of other young people who had also suffered: British soldiers, Dutch and Belgian civilians, her colleagues in the Red Cross. She worked hard, slept little, went dancing, wept, drank champagne as victory approached; worried and wondered. A whirlpool of emotion closed this chapter of her life.

1. Betty Jacobsthal, probably Berlin circa 1910.
2. Jo and Hilde Jacobsthal, Berlin circa 1928.
3. Helgoländer Ufer 5, where Hilde lived (second floor – European style).
   Picture taken in 2010.
4. Walter Jacobsthal, date and place unknown.

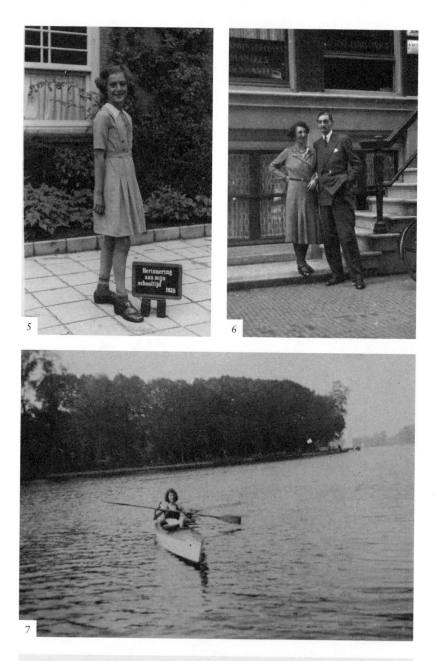

5. Hilde, Amsterdam 1935.
6. Betty and Walter in front of their clothing business, Amsterdam 1930s.
7. Hilde in her "canoe," 1941.

8. *Front row, l to r:* Lou, Charles, Betty. *Back row, l to r:* Jo, Hans, Walter, Hilde. The Jacobsthals' living room, 1938

9. *L to r:* Jo, Walter, Betty and Hilde with friends, Holland, possibly the mid-1930s.

Judentransport nach Theresienstadt am 14.September 1943.

51. Gutmann	Max	26. 1.90	Angestellter
52. Gutmann-Fabian	Hanny	11. 5.05	Ohne
53. Gutmann	Irene	23. 7.30	Ohne
54. Hayman	Hugo	4. 5.73	Ohne
55. Hayman-Ury	Kaethe	7.10.81	Ohne
56. Hertz	Ernst	2. 9.96	Kaufmann
57. Hertz-Freund	Martha	12. 9.99	Ohne
58. Heumann	Gustav	7. 7.74	Ohne
59. Hinfeld	Simon	26. 5.92	Friseur
60. Hinfeld-Gottschalk	Bertha	11.11.98	Verkäuferin
61. Hirsch	Friedrich	4. 5.89	Ohne
62. Hirsch-Hartog	Jenny	25. 2.91	Ohne
63. Hirschfeld	Willy	11. 9.89	Ingenieur
64. Hirschfeld-Neustadt	Charlotte	2. 3.91	Näherin
65. Hirsekorn	Martin	26. 5.97	Zimmermann
66. Hohenstein	Max	12. 2.89	Spiels.Fabr.
67. Hohenstein-Levy	Klee	3.12.02	Ohne
68. de Hond	Sientje	21. 4.20	Fabr.Arbeiterin
69. Horwitz	Abraham	21. 4.75	Angestellter
70. Horwitz-Stahl	Fanny	26.11.78	Ohne
71. Hohenhuser	Elias	6. 7.78	Angestellter
72. "ohenhuser-Asscher	Rachel	13. 8.86	Ohne
73. Intrator-Reisinger	Kindel	25.11.75	Ohne
74. Jacobs	Adolf	26. 1.94	Kaufmann
75. Jacobs-Gordon	Margot	31.12.01	Ohne
76. Jacobs-Cohen	Esther	21.11.04	Ohne
77. Jacobsthal	Walter	4. 5.90	Betr.Leiter
78. Jacobsthal-Littauer	Betty	6. 1.92	Handarbeiterin
79. Jacoby	Max	30. 7.92	Kaufmann
80. Joseph	Fritz	10. 7.95	Angestellter
81. Joseph-Hirschfeld	Betty	23. 1.92	Angestellter
82. Kalksens	Anna	8. 4.15	Verkäuferin
83. Kamp	Joel	16. 3.86	Jurist
84. Kamp-Meijer	Lilli	12. 5.00	Schneiderin
85. Kantein-Fler...Noris	Marianne	6. 6.95	Ohne
86. Kantorowicz	Ernst	14. 9.92	Hochschullehrer
87. Kantorowicz-Prins	Margaretha	13. 9.05	Angestellter
88. Katz	Gretel	13.12.29	Ohne
89. van Kleef	Mietje	9. 6.10	Näherin
90. Koerpel	Moritz	5.12.94	Schneider
91. Koerpel-Dobrin	Paula	23. 7.03	Ohne
92. Kok ke	Kurt	5. 3.96	Kaufmann
93. Lebenstein	Josef	31. 5.86	Ohne
94. .ebenstein-Friedmann	Paula	8. 8.94	Ohne
95. .ebenstein	Guenther	9. 9.28	Ohne
96. van Leeuwen	Joseph	20. 7.60	Ohne
van Leeuwen	Max	10. 4.97	Lehrer
van Leeuwen-Leons	Therese	14. 3.07	Kontoristin
Levita	Ellen	19. 4.28	Ohne
Levita	Frank	15.11.23	Angestellter

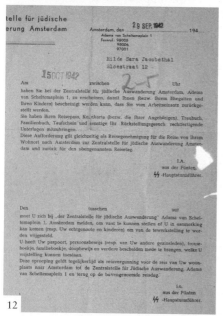

The coveted "exemption stamp"

10. Hilde, winter/spring 1943.

11. Nazi "transport" list including the names of Walter and Betty Jacobsthal. They are being sent from Bergen-Belsen to Theresienstadt, January 25, 1944.

12. Hilde's call-up notice, September 22, 1942.

13. Hilde's notice of deferral from call-up, September 25, 1942.

14. Hilde aged 19, after liberation, perhaps in early autumn 1944, after she had joined a Red Cross unit with her brother Jo. She is writing to François-Xavier Gérard, a Belgian suitor.

15. In the crèche on the Plantage Middenlaan, Amsterdam 1942 or 1943. Hilde's apron is in the background.

16. Remi van Duinwijck, the doomed foundling baby, in the crèche on the Plantage Middenlaan, Amsterdam 1943.

17. Children in the crèche, Plantage Middenlaan, Amsterdam 1942/1943.

18. Jo, *far left*, with colleagues in a Dutch medical rescue unit in what is evidently a recently vacated Nazi headquarters; on the Dutch/ Belgian border, end of 1944 or early 1945.

19. Uncle Whitehead, a British officer at Bergen-Belsen shortly after its liberation, April 1945.

20. Dutch medical rescue unit ID photo of Jo, 1944.

21. Notices at Bergen-Belsen in English and Yiddish warning of the danger of typhus carried by lice, spring or early summer 1945.

22. Grave marker at Bergen-Belsen.

23. Hilde, *top right,* in dark clothes, with nursery workers at Bergen-Belsen, probably spring/summer 1946.

24. Exercise time at Belsen day-care center, probably spring/summer 1946.

25. Hilde, *fourth from left,* with orphans at Blankenese, probably winter 1945. Helmuth, *third from left,* shows the effects of the camps in his stunted growth and uneven hair.

26. Birthday cards from Blankenese children, February 18, 1946, Hilde's twenty-first birthday.

27. Hilde in March 1946, in her American uniform, potty in hand, preparing to accompany the Blankenese children to Marseille.

28. Hilde at a British army Seder in Brussels, April 3, 1946, with the Alexander twins: Hanns (*right*) and Paul (*left*).

29. Wedding portrait of Hilde and Max, August 1947.

30. Hilde on her honeymoon in her idea of hiking gear, Arosa, Switzerland, July 1947.

31. Max, *left*, and Hilde, with (probably medical) colleagues in the Golani Brigade, Israel summer 1948.

32. Max, *center*, with fellow doctors on supposed basic training with the American army, Fort Sam Houston, Texas 1953. Note my father's dress shoes.

For this reason: _She wishes_ to use this Document in Lieu of a Passport, to travel as follows:

Countries to be visited: | Periods of visits: | Purpose:
HOLLAND | 2 PERIODS 9 DAYS | VISIT BROTHER
SWITZERLAND | 1 MONTH | VISIT
GERMANY | TRAVEL THROUGH (ROUND TRIP) |

Re-entry Permit issued on _SEPT. 23, 1951_ _____ Number _____

The affixed photograph is a true likeness of the affiant, whose personal description:

Height: 5 feet 6 inches   Age 26 years
Color of hair BROWN Eyes BROWN Complexion
MEDIUM Distinguishing marks _____

Subscribed and sworn to before me in _New York N.Y._
this _11th_ day of _December_ 19 51

_Hilda G_____ (Signature)

Hilda Goldberg L.S.
(Picture affixed of over purple frame)

On this _5th_ day of _April_ 195 _4_ before me,
officer, personally appeared _HILDA GOLDBERG_
being duly sworn did subscribe the name to the within instr
acknowledged to me that she did execute the same freely and
for the purposes therein contained and that the facts rect

_____ (Summary Court Officer)
THE NAVY DEPT.
STAFF JUDGE ADVOCATE SECTION
NAC APO 763, % FPO N.Y., N.Y.

UNITED STATES LINES
Affidavit of Identity and Nationality

State of _New York_
County of _New York_ } SS
City of _New York_

HILDA GOLDBERG (AND DAUGHTER HENRIETTA), formerly known as
JACOBSTHAL, being duly sworn states that _SHE_ resides at
STATE HOSPITAL HOWARD, R.I. Occupation: _HOUSEWIFE_
Date, place and country of birth: _FEBR. 10, 1925 BERLIN GERMANY_
Names of parents: Father: _WALTER JACOBSTHAL_ Mother: _BETTY LITTAU_
Date of entry into country of present residence: _MARCH 13, 1930_
Periods and places of residence in such country: _74 HOWARD AVE. BROOKLYN N.Y._
STATE HOSPITAL HOWARD, R.I.
Periods and places of residence in other countries: _SWITZERLAND_

Wife of husband's name: _MAX GOLDBERG_   Address: _STATE HOSP. H_
Nationality: _STATELESS_   Date and place of birth: _GRENCHEN 14 JUNE 19 2_
GRENCHEN SW.
Passport or other travel documents cannot be obtained because: _NON RENEWAL OF
EXPIRED PASSPORT_
Documentary evidence attached: _____

33

33. Part of a document authorizing Hilde to travel with me to and from the US and within Europe at a time when we were stateless but protected by my father's US green card.

COPY TO DR.GOLDBERG.

13th December,1946.

TO: Dr.William Schmidt.
A.J.D.C. PARIS.

FROM: Mr.David Wodlinger.
Belsen.

RE: DR. MAX GOLDBERG.

The above named, who is UNRRA Medical Officer at Camp Belsen, is anxious to join the A.J.D.C. He will be going to Paris shortly in order to discuss this matter with you.

Dr.Goldberg comes from Basle, Switzerland. He speaks German, French, English and Yiddish and has had good experience in the field. He expects to be terminated by UNRRA in due course and would like to continue to work among his co-religionists.

I think that after speaking with Dr.Goldberg you will come to the same conclusion that I have, namely that he would be a most desirable recruit to our programme.

D.Wodlinger.

U.F.15 (British Zone)

UNITED NATIONS
RELIEF AND REHABILITATION
ADMINISTRATION

TRAVEL AUTHORISATION

Date 10th Feb. 1947 No. UK/X/4029
Name Mr. Max GOLDBERG
Nationality Polish
Grade 10- Medical Officer
Military Entry Permit No. 80141
UNRRA Identity No. 7086
Official Station Berne, Switzerland
Unit UNRRA Team 806, Belsen

The person named herein is authorised to travel, in accordance with UNRRA regulations subject to undermentioned conditions. Date of this authority to appear on each expense sheet.

1. PURPOSE OF TRAVEL: The above named person will proceed from present station on dates indicated below for approximately 8 days for the purpose of: Annual Leave.
(If duty state duty)

2. ITINERARY: From Belsen to Basle, Switzerland
Frontier to be crossed at Basle
Vehicle No.

JOURNEY TO COMMENCE APPROX 14th Mar.1947.
CONTEMPLATED DATE OF ENTRY, STAY AND MUNRRA Team 806, Belsen
CONTEMPLATED DATE OF leaving to return

3. DURATION: Beginning 3rd Mar.
Ending on or about 9th Mar. 1947

4. PER DIEM IN LIEU OF SUBSISTENCE expenses the travel time.
Any subsistence allowance payable will be in accordance with rates laid down for respective areas. Where no specified rates have been laid down, reimbursement will be of actual expenses incurred and not exceeding £1. 15s per day.

5. OTHER CONDITIONS:
TDN. Travel authorised by Earl.
This travel has been approved by H.Q. concerned.
Documents issued in connection with journey:
Leave in Switzerland in accordance with UNRRA-Swiss Leave Programme. All expenses to be borne by Traveller.
Rations have been supplied up to: -

AUTHORISED:

To:

Approved for conformance with travel regulations.

NAME
TITLE
Funds Available

THIS SPACE FOR ACCOUNTING OFFICE

ESTIMATED COST:
Transportation
Per Diem
Incidental
Total

ACCOUNT
SYMBOL AND TITLE   NOTATIONS   AMOUNT

On completion of journey this order will be returned to office of issue.

34

34. *Top*, letter of recommendation for Max when he was trying to get a new job after his stint with UNRRA at Bergen-Belsen, December 1946.
Bottom, Max's travel authorization from UNRRA for his first visit to Switzerland with Hilde, February 1947.

35. M. Dupuis with me on the banks of the Meuse, Lustin, Belgium, probably spring 1953.

36. Jo and Zus Scholte, Amsterdam, mid-1950s.

37. A merry Mme Dupuis and Hilde, with Max in the background, on one of our visits to Belgium, probably 1953.

38. Susie, *left*, with me, Frankfurt, Germany, probably 1954.

SCHWEIZERISCHE
EIDGENOSSENSCHAFT

446   Nr. E.F.P. 16021

EINREISEVISUM
tig zum ...-maligen Grenzübertritt
die Schweiz bis 31. Juli. 1953

auer des Aufenthaltes: ...
... Basel, 3-18. Juli 1953
ufenthaltsort: Basel
weck: Besuch

ebühr Fr. 5.- (fr. 4. 50
r das Schweiz. Konsulat in Amsterdam
en 30 JUNI 1953   19...

Anmeldung 24 Juli 1953
Aufenthalt bewilligt
bis 18. August 1953
Kontrollbureau Basel-Stadt
Kantonale Fremdenpolizei
31.10.50

Affidavit of

Identity and Nationality

To Serve in
Lieu of Passport

U. S. DEPT OF JUSTICE
APR 5 1955
ADMITTED
NEW YORK N.Y.

Name

Address

UNITED STATES LINES

BUNDESREPUBLIK DEUTSCHLAND
1014
31.07.53
EINREISE
PASSKONTROLLE

1016
15.07.53
EINREISE
PASSKONTROLLE

1038
-9.08.53
EINREISE
PASSKONTROLLE

28.02

Nr.: 33935   Gebühr
Einreisesichtvermerk
für H. GOLDBERG
(Name des Inhabers)

für mehrere Einreisen in die Bundesrepublik Deutschland
(einschl. des Gebietes des Landes Berlin)

bis zum 31. DEZ. 1953
über jede für den großen Reiseverkehr zugelassene deutsche
Grenzübergangsstelle — über die Grenzübergangsstelle(n)

Der Inhaber dieses Sichtvermerks bedarf für den Aufenthalt in der Bundesrepublik einer besonderen Erlaubnis,
wenn er sich als Arbeitnehmer, Gewerbetreibender oder
Betriebsführer betätigen will oder wenn er sich sonst länger
als 3 Monate im Bundesgebiet aufhalten will.

Amsterdam, den 1. JUL 1953 195

Generalkonsulat der
Bundesrepublik Deutschland
Paßstelle
im Auftrag

(Unterschrift)

DER BUNDES
GEBÜHREN
GRATIS
PASS-STELLE

BUNDESREPUBLIK DEUTSCHLAND
1014
AUSREISE
-5.07.53
PASSKONTROLLE

9.02.58

Gültig für Hilde Goldberg
zur einmaligen Ausreise und Wiedereinreise in die Schweiz
in der Zeit vom 31.7.53 bis 3.8.53
Basel, den 29. Juli 1953   Kontrollbureau
Kantonale Fremdenpolizei

SCHWEIZ
E-2 AUG
BASEL

POLIZEIDEPARTEMENT
BASEL-STADT
KONTROLL

AUSREISE
-7.07.53
PASSKONTROLLE

Abmeldung -7. Aug. 195
nach Stuttgart
Kontrollbureau Basel-Stadt
Kantonale Fremdenpolizei

Visas

39

39. Another page of Hilde's postwar "crazy quilt of a document" with which she traveled
from and to the US and in Europe in the early to mid-1950s.

READING TOGETHER — Mrs. Hilda Goldberg and her daughter, Dottie, catch up on Mickey Mouse in the Goldberg home at 961 Wilson Avenue, Teaneck. (Staff photo.)

From Belsen Nazi Death Camp, She Comes To Day-Care Center

Former Underground Nurse Has Wide Experience With Children

By PETER BERNSTEIN
(Staff Writer)

Hackensack — A World War II partisan nurse who became a foster mother to the children in Bergen-Belsen Concentration Camp is now taking a leading role in the establishment of the Hackensack Day Care Center.

Mrs. Hilda Goldberg, a Teaneck resident, whose teen-age years were spent in the Dutch and Belgian underground and whose 20th year began as a nurse who sifted the living from among the stench of Bergen-Belsen's dead, is anxiously awaiting the Day Care Center's opening late in January.

The Center, located in a public housing project at the corner of Central Avenue and First Street, is the first State-supported project of its kind. With additional aid from the Hackensack Housing Authority, and the Federal Bureau of Children Services, the Center is being cosponsored by the Teaneck section of the National Council of Jewish Women and the Bergen County Chapter of the National Council of Negro Women.

Mrs. Goldberg is responsible for selecting and hiring the professional staff who will man the Center on weekdays from 8 A.M. to 4 P. M. She said the Center will enable mothers, many of whom would otherwise be on welfare, to leave their homes and take full-time work. Likewise, many of the children to be cared for would previously have been sent to foster homes.

HAS THREE GIRLS

Hilda Goldberg has done all that is possible to survive the nightmare of having seen chil-

The 60,000 bodies that the Red Cross found at the camp were to be a horrid reminder of the war. Among them were some of Hilda Goldberg's closest childhood friends — Margo and Anne Frank. Anne, the younger of the two sisters whose diary was preserved, died 10 days before her friend entered the camp.

MOUNDS OF BODIES

Mrs. Goldberg, who has three children attending Teaneck schools, recalls searching for her parents through the mounds of bodies that lay scattered inside and outside the death-camp dormitories.

She had had memories of a happy childhood in Amsterdam. In the winter, when the canal outside her parents' apartment at Sloesstraat turned to ice, she would skate across the city to the home of Anne and Margo Frank, whose father, Otto, had recently founded a liberal synagogue, where the youngsters would often meet at night.

During after-school hours, Hilda Goldberg, whose maiden name was Jacobstahl, wrote children's stories which she sold to the local Amsterdam newspaper. With these funds she bought a canoe and traveled through the City's canals during the spring and summer months, explaining neighborhood that she had never known

old when the Nazis began their arrests and deportations. It was then that she volunteered as a nurse in a day-care center established by Dutch partisans to house the children of deported adults.

Eventually, 2 days after she herself was sent into hiding, her parents were arrested and deported.

V-2 ROCKETS

During the next 4 years, Mrs. Goldberg miraculously escaped the Nazi net, posing first as a kitchen maid in Belgium with false papers, then as a Catholic nursemaid in France. When she was 19, she joined the Belgian partisan army as a nurse, and later served as an ambulance driver in Antwerp during the days and nights when the Belgian city was being bombarded by German V-2 rockets.

Toward the close of the war, Mrs. Goldberg joined the British Red Cross and with it moved through German-held territory toward Bergen-Belsen.

"Among the survivors were about 80 Jewish and Gypsy children. The 9-year-olds looked like 3-year-olds. They had no trust at all in adults and some of them had bodies so thin that their tongues showed through the holes in their cheeks," she said.

AIDED BY DOCTOR

Together with a young Swiss doctor (Dr. Max Goldberg, who later became her husband), the 20-year-old nurse established a hospital for the children.

"I became tied to them, and for 4 months, day and night, I never left them. It was vital for us to give the children confidence in adults."

Mrs. Goldberg later founded a day-care center in Marseilles, from which many of the chil-

40

---

40. Hilde with Dot, 1964. The article is from a local paper, *The Bergen Evening Record*, published in northern New Jersey.

—Journal-Bulletin

Otto Frank–Guide for a Diary

By LUCILLE ELFENBEIN

Outside of the diary of Anne Frank, very little has appeared in print about her father, Otto Frank. Yet Anne Frank died more than a dozen years ago at Belsen at the age of 15.

Otto Frank today is a mature and handsome man, who has built firmly a new life for himself, with enriched ideals, and an ever widening scope.

He is a modest man. Although it was he who found the remarkable diary when he returned to Amsterdam from the concentration camp at Auschwitz, he has avoided the limelight with remarkable success.

Altering his habit of avoiding reporters, the other day he consented to his first interview with any American reporter.

He was here on a visit from his new home in Basle, Switzerland, with his second wife, Fritzi. They were the house guests of Dr. and Mrs. Max Goldberg. Mrs. Goldberg was a contemporary in Amsterdam of the daughters of Otto Frank.

Dr. Goldberg is the clinical director at the State Institutions at Howard. The family resides in Cottage 2, a roomy comfortable brick two-story dwelling located on the north end of the grounds.

The cottage living room made a good setting for Otto Frank and his wife. Mrs. Frank is a pretty, fresh-looking middle aged brunette who dressed sensibly in a dark suit, white blouse, and low European suede walking shoes. Everyone and everything in the room seemed endowed with warmth and serenity.

Tall and white haired, 68-year-old Otto Frank has bright brown eyes that are at once sharp and soft. A glowing pinkness underlies his complexion, and a slight smile is at home upon his face.

He was dressed in a dark woven worsted suit, cut loosely from his broad shoulders, a white shirt, red tie, snug grey woolen socks and sturdy highly polished shoes that indicate a man who enjoys walking. He speaks English with just the barest undertone of a German accent.

In manner, coloring and style he seems exactly like Joseph Schildkraut's interpretation of Otto Frank in the Pulitzer Prize winning Broadway version of "The Diary of Anne Frank."

Otto Frank however cannot appreciate this fact. He has never seen any version of the play although it has played in 19 languages in 95 countries. It has been presented by both amateur and professional groups in places as varied as Japan and Argentina.

Despite the fact that he has been typecast by life in the role of himself, a wise, kindly,

Continued on Page 3, Col. 1

Frank

42

Salt Lake City—(AP)—A figure of a frontiersman at the base of a Brigham Young statue in downtown Salt Lake City got an extra

heard from yesterday almost two and a half hours after taking off from Hickam. The plane gave its position as 385 miles southwest of Oahu. It carried only enough fuel to stay aloft

Nassau Losing
$112,000 a Day

41. Article from the the *Evening Bulletin*, Providence, Rhode Island, January 20 1958.

42. *Inset:* Family photo on the same occasion, *l to r:* Hilde, Otto and Fritzi Frank, with Susie, *right*, and me on the hassock.

43 Jo and Hilde on Hilde's 70th birthday in 1995. He was a surprise guest.

44. The family gathered in the VIP suite of the New York Hilton in celebration of my parents' 60th wedding anniversary in 2007. *Seated:* Hilde, Max.
   Front row, l to r: Ellen, Gabriel and Daniel Hart, Benjamin Hart, Rebecca Ross Russell, Edward Brubaker. *Second row, l to r:* Oliver Hart, Melanie Brubaker, Rita Goldberg, Susie Goldberg Brubaker, David Ross Russell, Adam Ross Russell.
   Back row on staircase, l to r: Dorothy Goldberg (Ross Russell), Michael Brubaker, Heather Brubaker.

Chapter 6

Bergen-Belsen, April 1945

THE STORY OF my family, like many stories in modern America, is about the formation of identity by the volcanic pressures of war and emigration. For our dead and for our survivors, the period before we arrived in America was a trial by fire, and for me, still enough of a presence to qualify as a haunting. But for our children, the fires of the past have started to smolder, though occasionally their eyes still tear from the smoke. The great-grandparents who were thrown, like Shadrach, Meshach and Abednego, into the fiery furnace of Auschwitz, and were not redeemed to walk unscathed another day, have become legendary and remote. They simply perished like so many millions of others; no miracles for them. Our sons talk of them with awe because they lived and died in a time of incomprehensible violence. Though the war seems almost biblical to them in its distance, they share our emotional inheritance in their sense that our good fortune is also our diminution. How could we have come to such a pass, generations after the event? It taints our gratitude, our freedom, this It, this massive cruelty retreating at the edge of memory, like a mountain borne away by a glacier. The events of September 11, 2001, it's true, have intruded on our warm sense of survival, and have returned to us the resurrected doomsday instincts of our ancestors. Time is not always so glacial, nor is the fiery furnace so far from us. Perhaps memory will help to steer us after all through the extremes of suffering and forgetting.

In April 1945, the revelations still lay ahead, or were just coming to light. Hilde rode in the front seat of an ambulance as part of a military convoy for three days and nights, her head lolling on her shoulder, or on the driver's, during fitful periods of sleep. They must have stopped to sleep, she says, but she doesn't remember. The rigors of the journey, the emotional demands of it and the dread of what lay ahead, dazed her. The convoy crossed the famous bridge at Remagen, twenty miles northwest of Coblenz, where the Rhine had first been breached by American troops on March 7. The countryside near the border with Belgium was blasted and devastated where bombs, mines and battles had done their work, but soon they were in the blooming fields of mid-spring, and the landscape was tranquil, no mark of war on it anywhere. Later, my mother would look back on that first sight of an untouched Germany and wonder if the farmers and townspeople really hadn't known what was going on, despite their active involvement in other ways, with all their men at the front. They were in the grip of an evil idea, and had, at the least, countenanced persecution, violence and theft. Did it matter, at that point, whether they knew about the camps or not?

Slowly, Hilde made her own journey into the heart of darkness. First the procession of ambulances and trucks moved through the Rhineland, where the front line had been only weeks before. Now the front lay directly ahead, and the medical people followed in its wake. They were traveling up to Belsen on an indirect route, moving southeast rather than northeast from

Antwerp. Hilde had plenty of time to think. I imagine, too, that the sheer physical discomfort of the journey, and the enforced leisure, must have had a hypnotic effect on her, very different from the two years of overwork she had just passed through. "We sleep in the ambulance. We drive through clouds of dust," she wrote in her little book. She began to ask herself questions as she encountered the nation she had hated and fought so long. She saw German soldiers, starved and scared, emerge from wooded areas as the convoy passed through, to turn themselves over to the Allies. She wondered whether she might like to try shooting one or two, but she never came close. Killing wasn't in her. She wondered where her parents were, and whether they could possibly have survived; but at that point she had not yet encountered the dark center of the Nazi death-system, and didn't know how massively the odds were stacked against the tiny engine of her hope.

These were strange, even hallucinatory days. The area between the front and the Belgian border was a sort of no-man's-land, neither defended by German soldiers, who had surrendered, retreated or fled, nor yet occupied by the Allies. The medical convoy had an escort of tanks and armored cars for protection, but there was no need to do battle. The ground battles had occurred on the western borders, an area Hitler and his generals liked to refer to as the Western Wall, and around some of the big cities. But here in the rural heartland of Germany, nothing but an unearthly quiet.

Bergen-Belsen lay in an area of northwestern Germany known as the Lüneburger Heide. It is heathland, a rolling landscape full of heather and juniper and stands of pine and birch, the ghostly silver birches the inmates sometimes mentioned; it was a beauty spot before the war, and has become one again, the kind of place where you can take your children for a picnic, if the weather is neither too cold nor too hot. The straight-trunked trees don't offer much shelter from the elements. The heath made a convenient Sunday excursion for the citizens of Hanover and Celle, the cities nearby, because it was close. It was on this heath, near the village of Bergen, that the camp was constructed. My father, who was quartered in the picturesque inn there when he arrived at the camp a year after the Liberation, says that from the dining room windows he could see the ramp where the trains had delivered their prisoners. The stench over Bergen and over the outlying suburbs of Celle, whose town center was only twelve miles away, must have been overwhelming.

I imagine all this as I imagine the convoy finally approaching Bergen-Belsen on the third day. This is also my journey into darkness, my way into my own future, but imagination is my only guide, and secondhand images stand in for memories. The trip frightens me, but my mother, who is telling me today about her first impressions of Belsen, has never admitted to fright, only to a sense of dislocation, of distance and inadequacy. She begins gamely enough, telling the old grim tale. Her tone is usually calm, even when she talks about the most difficult days of the war. But then suddenly she says, in the same matter-of-fact voice, that she'd like to stop now. Something is happening to her inside, and she knows that we have talked enough for one day. I apologize to her again for putting her through this torment, and she apologizes to me when I say that I find it hard, too, to explore these things; and I get mock-angry at her for her apology.

This little ritual has become a kind of competition between us over the nature of our experience. It's one of the things that makes my sister Susie so angry. She doesn't like the emotional uncertainties of the history we have inherited. It feels to us at times as if my mother's story has manipulated us, ensuring that we can never do as much with our lives as she has done with hers. But how can we blame her for what history has made of us? Oddly enough, her suffering has given her a kind of invulnerability to argument and anger. Certainly, we know, we can never win on this territory, and we are ashamed that we have such feelings at all. In a way, we have never been allowed to have them. Reverence, admiration, compassion, these must always come first. Even as adolescents, we had to live up to the myth we inherited. Our teenaged obnoxiousness and egoism were measured against our grandparents' martyrdom, on the one hand, and our parents' exceptional courage, on the other. The routinely awful behavior of teenagers in peacetime was silently compared to that sublime standard, and of course we failed abjectly, again and again, to live up to it. The trouble was that we had swallowed these comparisons along with the stories we heard from earliest childhood, and they were inside us. It took us a long time to realize that our mother herself was a survivor, and that her own feelings of guilt had taken the form of active, energetic engagement in the business of healing the sick. But the road of action, the epic road to self-acceptance, was not open to us. We were driven back upon ourselves, or rather into ourselves. We could not bring the near-dead back to life, as she had done.

So this history is painful for my mother and for me, though in different ways. I find myself traveling with her because I must; I have no choice in the matter. I began that journey, through her telling of it, from the earliest moment when language became coherent for me. I don't even know which language the tale was told in first, probably German, perhaps English, but I can't be sure. As she travels back, in her mind, to the shock of discovery, I travel to find if I can unlock the prisoners held in my imagination, restore their voices, and free myself to make new things out of the shards of the past. For both of us, this retelling, this conversation with each other and with our shared past, is our journey to the underworld. We hope that our passage through this heathland of death will restore us to the living world, but it's risky. We know that such metaphors did not help the dead of Belsen.

My mother tells me that signs began appearing about ten miles out. My guess is that they were not quite that far away from the camp, and other witnesses have written that the signs were posted on a perimeter about three miles from Belsen. They featured a skull and crossbones, and warned passersby not to proceed on that road. *Achtung! Attention! Do not proceed! Typhus!* they said. These signs had been put up by the Nazi authorities as part of their agreement with the British for the peaceful takeover of the area. They are mentioned in a number of memoirs by medical and British army personnel. But the signs did not prepare the voyagers for the stench. It was the smell of the dead. Although the British had entered the week before, there were still thirteen thousand unburied bodies in the camp. The needs of those still living were too urgent, the demands of the situation too great, for even an army to find a way to organize the rescue.

Thirteen thousand bodies – that such figures can be written down makes them seem manageable, somehow. Thirteen thousand bodies don't seem so many, compared to the tens of millions of lives lost in those years. Eichmann, in his trial at Jerusalem, describes his horror at seeing blood bubbling up from the ground after one of the mass shootings he had ordered somewhere in the East. Perhaps just as many people were shot in a weekend in one of the forests of Poland or gorges of Ukraine. But thirteen thousand bodies at Belsen, among nearly sixty thousand still barely alive, meant bodies everywhere, draped in every grotesquery of death, stacked six deep as if by some distracted Polyphemus for cordwood or storage, bodies squatting at stool, bodies begging by the roadside, bodies asleep, their arms around a living bunkmate, bodies underfoot, carpeting the dirt floors of the huts, bodies pulsing with a life no longer their own of maggots and lice and bedbugs. One week before the British arrived, there had been sixty thousand prisoners in the camp, and more than thirty thousand others had died in the previous two months. Within the barbed wire of that barren, treeless space, between the barracks and the cemeteries, in an area less than a mile wide and half a mile deep, a population the size of a large town, the size, say, of Newton, Massachusetts, hovered on the edge of death or crossed over. Perhaps we can better understand the thirteen thousand dead who happened to be lying around unburied on the day of Liberation by understanding the magnitude of their company, the legions underground or dissolved into ash.

Then came my mother's note in her little book for April 21: "Arrival Belsen. Horror camp." I ask her if she can remember exactly what the first moments were like. She describes the way the daze of long and arduous travel was replaced by the daze of shock. As the convoy approached the camp, she saw skeletal creatures in striped pajamas, or naked, wrapped in blankets. They were the strongest inmates, but they, too, were dazed, dazed by hunger and privation and by the sudden recognition that they might survive the war after all. They stood in small groups, watching the convoy arrive with a blank, incurious expression that Hilde came to associate with the long misery of existence in such a place. We who come after have seen it countless times on our television screens, beamed by satellite from Ethiopia and Cambodia, Bangladesh and Ruanda, Bosnia, Liberia, Congo, Sudan. But these abject creatures had once been active and enthusiastic citizens of a mostly urban world. It was not deprivation that had brought them to this predicament. The most modern methods of operations research and technology management had deposited them amid the dirt and puddles of Belsen, only yards from the cozy inn of the quaint village of Bergen.

The group was taken directly to the former SS barracks, just inside the perimeter of the camp. My mother thinks that she and her colleagues might have been housed in tents for a night or two. She remembers a central bathroom with showers, tubs, and hot water. Later on, they had rooms in stone barracks that had private bathrooms and had housed German officers, she thinks. They were given dinner, and then, at last, they stretched out for a proper sleep. Perhaps physical exhaustion had been part of the Army's program. It was not easy otherwise to come upon Belsen and resume the normal routines of life.

The British authorities were careful of the physical and mental health of their staff, as Hilde found when she reported the next morning for a briefing and the first day of work. The newcomers were inoculated against the diseases they were likely to encounter. In addition to the routine dusting from head to toe with DDT powder every day, to protect them from the camp's ubiquitous lice, each nurse, doctor and orderly was required to drink half an ounce of rum under the supervision of a staff sergeant. The rum was part of the British Army's ration for troops serving under unusually trying conditions. For the most part, my mother says, it was gratefully received and often supplemented during those difficult days.

The staff worked, at first, for two-hour periods, interrupted by coffee and tea breaks. The breaks were ordered by Colonel Whitehead, whose name was particularly well-suited to his snowy hair and handlebar mustache. There was some doubt as to whether he was really a colonel, but he was universally beloved and known as Uncle Whitehead, because he was the oldest person there. He was in his fifties, my mother thinks. Later on, he helped my mother begin a sort of post office through which survivors could find each other as they wandered across Europe in the years after the war.

All of the British Red Cross nurses who arrived with Hilde were assigned work at the German hospital, later renamed after

Glyn Hughes, the general who oversaw the rescue operations. This had been a well-equipped modern hospital, located at a military base about a half-mile from the camp. The British had requisitioned it immediately, and it was in the process of being transformed into a center for the treatment of patients who required more than palliative care or simple nutrition. But at this point, a week after Liberation, inmates were still dying at the incredible rate of 400–1000 a day. The first job, for Hilde and other workers at what was called the Horror Camp or Camp 1 – the heart of Bergen-Belsen, where Jewish prisoners had been left to die through neglect and brutality – was to sort out the living from the dead. After that, the living corpses, as most of them were, were cleaned up and transported to proper beds. All this was organized within a matter of a week or two by the British forces.

The condition of the camp and its reorganization was dramatically described by Robert Collis, a Red Cross pediatrician with a flair for words, in the *British Medical Journal* of June 9, 1945 (two years later, together with his future wife, he co-wrote a book called *Straight On* about his experiences at Belsen). He began his report with notes scrawled not by him but by the chief medical officer, Lieutenant-Colonel J.A.D. Johnston, on April 17, four days before Hilde arrived. These notes were later modified to become part of Johnston's deposition during the Belsen trials in September:

> The camp is separated into two distinct portions – Camps 1 and 2. Camp 1 is a hutted encampment housing approximately 22,000 females and 18,000 males. Camp 2 consists of a series of brick buildings and houses approximately 27,000 males. The inhabitants of these camps are of mixed nationalities, with Russians and Poles predominating. Czechs, Belgians, French, and Italians are also present.

...Camp 1. – A dense mass of emaciated apathetic scarecrows huddled together in wooden huts without beds or blankets in many cases, without any clothing whatsoever in some cases. The females in worse condition than the men, their clothing generally, if they have any, only filthy rags. The dead lie all over the camp and in piles outside the blocks of huts which house the worst of the sick and are miscalled hospitals. Approximately 3000 naked and emaciated corpses in various stages of decomposition are lying about in this camp. Sanitation is non-existent. Pits, with, in only a few instances, wooden perch rails are available in totally inadequate numbers, but the majority of inmates, from starvation, apathy, and weakness, defaecate and urinate where they sit or lie, even inside the living huts. There is no running water or electricity. All water is being brought in by our water trucks.

Collis went on to say that things were much worse than this first impression suggested. Inmates were dying by the hundreds every day from disease and starvation alone. Guards murdered many more until the hour the British arrived and for some days afterward, according to *Belsen Uncovered*, a memoir written in 1946 by Derek Sington, one of the first British officers to enter the camp. On that day, April 15, the inmates had had no water for a week. There were many more corpses than had at first been thought.

There are variations even now in the estimates of how many living and dead the camp contained in the weeks just before and just after Liberation. There were simply too many bodies, and too much confusion among the living, to keep track. Unlike the Nazis, the British and other rescue personnel seemed to float in a state of permanent shock. They were capable of hard work, and, I suspect, fell into the colonial reflexes they knew so well when confronted with a massive organizational task; but I cannot imagine that they were as interested as the Germans had been in recording the exact numbers of living and dead.

Hilde had asked to be sent straight into the Horror Camp – again, the part that housed the Jewish prisoners, and where disease and death had claimed most lives –because she wanted to look for her parents. This wish was granted not only because her superiors respected her reasons, but because Hilde's facility in languages was useful to them. The English-speaking rescuers could not communicate with the people they were trying to help; this comes out in memoirs of the period. Thus Hilde, who was the youngest member of the rescue team as well as its only non-British member, found herself working with regular British soldiers, Hungarian guards impressed into service by the occupiers, and doctors detailed for this most gruesome task of sorting the living from the dead. She was certainly the only woman from her unit to be "allowed" into the Horror Camp, and perhaps the only woman rescuer from any group, in those first few weeks. Recent research by Joanne Reilly on the liberation suggests that the British command thought the camp too upsetting for the nurses and other women working there, despite the fact that they were seasoned veterans of the Normandy invasion.

Hilde turned bodies over, trying to recognize familiar features. Each time, she wondered whether she would discover her parents. The faces of these thousands of strangers were so distorted by fleshlessness and pain that at times she couldn't reconstruct a human personality from them, and, almost more than finding her parents there, she feared that she wouldn't be able to recognize them if she did. She says that she wasn't repelled by what she saw: the feces and urine, six inches deep in places, in which people lay, and which encrusted the bodies of the living and the dead; the sores thick with lice, and swellings that oozed pus at a touch. She says that it was the skull-like faces that haunted her, and the fear that she would break the poor arms and legs she held. Often a feeble groan issued from a pile of bodies about to be removed. Other witnesses have reported occasions when one of the corpses clapped its hands just enough to be heard. Hilde and the other staff ran to unstack the living person from the corpses on top and below. If the dead were inside, in the huts, they were piled on boards, three or four to a bunk, three bunks high, as we who come after have seen in photograph after photograph: it was the standard Nazi architecture of misery for Jews. In many of the huts, there were not even bunks. Seven or eight thousand people had been crammed into sheds with no doors or windows, and bare floors strewn with straw. The newly dead lay in heaps on the dirt floor of the huts, or outside, where they had crawled in search of water.

The British filmed some of the cleanup in the first days after Liberation. Sometimes the films are shown on television, to commemorate an anniversary day of one sort or another. There they are, the SS and Hungarian guards who are now prisoners of the British, carrying one corpse at a time to the mass graves for burial. The skeletal arms flop sickeningly as the guards hoist them on one shoulder; the stains of their last agony darken the corpses' pelvises, now all bone, the hips jutting out as if the skin itself were a last attempt at modesty. Yet, for the cameras, they are carried carefully and laid down carefully upon the thousands of dead who preceded them into the huge pits. This care was expressly ordered by Lt.-Col. James Johnston, the officer in charge of the cleaning and rehabilitation of the camp, and his disgust at what he saw translated into standards of humane tenderness that were difficult to adhere to. Inmates reported the unceremonious way the now-imprisoned Nazi guards handled the corpses, unless they were constantly admonished.

Some of this care was factitious, since trucks and bulldozers were soon impressed into service to hasten the overwhelming task. Quickly enough, the bodies were thrown into the pits, and bulldozers were used, not only to dig the graves, but to push the heaps of bodies in; though in fairness eyewitnesses testify that the bulldozing occurred only twice, when the bodies were in too advanced a state of decomposition to be handled in the usual way. The ordinary British soldiers assigned to such tasks suffered doing them, as accounts at the Imperial War Museum permanent exhibit in London make clear. Before each pit was filled in, a team of British army chaplains, including rabbis, priests and ministers, said prayers for the dead. One of them, Leslie Hardman, a British rabbi who went into Bergen-Belsen the day after liberation, describes how he pleaded with the soldiers to take care with the bodies at first:

> The bulldozer had been at work again, and at the far end of the camp another mass grave had been dug to contain 5000 bodies, and five or six graves to contain a thousand bodies each. Again I pleaded for reverence, and the bodies for the smaller mass graves were taken to the edge on lorries; then the SS were made to take them down one by one, and lay them side by side in their last resting place.

My mother testifies to the extreme gentleness with which the living were handled. And the guards, who continued to shoot prisoners for some days after the Liberation, as if they had forgotten what civilized behavior looked like, were severely punished if their work with the dead did not conform to the code. If they contracted typhus from the lice on the bodies they carried, they were treated as they had treated their prisoners; the requisitioned German Hospital was no longer open to them. Several were shot, to the applause of watching inmates, when they tried to escape the burial teams.

During the first week or two of her work at Belsen, Hilde tried to find out the fate of her parents and of friends and neighbors from Amsterdam. She soon learned that whatever had happened to her parents had not happened here, though indeed, she discovered later, they had spent some time at Bergen-Belsen. She saw one Dutch woman who had been a neighbor in South Amsterdam. The woman was lying on the floor of a hut, delirious with typhus. Somehow she recognized my mother, despite her high temperature and the unexpectedness of the encounter. "Hilde, your parents are dead, your parents are dead!" she shrieked. My mother ran out, never to return. She cannot remember the woman's name, nor did she go back to help her. That moment is one of several that fill her with unresolvable guilt. My mother will never know whether the woman lived or died in the end. She was unable to tolerate what the woman said, and could not decide, at the time, whether she was simply raving, or knew the truth.

When she asked about other Dutch Jews, the women inmates pointed her toward a hut they called the Dutch Children's Barrack. There, Hilde learned from the desperately ill young women on adjacent bunks that Margot and Anne Frank had never gone to Switzerland, but had been arrested in their hiding place in August 1944. They had died at Bergen-Belsen the month before, only weeks before the camp was liberated. In that month, March of 1945, over eighteen thousand people perished. The monthly death rate was by far the highest of the war until April approached or surpassed it, despite the best efforts of the relief workers. The young women in the barrack told Hilde about the deaths of the sisters in as much detail as they could remember. They told her how Margot, almost unconscious with typhus, had fallen out of an upper bunk and died; and how Anne, through the fog of her own high fever, had sensed what had happened, and had given up hope. She did not know that her beloved father,

Otto, had already been liberated by the Russians at Auschwitz on January 27, 1945, and was searching for her.

The Dutch girls told Hilde all about the early days of the Franks' arrival the previous October: how the girls had been torn away from their mother, who had remained behind at Auschwitz-Birkenau; how they had been housed in tents on an exposed, open part of the heath; how the first storm had knocked the tents over, and how they and other Dutch girls had wandered through the night, drenched and freezing, wrapped in a single blanket quivering with lice. They told Hilde that even under these hellish conditions, Anne was so repelled by the lice crawling in her hair and in every crevice of her skin that, in the wintry weeks before her death, she threw away her clothes, preferring the single flat surface of her blanket to the seams and wrinkles that harbored insects. They told about her growing depression, and about conversations they had had. Hilde was overwhelmed by the way the Dutch girls had held onto their humanity and their kindness. Anne and Margot were still individuals for them. The group still protected its members.

Decades later, these women appeared in a television documentary and then, in 1995, in a film by Jon Blair, *Anne Frank Remembered*, which eventually won an Academy Award. My mother and I watched the television version at the same time, though separated by hundreds of miles. I called her during a break at one point, and she answered, her voice heavy with tears. She was gasping, sobbing in great breaths. "I recognize so many of them. Aren't they amazing?" she said. I agreed through my own tears that they were amazing. They had grace, stoicism, dignity, warmth, even humor, when they could so easily have turned their backs on the nightmare of their adolescence. One woman, Janny Brandes, round-faced and solid, told the story I had heard from my mother with a mixture of composure and deep feeling which gave me absolute confidence in the accuracy of what she said. She described the stormy night on the heath with a kind of Dutch drollery that made the girls, starved and bald-headed, sound almost cuddly as they trudged in the darkness shawled in their blankets. Her loving tone as she painted the scene of horror made it all the more affecting. But when she tried to describe the scenes of cannibalism that she had witnessed at around the time of the sisters' deaths, her voice failed her. She tried once; she tried twice; her mouth opened and closed on silence; she looked down at her lap and swallowed hard.

It took three weeks to empty the Horror Camp and bury the dead, over thirty thousand people by the time the death rates had slowed. The huts were burned one by one as they were emptied. On May 21, a ceremony was held to mark the burning of the last of the barracks. My mother has pictures of the occasion, which the entire camp attended, inmates and relief workers alike. Colonel Bird, the commanding officer, made a short speech before the flame-throwing tanks began their work. The speech was recorded by Rabbi Hardman:

> We are now going to burn Camp No. 1. Let it be a symbol, and a beginning of the effacement from this world of evil such as has been perpetrated here. These terrible things must never happen again.
> When this camp is burnt down, the British flag will fly over it – the British flag does not fly over brutality, disease, and murder, and that is why we have not yet raised it here. But after this camp is burned you will see the British flag, and you will know these horrors are over.

Rabbi Helfgott, a former prisoner, said the final prayers for those who had died in that place. Then it was razed to the ground. In the photographs the flames leap high above the heads of the spectators.

*

During and after the destruction of the Horror Camp, the staff turned its full attention to the rehabilitation of the survivors. This had been no easy task, for most of the medical people had never seen the diseases prevalent at the camp, and had not known how to treat them at first. Many inmates had died in the first week or two, trying to eat the rations that well-meaning British soldiers gave them. My mother remembers soldiers handing out boiled potatoes, for example, which acted violently on the inflamed and sometimes raw linings of starved stomachs and intestines. The food was too rich or too hard to digest, and the shock to the feeble bodies of the newly liberated often killed them. The starving inmates fought over every scrap of food for the first few days, and they rejected a concoction a British expert had developed for famines in India, a nutritious but unpalatable paste called Bengal Mixture. Such problems persisted only at first. After a couple of weeks, it became clear that the real problem was the lack of calories the British allocated to each inmate; the official food supply had to be augmented by other means, and a flourishing black market developed.

In the initial weeks, even the operation of cleaning the prisoners in an area that became known as the Human Laundry carried off many of the weakest, though it was a necessary process humanely carried out. My mother describes how patients were laid on tables, gently washed from head to toe and the dead skin scraped from their filthy feet and other parts of their bodies where dirt was too encrusted to be removed with soap, or where scabies and other skin infections required more than washing. Then they were dusted with DDT powder and put to bed. Hilde supervised nurses brought in from regular German hospitals, since the British were perpetually shorthanded for the mammoth task of burying the dead and rescuing the living. The German nurses professed to be shocked by what they saw and to have no prior knowledge of it, but my mother caught them treating the patients roughly just the same. She shouted at them with all the fury that was in her. She thought of the gun that she had in her room, but still could not imagine using it. It was better, she says, to think of the nurses as robots whom she could command at will. She hated to think of them touching those brutalized Jewish bodies, she said, and often the patients flinched and screamed; they expected only torture and death from Germans. A number of medical students later described the hysteria aroused by the sight of hypodermics, needles and intravenous gear, because at Belsen people had been injected with benzene and observed as they languished in their death agonies. But Hilde, young, fresh and Jewish, gave the patients confidence that they could submit themselves safely. They believed her, and let German hands perform the ironies of healing.

The first relief personnel to arrive were bewildered by the nature of typhus, another disease that had disappeared in Britain and America after World War I. They didn't understand, at first, that delirium was part of the illness at its crisis; that the people running, shouting and sobbing their way through the camp were not permanently deranged, but in the grip of high fever. Many, of course, dropped in their tracks as they ran, but later they were kept cool and restrained, and many more survived the crisis and quickly recovered. Scurvy, pellagra and the other signs of severe malnutrition were not well-understood at first, either. For the doctors, nurses and orderlies of Belsen, it was as if a time machine had suddenly deposited them in Germany at the time of the Black Death. But this disaster was created entirely by human ingenuity, and fed by hatred. It was unprecedented in the world. The beleaguered rescuers felt this, and were changed permanently by that knowledge.

These first rescuers, softened by shock and by the brutal pace of the first few weeks, were soon replaced by the bureaucracy of the regular British army. Robert Collis, the pediatrician, writes that a wag called this new order "the Colonel Period." Lt.-Col. Johnston had been universally beloved for his humane treatment of the inmates during the heroically efficient rescue effort he superintended. After a few weeks, he was replaced by an almost comical succession of career officers who saw Belsen as a problem in logistics. They thought of the former prisoners as prisoners still, or as an exceptionally unruly lot of colonials, and they were more concerned with enforcing the dozens of rules they imposed and with obeying the dictates of the Foreign Office in London than with the rehabilitation of broken human lives. Indeed, a certain number were anti-Semitic. Hardman tells of overhearing someone among new arrivals in the officers' mess say "Bloody Jews, it's good for them." Other organizations arrived, too: UNRRA (the United Nations Relief and Rehabilitation Agency), for one, which eventually brought my father to the camp; and Jewish organizations like ORT (the Organization for Rehabilitation through Training) and the American Joint Field Service, which my mother joined when her British Red Cross unit disbanded. The Jewish workers, who were still in a tiny minority, had a very different attitude toward the camp from the British career officers, and the inmates themselves quickly began to protest the treatment they received from an often misguided British administration.

In many ways, real Jewish recovery began with these protests against the condescension and meanness with which the inmates who survived the first few weeks were treated. A Central Committee was set up on April 18, only three days after liberation and three days before Hilde got to the camp with the first Red Cross units (see Imperial War Museum exhibition chronology). It consisted of former inmates and was supposed to act as a liaison with the British administration, but it rapidly became much more. Under the leadership of the extraordinary Josef Rosensaft, who is mentioned in every memoir and whom both my parents knew well, the inmates organized a government that operated in every sphere of camp life.

There was the question of repatriation, for example: the British thought that everyone ought to go home as soon as possible. Although they did send convalescent TB patients to sanatoria in Sweden and Switzerland shortly after liberation (a massive rescue effort chronicled by Collis in his memoir, *Straight On*), in general they refused to acknowledge that being Jewish was a special case. Most Jewish former prisoners had nothing to go home to, and were no longer citizens of their countries of origin. The British argued, partly out of genuine liberal conviction and partly out of less honorable motives, that acknowledging Jews as a separate group from others would be to concede a victory to Nazi bigotry.

Though the vast majority of camp residents had come from Eastern European countries in which millions had been murdered, often with the enthusiastic help of residents, and though the vast majority expressed the desire to emigrate to America or to Palestine, they were shipped off almost immediately. A contingent of Czech women and children left by truck in early July, for example, although there was no clear destination for them. Others were forcibly moved to "holding camps" often in worse condition than Belsen itself; one of the first demonstrations at Belsen involved the forced removal of over a thousand inmates on May 24 to a camp near the Dutch border. Most of them returned to Belsen right away. Soon former prisoners from other camps began arriving, followed by returnees to Eastern Europe who fled back to the West after renewed pogroms and before the imminent thud of the Iron Curtain.

By June 2, in fact, the Dutch girls Hilde had seen in the hut on first arrival had already been flown home. By then there were only twenty or twenty-five of them left, she thinks. Belsen became the largest Displaced Persons camp in Europe, home to a sizeable percentage of Jewish survivors of the Holocaust. The British found that, through their own mismanagement at the outset, they had a much larger political problem on their hands than they began with. Most former prisoners remember the British administration with a mixture of affection and irritation. There were many kind hearts among the soldiers, but increasingly rigid policies imposed from London often made recovery an exhausting and complicated business.

In the meantime, inmates were desperate to stay put so that they could find relatives who might have survived. Hilde's diary for the late spring and summer of 1945, written in hasty Dutch, becomes helpful in untangling the skein of events. As the patients began to recover, she devoted less time to the hospital block and more to putting inmates in touch with each other. By the beginning of June, the work of contacting former prisoners had become the primary task. On May 31, she wrote that a man called Duncan, from the American Field Service, offered to go to Buchenwald for her to look for survivors with relatives in Belsen. On June 2, he arrived in camp with a truckload of people, and Hilde wrote (still unconsciously using the language of the war): "transport was a big success." Duncan disappeared before the month was up. Hilde never had a chance to thank him; such was the chaos of the period.

With the arrival of this first group of former prisoners, an informal postal service was set up between camps. It involved the mostly illegal use of military channels, and a network of friends and acquaintances who served as couriers. The British Quakers, and the American Field Service, their American counterparts, became particularly useful, loading up trucks and ambulances with people who wanted to travel from camp to camp. Hilde, with Uncle Whitehead, was actively involved in this project.

The aid workers tried to set up a means of registration so that they could confirm that a person had survived, or had been identified. People began to sign up at what became an information center. Slowly something of a system evolved. Hilde made contacts wherever she could, and followed up leads from abroad as letters of inquiry about survivors began pouring in from around the world. On June 7, Hilde wrote: "Giesi and Flora are coming to work in our office." They were young former inmates who knew Czech and Hungarian, and they doubled the manpower of the office within a few days of the arrival of the Buchenwald prisoners. On June 14, Hilde added: "Post office is working very well. We are now getting responses."

A second little book she has given me, not her calendar but one made up of blank pages, has been filled with hastily scrawled notes, written in a mix of Dutch and English, occasionally even French. There are shopping lists for chocolate, writing paper, women's underwear, and books and more books, "books for patients," she writes. Some of the lists contain such apparently random items that they might be taken for those vocabulary lists people memorize when they're learning a new language, were it not for the mix of languages within each list: "post letters. Jopie apart. Horloge." Or this one: "Lighter. Buttons. girdle. bathing suit. bicycle. scarf. broche [brooch]. necklace. shoes. shampoo. washandjes. note book. manchetknopen." My mother has told me that she was constantly buying things for women inmates, but also, occasionally, something for herself or for a friend when she went on leave. I am intrigued by the fact that on this last list, she has crossed off "bathing suit, bicycle, broche, necklace, shoes and shampoo." Did she manage to find all of those things successfully on one shopping expedition?

There are more notes – so many notes. "What about women with sick children. Russians in Auschwitz. contact for children. Hung. prisoners in Russia." And dominating every page, carefully written but with an urgency which still comes through after all these years, are names and addresses: "Otto Ballek, 32 years,

Czechoslovakian from Prag. Went to England in Febr. 39, to London. Herz, Ilse. Block 66. Has husband in Neugamme near Berlin. Herman Jansen. 11-6-77. Stateless. Bergen-Belsen." There are addresses in Holland, in England, in Belgium, in France, in Israel, in America. Notes in other hands, in Czech, German and English. Someone has written in a minute script: "Bl. 49. Regina wants her sister. German Gypsy." Then an illegible name, followed by a note in the same tiny hand: "Mother and sister. Friend found in MB 1." Addresses of a French liaison officer, a rabbi in the American army, a British Red Cross officer in London, a contact at Dachau, Jewish refugee organizations in London and Amsterdam are scattered throughout. I can't look at these pages without tears. The evidence of chaos and devastation is so great, hardly matched by the haste and energy with which my mother and her friends jump in to repair the world; it is just too much.

Hilde's most immediate tasks after the first days of sorting the living from the dead and supervising the first stages of their cure still required her medical talents. She was put in charge of nursing in one of the wards set up in a former SS barracks on two storeys. The building housed, altogether, about 150 people in fifteen rooms. British doctors and medical students made the rounds twice a day. Most of them were young and heroically dedicated to the task at hand, but not always terribly experienced.

Hilde, at those times, acted as an interpreter. Her little notebook confirms this. A common form of surgery, she explains, was the resetting of untreated broken bones. Such inmates expected to be crippled for life, but British doctors could rebreak the badly healed limbs surgically and put them into proper alignment. This took much explanation, and on such days Ian Paterson, one of the surgeons at the Glyn Hughes Hospital, arrived on his motorcycle and gave Hilde a ride to the operating theater.

The women patients, especially, liked to have her at their

bedside to reassure and explain. Sometimes, if it had been decided that they needed surgery, they asked her to accompany them, so that they could see a comforting face before and after the anesthesia. Such patients were not in immediate danger of death, but many of them perished eventually because their immune systems could no longer cope with the overwhelming wounds and infections that burdened their bodies. My mother describes delirious patients who died in her arms in mid-sentence.

Rapidly, however, life returned to Bergen-Belsen. After the first terrible weeks, when the death toll mounted higher than it had been even in the month before liberation, the survivors were able to eat again, and within an astonishingly short time, my mother says, they regained flesh, color and strength. The Gypsies were among the first to leave. They had suffered terrible atrocities at the hands of the Germans, from forced sterilization to wholesale murder. In the last days, when the Germans ran their makeshift crematorium day and night in an attempt to hide the evidence of their crimes from the advancing Allies, they had forced the prisoners to drag corpses across the camp to waltzes by Strauss and Lehar, played by Gypsy bands; that peculiarly demonic twist of art and sadism has become legendary.

Leslie Hardman, the British rabbi, also reports that the Gypsies left on May 21, the day the Horror Camp was burned. On that day, in fact, the first open-air dance was held at Belsen. Several memoirs contain pictures of young girls, already outfitted with clothes from the supply hut which the survivors dubbed "Harrods," dancing with British enlisted men; for rank was always observed under British rule.

My mother remembers theater performances taking place quite soon after the liberation. All the memoirists recall how many talents the inmates had. There were singers and actors, doctors and professors, carpenters, electricians, tailors and people skilled in stagecraft. The inmates erected a tented theater. In the pictures

I have seen, it looks like a professional structure. Soon singers and orchestras entertained the residents of Belsen. Productions by once-imprisoned playwrights and composers were performed by once-imprisoned actors and musicians, with costumes and lighting by former inmates. The actors of the Old Vic came, too. My mother and other memoirists remember seeing Peggy Ashcroft, in particular. It had been the actress's idea, I think, to tour the ruined places of Europe so soon after the war.

During that summer, as food, medical treatment, clean beds and kindness began to do their work, people rediscovered each other. My mother remembers the first birth, the first *bris*, or circumcision, the first marriage, the first signs that the Orthodox residents at the camp had resumed their traditional dress. Services were held, letters written, and people began to lift their heads and look about them again. Belsen became a community. Its residents could not know how long and hard they would struggle to find a home. Joseph Rosensaft and his wife Hadassah would not leave until 1950, when they were sure that everyone had been safely repatriated. In the meantime the camp had become a small town, with more residents arriving daily from the East.

Hilde's life, too, resumed the entanglements of ordinary life – hardly ordinary, given the circumstances – but a life in which the sea of young men surrounding her acquired faces and personalities once matters of life and death had begun to recede. "What must you think of me?" she says to me now, when I tease her about the number of men she mentions in the hasty amendments to her pocket calendar. Beyond a few chaste kisses, she never succumbed to the blandishments of the much older, mostly married men who surrounded her. She remembers a kind of chivalry that prevailed when people realized how young she was – she was twenty when she arrived at Belsen, and twenty-two when she left in the company of my father. Her colleagues felt protective of her. Besides, she smiles, there were plenty of women around who didn't share her hesitation, and perhaps that was a piece of luck too. Several times she has repeated a joke told among the British troops. A soldier gets a letter from his girlfriend back home after he has confessed to having strayed. "What's she got that I haven't got?" the girlfriend wants to know. The soldier writes back: "Nothing, but she's got it right here!"

Ian Paterson, the Scottish surgeon who took Hilde by motorcycle to interpreting jobs at the hospital, was the first of her gallants at Belsen. He was married, and their relationship was tender but decorous. He helped her set up a well-baby clinic in the camp in the earliest weeks as orphaned children were found and newly delivered women arrived in the camp. The Gypsies had abandoned some babies when they had left the camp in late May. No one knew why, exactly, but it was speculated that they thought the children would die anyway and would not survive the rigors of the adults' journey. Hilde looked after them and nursed many back to health; some Gypsy parents actually returned to reclaim them later on. On June 9 Ian Paterson was transferred to Hamburg, and the close relationship of a few weeks came to an end. Although he and Hilde never met again, I have learned that he died in 2008 at age ninety-three after a long and happy marriage that produced four children. He spent the rest of his life in Scotland as an orthopedic surgeon, still fearless and still dedicated to hard cases.

Because the work was so intense and difficult, time off was crucial to the sanity of the workers at Belsen. There were late-night gatherings in people's rooms, Sunday excursions, and frequent trips to the officers' club in Celle. The club was particularly important as a sort of informal networking center as well as a place to relax. My mother mentions meeting a liaison officer from Poland there on June 11, as well as a dentist she had worked with in Belgium, old contacts as well as new. The Polish officer helped her to reunite survivors from that area, and the dentist supplied news on events in the countries she had so recently left.

At the officers' club, Hilde discovered that her brother Jo was still alive. It was May 31, the same day on which Duncan had decided to make the trip to Buchenwald to look for survivors. The entry in her little notebook gives an idea of the intensity and dislocation of life at Belsen in that period: "May 31. Duncan, from the AFS, is going to Buchenwald for me. Then we had a party in the officers' club in Celle at night. There was a Major Maher I talked with, and he knew Jo. In the afternoon I had a picnic with Pat."

Jo had been liberated at Fallingbostel, the German prisoner-of-war camp only fifteen miles northwest of Belsen (this was the camp that Jo couldn't remember; nor did he remember the reunion with his sister). By June 1, Hilde had been given permission to accompany him home to Amsterdam. He was being resettled, and she had a weekend pass. Hilde looked forward to the time in Amsterdam with an anxiety that I can only try to imagine. Meanwhile she was developing some emotional support from her relationship with Hanns Alexander, an important figure in her life at Belsen. On May 15, she wrote in her diary, using the British nickname derived from his last name, "Alex arrives. I can't stand him." This was not a very promising start. The entry contains some of the ambivalence she felt toward Hanns right through their relationship. My mother explains that the British War Crimes Commission, of which Hanns Alexander was a member, was billeted across the way from her own unit of the British Red Cross. They shared a mess tent, and since only a few dozen people ate there, everyone met quickly.

Hanns was a German refugee from Berlin who had become a captain in the British army, and he was in the process of assembling prisoners and evidence for the trials at various venues in Germany. The trial of Belsen personnel, for example, was held at Lüneburg between September 17 and November 17, 1945. Perhaps Hanns Alexander had been recruited for the work because he spoke fluent German, since he had no other special training; at any rate, it must have been a satisfying job. Leo Genn, a British Jew who was trained as a lawyer but worked as an actor with the Old Vic, was another member of the commission. When the Old Vic came to Celle to perform *Of Mice and Men* that summer, Leo Genn introduced my mother to Laurence Olivier.

Despite that first impression, Hilde took to Hanns quickly, because she wrote on May 20: "Picnic Gordon, Godfrey, Woody, the Swiss Red Cross workers, and Freddy. Met Alex, cancelled Woody."

"Poor Woody," I say to my mother as we sit side by side on the deck in Cape Cod in the summer of 1995, poring over the tiny books she has given me. "I must have been quite awful," she says, looking extraordinarily pleased with herself all the same. I ask about the men at the picnic, but of course we talk most about Hanns. She describes him as handsome and gallant. He had good manners, but he was bossy and arrogant at times, and they had a pattern of quarreling from quite early on. She soon learned about his fiancée in England, to whom he had been engaged for seven years or so. The fiancée had been handpicked for him by his mother, and he had never questioned her choice – that is, he told Hilde, until meeting her. He was some years older than Hilde, too, twenty-eight in 1945, but she was used to that.

In the meantime, she took her leave to Amsterdam from June 3 to June 7, writing a word or so here or there in her notebook during that period. Then, a few days later I suppose, she adds: "Amsterdam was great. It was less bad than we anticipated. We thought it would be very depressing and full of memories, but we were received so generously. We had lunch at Habbema" [Jo's school principal]. Then she mentions various names she can hardly remember now – neighbors, she thinks? and that they spent a night on their return in the town of Hengelo. Then one name: "Otto Frank. June 7." She adds: "I am back in Belsen. I'm happy to be in Belsen – what a strange contradiction! Freddy was disappointed because I had been away."

This sketchy account hardly does justice to the events of those few days. My mother has described for me the reception she and Jo got from Zus Scholte, their rescuer on so many occasions. Zus opened the door, threw her arms around them, and burst into tears. They stayed with the Scholtes, who treated them with their customary kindness and tried to press on them all the objects they had kept safely for them through the war. Hilde refused everything, but Zus told her to wait; some day she would want them.

My mother says that this period passed in a fog. There was a whirl of trying to find out who was alive and who was dead. She can hardly remember whom she saw, only that everyone was kind. She was invited in for the obligatory *kopje tee*, cup of tea, no matter how painful the information her hosts had to impart to her, or how shabby their circumstances. She met former members of her parents' congregation, and others from whom she was able to piece together the story of their fate after their arrest. She didn't get exact dates until 1958, but at the time Hilde found herself unable to pursue the story of my grandparents' last days in any detail. She learned from the returnees that her parents had been in Westerbork (the documents confirm that they were kept there from July 24 to September 14, 1943). They were deported to Bergen-Belsen, and then, on January 25, 1944, to Theresienstadt.

From survivors who had seen them at Bergen-Belsen, Hilde learned that her parents had been put to work making *Glimmer*, strips of shiny material which were used to disrupt aircraft communications and to intercept radar. Walter, like so many others at that time, had to tear shoes apart to recycle the usable materials they contained. The shoes came from murdered victims at other camps. The survivors recollected that, even in the camps, Walter was a leader of the Dutch group. He remained cheerful, and had earned their admiration for the many ways he showed a quiet heroism. During roll call, the notorious *Appell* during which inmates had to stand at attention for hours outside their huts in all weather, Walter often replaced people too sick to manage the task, and thus saved lives. I think of what the historian Jacob Presser has written about the Jews who had become used to Holland and its civilized ways – that their survival rates were low because their human expectations, of themselves and others, were high.

Later during that same leave, Hilde met her Aunt Jenny, who was living in a Jewish *pension* for returnees. She helped out in the kitchen and got some support from the AJDC, the American Joint Distribution Committee, the organization for which Hilde herself would be working in a matter of weeks, though she didn't know it at the time. "Jenny knew by then that her husband and her daughter were dead, and that her sister and brother-in-law were most likely dead too," my mother says. "There was a lot of crying going on all around, but Jenny didn't cry."

Jenny had been reunited with my grandparents at Theresienstadt. She reported that a Jewish doctor at that camp had told Walter that he had contracted tuberculosis, stimulated by his dusty work with the shoes at Bergen-Belsen, but that it was only a light case. If his wife could somehow get him decent nourishment, and if he could keep alive long enough to get to Sweden or Switzerland when the war ended, he could recover. Betty, on hearing this, found a job as a cleaner for the camp commandant and was paid in food. But in the end, she couldn't save her husband. His tuberculosis was discovered, and he was "selected" for deportation to Auschwitz in October 1944. And then, Aunt Jenny told Hilde, my grandmother Betty did a really silly thing. She elected to go along with Walter. *"Das war doch ein*

Blödsinn! How stupid of her!" Jenny said. "She could have saved her own life at least!"

Hilde left without saying much. She was unable to speak to Jenny for some years. "Where could I get the charity to spare for her at that time? But I felt so badly for her. How angry can you be? Still, inside I never really forgave her," she says to me now. We are sitting on the deck as before, but two years later in 1997, looking over the waving junipers in the backyard of the Cape Cod house. After ten years during which it swarmed with grandchildren and visitors, my parents are putting the house up for sale. It is too much of an expense to justify a few weeks of use each summer

My parents have grown older. My father has to be careful of the sun where a skin graft is healing over a once-cancerous spot on his face. My mother limps from sciatica. The long walks on the beach of a few years ago have grown suddenly more difficult. And the grandchildren are beginning to scatter: one of my sons has already reached adulthood, and spends his summers thousands of miles from here.

I remember *Tante* Jenny vividly from my own childhood. She spent her last years living in a residential hotel, the Hotel Paris, on the West Side of Manhattan. She looked like a superannuated Zsa Zsa Gabor, before Zsa Zsa herself reached that category. I remember her in pink knockoff Chanel suits, with rhinestone rings on her wrinkled fingers and perfumed white powder in the deep folds on her face. She was what they call *appetitlich* in German, an appetizing old woman, sweetly scented and groomed, her white hair tinged with blue and perfectly waved, like one of those dolls with a pomander for a head. She spoke an excruciating English that we took up with enthusiasm. In restaurants, she asked for *smashed potatoes* (now a fashionable description, but not then), and when she traveled she stayed in suddenly Yiddishized hostelries known as *MOtles*, with the accent on the first syllable.

She thought everything we did was marvelous, and when she died, my mother found poems and letters from my sisters and me annotated in her vigorous copperplate handwriting: *ONLY TEN YEARS OLD!!!* She was fun, but we absorbed our mother's ambivalence right away. She had committed some sort of sin for which my mother could not quite love her as she had loved her once. I didn't know the nature of it until my mother told me the story of that first weekend in Amsterdam after the war. My parents cared for Jenny anyway, and we saw her frequently. I learned her accent so perfectly that, when I was thirteen and in summer camp, my bunkmates asked me to imitate our German refugee camp director. I stalked among the cabins, demanding that the lights be out by seven p.m. Everyone obeyed us and went to bed.

There was another reunion in those eventful four days. Coming out of Zus's house, Hilde bumped into Otto Frank on the street. He was staying with Miep and Jan Gies, who lived on the same block. They embraced and cried. Hilde told Otto what she had heard at Belsen about his children. For a long time, she thought that she had been the first to inform him of their fate. But since then, we have learned that he had had word only days before from the same Belsen inmates who had talked to my mother, when they finally found each other among the returnees to Amsterdam. He, in turn, was able to tell her more about what had happened to her parents. He was already at Auschwitz when he heard from other Dutch inmates that her parents were thought to be on a transport from Theresienstadt that had gone straight to the gas chambers. But that wasn't proof, he told her. Perhaps there was still a chance that they were alive. Then what was there to do but weep in each other's arms, there on the street? Or was this another of those conversations held over a cup of tea, either at Zus's place or at Miep's? I cannot imagine this talk, nor can I quite bring myself to ask my mother the details of it, though she would be quite willing to provide them. When she talks about that long weekend, I can almost taste the cold fog of grief. It still wraps her like a shroud.

Her little notebook doesn't say much about the important things. She was unlikely to forget the news or the faces. It was enough to mark the coincidence of meeting Otto by scratching his name down, all by itself on the page. And it must have been difficult enough to hear what people said, really to hear, that is, after the blow of the first words. What else can one notice when hope is snatched away? Surely one's ears ring and ring, and one shudders involuntarily, as if with sudden cold. When I shivered like that in childhood, my parents used to repeat the folk saying that someone was walking across my grave. What voices, what footsteps, must my mother have heard in the ensuing months? But her conversations with Jenny and Otto hardly make it into her little book. The hangdog Freddy and the overbearing Hanns take up more space. Until now, nothing more has ever been committed to paper about those meetings, when my mother's future shattered.

She and Otto remained close from that moment. They corresponded, signing their letters for a time, "Your father" and "Your daughter." As it happened, they would be linked later on in more ways than they expected.

But with the almost certain revelation of her parents' death, Hilde had come to some quick realizations of her own. Amsterdam was empty. In fact the whole of Europe had become a wasteland for her. Her dream of caring for her parents when they returned from their ordeal had been buried with them. Now she would return to Belsen and commit herself to the rehabilitation of the remnant there. She planned to stay until all the survivors had gone. It had become familiar, even comforting, with its pathos and its intense friendships, its superfluity of energetic young men, its constant arguments, its black market, its struggle to regain citizenship in the world for its inhabitants.

She was still stateless herself. She had discovered in Amsterdam that she didn't officially exist. The municipal records office had been bombed by the Resistance during the latter part of the war, ironically enough to help prevent further deportations. Now that she was a member of the tiny group of Jewish survivors, her presence was not enough to convince the authorities that she had an identity at all. Otto had told her that rumors were not proof of death, and she learned that her body was not proof of existence, either. She was a ghost in Holland. For the moment, Belsen had become home.

Alex was waiting for her upon her return, and Hilde's notes concentrated on the ups and downs of their quickly developing relationship. There was no confusion about the news she had had from the returnees, but her predicament with Alex was very confusing, and distracting in a way that must have been useful at such a time. On July 5, she sounded like the twenty-year-old she was:

> People who are engaged are worse than married people because everyone sees them as single, and everybody wants to date them, and they themselves think of themselves as single. Alex's views on marriage and fidelity are awful, and he knows it.

She took advice from other young men who were also interested in her, and of course they counseled her to break off with such a two-timer. She wrote on July 10: "Gordon is very supportive in my battle against my feelings for Alex. Now I am over it." And on July 12: "I have to keep a clear head because he keeps saying that he loves me." In the meantime, there were little reports on her work, in which she immersed herself when she was not struggling with her mixed feelings for Alex. July 8: "Uncle [Whitehead] has returned from the trip to Mauthausen. The

Czechs have left. July 9: Hundreds of people are coming to the office."

Then, on July 19, Hilde saw her brother. He had gone to the Red Cross to track his parents down, and he came to see her in Belsen with the official confirmation of their deaths. "I'm depressed because Jo has come back from Holland," she writes, "and he brings news that our parents have definitely died. Alex turns out to be a good friend. We went to a service and he said *Kaddish*."

Kaddish, the prayer for the dead, is awe-inspiring in Aramaic, with its alliterative crescendo of cumulative praise uttered quickly in unison by the congregation. Oddly enough, it says nothing about the dead. It speaks of the praise of God, and of the future:

Let the glory of God be extolled, let His great name be hallowed, in the world whose creation He willed. May His kingdom soon prevail, in our own day, our own lives, and the life of all Israel, and let us say: Amen.

Let His great name be blessed for ever and ever.

Let the name of the Holy One, blessed is He, be glorified, exalted, and honored, though He is beyond all the praises, songs, and adorations that we can utter, and let us say: Amen.

For us and for all Israel, may the blessing of peace and the promise of life come true, and let us say: Amen.

May He who causes peace to reign in the high heavens, let peace descend on us, on all Israel, and all the world, and let us say: Amen.

Such words had no meaning for Hilde. She felt dead inside. It was far more important that someone cared for her enough to say the prayers on her behalf, to put his arm around her waist, and to walk with her when she could not hide her grief. And Hilde was very good at hiding her grief. She has always been a good laugher. It was her wide, innocent grin my father fell in love with when he finally arrived at the camp: that, he says, and her knees. That smile must have attracted other people as well. I think that she has always had the ability to separate one feeling from the other, like someone drawing in India ink.

She has always had a profound capacity to enjoy the actual business of living. That talent was sharpened, rather than dimmed, by the deprivations of her hunted youth. My sisters and I inherited much of her pleasure in the simplicities of existence, which comes as naturally to us from our mother as the breath of life. So I can understand how she could go on an excursion to a beach on the North Sea the following Sunday with a large group of young people. "We tipped over in the boat because it hit a rock and then we made a campfire. It was a wonderful day," she wrote. She smiles upon reading this as we go over her notebook. She doubts that she would enjoy being half-drowned and frozen as much today, but she was in the company of good friends, and unconsciously she must have welcomed the release from responsibility and the strong sensations of cold and wet; they rescued her for a few hours from her inner numbness.

That she was numb, I have no doubt. On July 25, she noted in her diary: "Today a year ago father and mother were arrested." In fact it had been two years since her parents' arrest. I wonder whether time had stopped for her in some way. In those two years, she had gained and lost everything: her name, her language, her country, her parents. She was orphaned and stateless. Except for her brother, whose interest in her was intermittent at best, she was alone in the world. The men who took her out were not the right men for her, but she didn't know that then. Perhaps that's all love was, a pleasant kiss from a pleasant person. Perhaps she should marry the importunate Hanns. What else was there? She had seen so much death. It would be nice to escape into a normal life.

Surely, in peacetime, that inner vacancy could be filled somehow, in some way less urgent than caring for the dying and displaced.

I try to imagine my mother at twenty, thinking such thoughts and pushing them away. I imagine her jumping to her feet to tidy something up, or to organize something. She has always been good at getting people to co-operate with one another. She's a natural manager, a practical person. And though all her daughters have inherited some of that skill, we are all watercolorists rather than draughtswomen. Our emotions are much closer to the surface, and can swirl like one of those radar hurricane maps. I wonder how we can be so different from both our parents in that way. Perhaps our mother's *wall,* that inner structure of separation and containment, sprang a leak in our generation, for whom peace and prosperity have created a more generous environment for feeling. The daughterly questions of our nightmares come up again: how would we, at the age of twenty, have managed the news of our parents' murder, in a death camp? Would we have survived the war? I, for one, have always been convinced that I don't possess the stuff of which survival is made. This conviction has influenced everything I have undertaken.

But Hilde had reached a sort of equipoise. She was at the zero hour of her growing up. Now she was alone, but still she was needed. The survivors clamored for her help, the young men knocked at her door. She would not give in to her sorrow. She would shake her fist at the non-existent God who had allowed so much destruction. She would have to rebuild her world somehow, though hope was gone.

Chapter 7

Displaced Persons, Bergen-Belsen

MY MOTHER'S NOTEBOOK contains almost as many lyrics as shopping lists. She wrote down the words to "White Christmas," to "I'm Always Chasing Rainbows," and to several love songs I can't identify. She still hums those songs, which are associated, in her mind, with the young men and women she worked with at Belsen. They became her family for a time, the focus of her most intense emotions, as the world continued on its course of recovery from war. Almost immediately after Jo told her that he had found the records of her parents' deaths, the circumstances of life changed for her again. The original rescue groups were leaving every day as they completed their tasks and were reassigned.

In the summer of 1945, preparations for the war crimes trials the following autumn were proceeding rapidly, and military commanders shifted in and out of Bergen-Belsen. A moving order arrived from the British Red Cross. It seemed that Hilde's unit was about to be sent somewhere else, and though that order was cancelled on August 9, she realized that she had to find a more secure position for herself.

The American Joint Distribution Committee was the central Jewish organization doing relief work in Europe after the war, and the director in charge of the unit at Belsen, David Wodlinger, invited Hilde to join just as the British Red Cross was about to withdraw. She was given an American uniform and a rank equivalent to lieutenant, more or less the same rank she had held with the British. Now she was free to carry on with her work among the former prisoners, and to stay, for the moment, in the only home she had. From then on, the inmates called her *Miss Hilde from Joint.* I remind my mother that the atom bomb was dropped during the flurried weeks of rumors and departures at Belsen. She tells me that people greeted the news with relief, but that they were indifferent, for the time being, to its human cost. "Hiroshima didn't seem as monumental as it really was," she says, "because we were in a monumental situation ourselves."

The Jewish workers who came to Belsen from America, South Africa and from other European countries were sympathetic to the refugees who wanted to get to Palestine. Practically all of them were involved in more or less clandestine work with the Jewish Agency, which was beginning to move former prisoners secretly to ports on the Mediterranean in preparation for their illegal immigration. Their activism rose largely in response to British policy on the postwar resettlement of Jews. Britain was not prepared to admit refugees, and its position on Palestine was hardening.

Clement Attlee's Labour victory over Churchill's Conservative Party on July 26, 1945 turned out to be a disappointment. The workers and internees at Belsen had thought at first that the Labour party looked favorably upon the plight of European Jews, and that it would lift the absurdly small monthly immigration quota of 1500 people a month that had existed since the end of the war. The infamous White Paper of 1939, imposed when European Jews were making their last frantic efforts to get out of Europe, had declared Zionism an illegal conspiracy. It allowed the entry into Palestine of 75,000 Jews over the next five years – when, as it turned out, the relevant population was trapped in the Nazi death machine – and thereafter handed control of immigration over to the Arabs, who stopped it almost completely. The White Paper had been the work of the Foreign Office under the Chamberlain government in the years just before the war. It was thought that the new Labour government would honor the terms of the Balfour Declaration, now almost thirty years old, which promised the establishment of a Jewish homeland in Palestine. But Ernest Bevin, a confirmed and widely acknowledged anti-Semite, became foreign minister. He was impervious to pleas even from President Truman, let alone from a scattered remnant of homeless Jews. As late as the winter of 1947, when the struggle for a homeland had become a major crisis, he told a delegation of American rabbis: "You Jews are the cause of all the trouble in the world – no wonder everyone hates you." It was at that point that he turned the whole matter of Jewish emigration to Palestine over to the UN.

Increasingly, Jewish relief workers at Belsen, and American workers at the camp as well, saw themselves as at odds with the British administration. The issue of rations was typical, as Joe Wolhandler, an old friend and American co-worker of my mother's, describes it. He tells me about a colonel in charge of the camp who insisted that former prisoners in one section were consuming too much food. "There can't be more than 2000 Jews here," he said, "but they're eating enough for 3000." To get to the bottom of this situation, he ordered a group of soldiers to go door to door, bayonets drawn, among the locked huts, and he discovered that there were 5000 former prisoners getting rations for 2000.

This state of affairs had, in fact, been the subject of a

vehement protest by President Truman's personal envoy, Erroll G. Harrison, who had insisted that the former prisoners be treated as free people and given proper food and help. He cited the British zone as being particularly stingy with calories (the allowance per inmate still stood at 1800, according to Joanne Reilly) and particularly inept in the preservation of what we would now call the civil rights of the people in its care. Harrison's visits and report are described in detail by Joanne Reilly, and are mentioned again in the documentary film *The Long Way Home.* Britain itself was still suffering from the shortages of the war, which would persist well into the 1950s, and the mood there was not particularly generous. It was on the basis of Harrison's report that Truman repeatedly urged the Attlee government, and specifically Bevin, to increase the immigration quota for Palestine to 100,000 a year, but his pleas were as repeatedly rejected.

Because of this increasingly hostile climate, Joe says, he and many others operated independently of the British. This meant, among other things, helping Joseph Rosensaft, the leader of the Belsen community, to make his case abroad. The British had forbidden him to travel, but Rosensaft had many other helpers at hand. Joe, for example, smuggled him out of Belsen and across the French border by flashing a New York Public Library card in lieu of proper documents. Eventually he got Rosensaft on a plane to New York.

At the national conference of the United Jewish Appeal in Atlantic City on the weekend of December 15–17, 1945, Rosensaft made an impassioned plea to Americans, and to American Jews in particular, for the encouragement of immigration to Palestine. A description of this event was the main item in the January 1946 issue of the *JDC Digest*, the newsletter of the American Joint Distribution Committee, and included a few lines from his remarks, in which he asked "in the name of the saved remnant, the Jewish partisan, the Jewish rebel of the ghetto...to rouse all the world to open Palestine to us." His speech made the front page of the *New York Times*, and the UJA resolved to raise one hundred million dollars for the relief of survivors in Europe. The case of Belsen could no longer be kept secret.

Meanwhile, back at Bergen-Belsen, Hilde still had breakfast with Hanns Alexander whenever they could manage it between trips away. She was thrown into confusion one morning when another Hanns came in and sat down on her other side. This was Hanns's identical twin, Paul. Her diary entry, typically, was much more sedate than the event itself: "Alex's twin appeared. It was very nice to meet him." Now the three of them went out together to the officers' club or to see a film. At the movies, Hilde sat between the twins, holding hands with both. Paul was stationed in the general neighborhood, and when Hanns was away on one of his missions, he instructed his twin to look after Hilde. Thus it happened, as Paul explained, that he fell in love with her as well. "I always fall in love with my brother's girlfriends," he told her humbly. "It's just fate. It's what happens when you're twins."

During that autumn of 1945, Hilde ran the ever-expanding "post office" in the morning, and the well-baby clinic originally suggested by her friend Pat, the Scottish surgeon, in the afternoon. The clinic took up two ground-floor rooms and served pregnant women as well as their children, who only began to be born toward the end of 1945. Before that, there had been the Gypsy babies and other orphans and strays who had miraculously made it through the war, or who had been brought there in the early days of the increasing movement of Jews back from Eastern Europe. The first patients at these clinics were young women from countries like Czechoslovakia or Hungary who had been deported relatively late in the war and had been in the camps for so short a time that starvation had not yet affected their reproductive cycles. Later on, the clientele came almost entirely from Poland and Russia. They were twice-exiled: first because of Hitler, then because of violence against Jews returning from the camps. The Iron Curtain fell, and thousands of Jews retraced their steps to the West. The children of the early marriages at Belsen and of the exiled Eastern Europeans became a substantial population at the camp during the next few years.

Until the end of 1945, this was a period of relative tranquility for Hilde. Her emotional life was another matter, and there I find my imagination stymied. She seemed to lead an unruffled life with her three principal admirers – Joe Wolhandler, Hanns and Paul Alexander – and a host of minor ones who pop up casually in conversation. When I write about her relationships with this string of young men, all of whom seem comically unable to detach themselves despite a certain evident lack of interest on her part, I can't find a woman I can understand. She was simply not in love with any of them. That would explain the ease of her detachment and her honesty in explaining herself, but why keep them hanging around? She talks sometimes about having come through with her "morals" intact, in a way I find both touching and dated. As the mother of three girls who came of age in the 1960s and '70s, she was much more relaxed than she must have been at twenty.

But there is a distinct air of unreality in her account of these early romances, or "friendships," as she always calls them, as if she and her beaux were children playing in the street. There was real comedy in the situation, and she has always made the most of it in her retellings. But I hear no strong emotion in her voice, and none of that edge of pain that comes with passion. My mother tells these stories as if she were outside herself looking on, not as if she had been the center of a swirl of feeling. My own relationships with men have, on the whole, been quite different, all anxiety and extrasystoles on my side. I can't imagine my mother stumbling around, as I did at her age and for years afterward, so blind with passion that the world looked as if someone had polished the trees and street signs and put them back in the wrong order.

Hilde was in mourning, of course, and she was busy with the restoration of life at the camp. But I can't understand the nature of her mourning, either. The only moment that stands out emotionally for her during this period is the Yom Kippur of 1945, the first observance of the holiday since the end of the war. Yom Kippur, the Day of Atonement, is the most serious day in the Jewish calendar. According to tradition, the book of judgment, which Jehovah has opened on Rosh Hashanah, is closed for another year on Yom Kippur. If Jews have not asked forgiveness from those they have wronged or hurt, or have not made an attempt to correct their faults, they will have to wait a year for another chance to have their names inscribed in the Book of Life. It is a fast day, particularly hard, I should have thought, on a congregation that had been starving until so recently. It is especially a day for remembering the dead.

The Belsen services were held in the former German theater. It was a harrowing scene, my mother says. The place was packed with people. Some wore the caftans and fur hats of the Chasidim, others skullcaps and prayer shawls, and others stood bareheaded in street clothes. They represented every degree of orthodoxy in the Jewish community. The people prayed and sang. They cried, of course. Then they began to wail, and then they screamed.

Hilde fled with Joe Wolhandler, who had come along, and they spent the day walking in the woods, trying to sort out their feelings. She could not understand how the survivors had kept their faith. For her, God had died long ago, and was buried with the innocent ashes of her parents and of so many others in some tainted corner of the earth where evil had finally won. Until Joe's death, he and Hilde met or talked on the phone on Yom Kippur, no matter where they found themselves. They could not get through the hours without remembering that first Day of Atonement, when the pain of loss was as raw as an open heart.

During my childhood, we trod as lightly as we could when we thought we were in the vicinity of my mother's unhealed heart. Our father had taught us not to put her in harm's way. If there were a program on television, or a magazine with pictures, she had to be forewarned or protected. It was not that the Holocaust was unspeakable. My mother herself became semi-professional at speaking about it, especially when our connection with Otto Frank became known. Still, we had to be wary, we had to take care. The worst thing was to take my mother by surprise, or so my father thought. He imagined that sudden revelations, the casual toss of a page on the coffee table, the sound of Hitler's voice in a documentary, could all be dangerous.

But since I have been talking with my mother so often about her memories, I have wondered about my father's protectiveness. It seems to me that my mother has buried part of herself very deep. There are certain areas that will always remain impenetrable, even when we see her tears. Along with her toughness, she has a real gift for apprehending comic possibility. Her wide grin suggests this too. So I have an odd archive to make a story of: the news from Amsterdam, the terrible Yom Kippur with Joe, interleaved with the prospect of my mother's holding hands with twins. These events form a knot of light and dark, skeins of laughter and suffering interwoven in what sounds like some kitschy lyric from *Fiddler on the Roof*. That knot of experience, the *way* in which it has become a story of experience, reflects my mother's personality, that self-protectiveness which is both her talent and her shield.

She soon needed all her armor for her next task. By the autumn of 1945, Hanns (called by his nickname, Alex, so often in her notes), had accomplished much of what he had been expected to do in Germany. The Belsen war crimes trial, the first of many, had begun on September 17 at Lüneburg. Forty-five Belsen guards and officers were tried. When sentence was passed, on November 17, 1945, eleven people, including the commandant, Josef Kramer, and Irma Grese, a wardress popularly known as the Bitch of Belsen, were sentenced to hang. The sentence was carried out on December 12. Hanns must have decided to return to England to marry his long-suffering fiancée, because he becomes less prominent in my mother's reminiscences, although he remained in Germany until he was demobbed in the spring of 1946. Paul, the gentler twin, was still serving relatively close by and took Hilde out when he was at Belsen, but Hilde had been far more attracted to the livelier Hanns. One twin was not a substitute for the other, however much Paul hoped that he could persuade my mother otherwise.

By December, Hilde had been called to work at Blankenese, an estate outside Hamburg that was being used to house and educate orphan children who had survived the camps, and the issue of the twins became academic for a few welcome months.

The estate had been donated by the Warburg banking family for the care and rehabilitation of children. It had survived the war intact in the care of the original staff who still looked after it. My mother describes it as a beautiful mansion, with extensive grounds. Reuma Weizmann, sister-in-law of Moshe Dayan (a dominant military commander, politican and diplomat during Israel's formative years), and future wife of Ezer Weizmann (later a president of Israel), was a worker there a little later than my mother, overlapping with her briefly. In a memoir, she writes that the estate had three "fine houses," a tennis court and a swimming pool. She was assigned there as a worker for the Jewish Agency, the group which was overseeing the immigration of survivors to Palestine. Hilde arrived as a representative of the American Jewish Joint Distribution Committee, which worked, technically, for the welfare and future resettlement of the same group, without making specific claims for Palestine.

The British had agreed that the handful of Jewish orphans who had survived the camps or who had emerged from hiding might be allowed to enter Palestine legally. According to Oscar Handlin in *A Continuing Task*, a brief history of the AJDC, the British set the number of child emigrants at six thousand. Blankenese was used to prepare them for their new life. The children came from all over Europe. Some teenagers had already made friends with Hilde and Joe Wolhandler at Belsen. These children had been brought or had made their way from the American zone. Soldiers had directed them to Belsen, which already had a reputation as a place where orphans were well looked after.

Hilde was enlisted in the task by two skilled workers from Joint, Charlotte Rosenbaum, from the Alsace, and Adrienne Schwimmer, from Antwerp. They were supported by young people sent by the Jewish Agency, first young soldiers from the Jewish Brigades of the British army who stayed in Europe after demobilization to serve as teachers of Hebrew and Jewish culture, and later by specifically trained civilians, like Reuma, who came from Palestine. All of these young people were there to help the children emigrate to the country which would come to be known again as Israel.

The young people were being prepared for the *kibbutzim,* or co-operative agricultural settlements, which the Zionists had set up as part of their vision of a new society in Theodor Herzl's old-new land of Israel. Some of these co-operatives would be populated entirely by children who had survived the war in Europe. My mother says that many of the first group went to a children's village called Ben Shemen, where they adjusted very well to the communal life of the kibbutz. It's now a lush town, and apparently has always contained an agricultural school that many of the orphans must have attended. The survivors soon found, however, that no one in their new homeland wanted to hear anything about the war or their early lives, and they learned to keep silent. It wasn't until the Eichmann trial of 1961 forced a public discussion that any aspect of the Holocaust was openly talked about in Israel.

My mother guesses that there were about sixty or seventy children in this first group. They were mostly Hungarian in origin. She was given the youngest to look after. They ranged in age from three to twelve. All were physically underdeveloped and emotionally devastated. "A nine-year-old looked like a four-year-old," she says. "They had only known adults who hurt, who took away their parents, and who did terribly cruel things. So they wet their beds at night, they had nightmares. They were sick a great deal. They wouldn't eat, they were afraid to taste food." Hilde moved her bed into the two downstairs rooms of the mansion that served as the children's dormitory. She stayed with them twenty-four hours a day, eventually teaching them how to play, how to use toys, how to trust adults.

One little boy of about eight looked perhaps four; the pictures show a stunted child with half-grown hair. He was called Helmuth, and he had not spoken for months. Hilde remembers his freckles and his curly red hair, and the way he screamed at night. My mother read to him, and sang, and carefully embraced him, and one day he looked at her and began to talk in the baby German of his brief childhood. Hilde never knew quite what had happened to him in the camps. Like many of the youngest children, he was simply too young to frame the enormity in his mind. He had no concepts, no language, for such a thing. The work was painful for Hilde. The Nazi barbarity had wrought such obvious destruction in the innocent spirits of the young. But it was satisfying, too, because the children showed signs of recovery and responded, in time, to the constant care and affection their new attendants showered on them.

Now Hilde was going back and forth to Amsterdam regularly

to see her brother and friends who had survived the war. Her American military papers gave her considerable freedom to travel. The survivors, on hearing about the work at Blankenese, gave her toys, clothes, children's equipment, and even carpeting to take back with her.

My mother has quite a few pictures from Blankenese. In them, the adolescent survivors outnumber the small children by about ten to one. Seven stunted children stand in a field with Hilde, their hair just growing in after the shaved-headed deprivation of the camps. Later on, when the trees are beginning to take on a promising look and the spring sunshine has some consistency, the children appear more solid and have begun to smile. They look healthy enough to be any children.

On Hilde's twenty-first birthday in February 1946, the children made delicate watercolor cards with all kinds of messages in French, English and German, according to the native language of the helpers who translated for them, where necessary, from Hungarian. The cards radiate eager affection, and the colors of the painted flowers are still bright. "Happy birthday to Hilda," wrote a little girl who knew she was a handful, "from Gentle Wilma. Whatever my whims, Wild or Wicked, I Love You." A boy named Peter wrote in German and (I think) in his own hand: "I am your oldest child and I promise you with best wishes from all of us to be very good in the future." Helmuth, the child who wouldn't speak, has a French-speaking scribe set down his wishes: "With the compliments and best wishes of a favorite with the ladies, Helmuth." So many of the cards promise better behavior that I imagine that daily life in the little group was quite rough. The care they got at Blankenese was gentle in the extreme, with not the slightest whisper of punishment, but it must have been a struggle for the children to relinquish the survival techniques of the camps, and to begin to grasp emotionally what had really happened to them. Where did the consciousness come from that they were difficult? Was it perhaps left over from the harshness of the only other life many of them had known?

But Hilde's stay at Blankenese soon came to an end. The goal of the children's re-education was, after all, departure, and her orders were to leave when her group did, though the work at Blankenese continued for some years. All the training in Hebrew, the singing and dancing, the Friday-night dinners and Shabbat candles, the restoration of trust in the outside world, had resettlement in Palestine as an ultimate aim. In March of 1946, only three weeks after her birthday celebration, Hilde accompanied her children on the long train journey from Hamburg to Marseille, the port of embarkation for Palestine.

The teenagers understood that they were on their way to Israel at last, and they were filled with hope and excitement; they held a celebration on the last night and danced the hora. The younger children were at the party, too, and there was much discussion about future events. My mother has a picture of the group about to leave Blankenese. She is in uniform with a chamber pot in her hand, for children who wouldn't be able to wait in line for a toilet on the train. The trip from the north of Germany to the south of France took four or five days, because the children's chartered train was sidelined whenever more important ones had to go through. When the group arrived in Marseille, the children realized for the first time that Hilde would not be accompanying them any farther. She had thought that she and the rest of the staff had explained this very carefully, but the children had chosen not to hear or not to believe what they had been told. The children clung to her skirts and wept, and would not let her go. "We lost our parents and you were our mother, and now you're abandoning us," one little girl named Agnes told her.

Hilde, deeply shaken but certain that she was not ready to emigrate herself, returned to Belsen via Brussels, where on April 3, 1946, she celebrated Passover with Hanns and Paul Alexander at a British army seder. She was certain that returning to Holland, "which was just a big cemetery to me," she says, would be a mistake. The bureaucratic rigmarole to which she would be subjected in the next year soon confirmed her sense that even the Dutch were tired of stateless people and victims of war. She felt that she was of most use at Belsen, but she wasn't sure exactly where to turn after the intense months at Blankenese.

Soon enough, her next calling came to her. She stuck with this role for the year that remained to her at Belsen. Until we talked about it in more detail, I had always thought that it had been her work there from the beginning, because it figured so prominently in her memories. By the time she returned from Blankenese, the flow of returnees from Russia and Poland had become a flood. Jews who had returned to their countries of origin in Eastern Europe, as prescribed by the well-meant but misguided policies of the British and UN relief organizations, found that they were not welcome. Their neighbors had profited from their absence, looting their belongings and taking their houses and businesses for themselves. The camp survivors were met with insults, pogroms, and killings. The most dramatic of these attacks occurred at Kielce, in Poland, where Poles were inflamed by the hoary libel that Jews had abducted and murdered Christian children to use their blood in the Passover matzohs. On July 4, 1946, mobs murdered forty-two returnees from the camps. There was a worldwide protest, and one hundred thousand Jews, over half the survivors, fled the country. The Polish and Czech governments were only too happy to see the last of their Jews depart, and 2500 to 3000 Jews left every day. They were joined by Polish Jews who had been moved by the Soviets to the interior republics of the USSR during the brief period of the Soviet-German friendship pact of 1940. They had survived the war, but had fled once it became clear that they were no longer safe under Stalin.

Directly after the war, anti-Semitism re-emerged on both sides of the Iron Curtain. Such Western figures as Bevin and certain members of the US State Department, as well as Polish cardinals and ministers, branded the Jews agents of Communism, just as Hitler had. "These damn Jews," said the American ambassador to Poland when a delegation of American rabbis came to Poland to protest the events at Kielce, "they create problems all the time." And a Catholic cardinal told them: "These Jews bring it on themselves. They are all Communists." The leader of the Communist party in Poland, to complicate matters further, actually was a Jew himself. Astoundingly, he took the standard Socialist line of the time: "What's the big deal about a pogrom? It's irrelevant in history."

As a result of such political complexities, and especially because of the violence, many of the survivors of this second struggle in Eastern Europe spilled into the former concentration camps, which were now officially relabelled Displaced Persons' camps. Of these, Belsen was by far the largest. Unlike DPs in the American zone, where there was the possibility of emigration to the United States, the DPs at Belsen were there to stay for the moment. They knew that there was no chance that they might enter Britain. Hilde looked about her, and saw barracks once more overcrowded with underfed, underclothed and understimulated children.

She asked David Wodlinger, the director of Joint activities at Belsen, if she could set up a day care center. She was given one building, and set to work. She found German carpenters whom she paid, according to the barter economy of postwar Europe, in cigarettes. They made small chairs and tables for the children. She got white flour for the children's breakfast rolls in the same way. The children rested on British army stretchers, which were used as cots. There were typically about fifty of them. They came when their parents wanted them to, and stayed until mid-afternoon, after a hot lunch and a nap. "We just tried to have as much fun with them as possible," my mother says. There were games indoors and out, singing, drawing, walks and affection. There was even a performance for the rest of the camp, in which, my parents remember with laughter, the tiny children marched around and sang songs in praise of Stalin. These had been the equivalent of nursery rhymes in their experience, and they had learned them in Soviet kindergartens.

Most of all, Hilde enlisted camp inmates as workers for the day care center. She began to train survivors who were too weak to work a full day, but who could manage shifts a few hours long. Some worked in the kitchen, others cleaned or used their infinite skills for everything that needed doing. Seamstresses made cheerful curtains; a fleet of artists covered the walls with murals, mostly of Disney characters. Other young women were trained as teachers, or already had the training, but needed to get used to regular work in peacetime. They wore nurse-like white coats supplied by the Red Cross. This was Hilde's idea, because it would give the young women prestige in the camp and self-respect. By the time Hilde was finished, the center had become a model of its kind. There were few toys or amenities, but it was a bright, joyful, well-organized place. The kitchen provided meals – a hot breakfast, snacks and midday dinner – for all the children under the age of six whose parents declared a need. My mother says that they managed their resources so efficiently that they ended up feeding whole families, parents and older children as well, with the leftovers that parents were encouraged to take home.

This is the kind of work that the American Joint Distribution Committee mentioned in its newsletter, which went out to supporters in the United States. Even at the height of the crisis in postwar Europe, the organization had surprisingly few employees. The same newsletter that described Joseph Rosensaft's visit to New York also reported that there were only sixty or seventy workers in the camps, of whom Hilde was one. But this little group of people was extraordinarily energetic, and so able that what it achieved seems miraculous. Young veterans of wartime relief like Hilde were especially good at harnessing the bureaucracies of other organizations – UNRRA, the British Army, the Red Cross – to achieve goals that might have been impossible with their own small numbers. And of course, money was pouring in from American Jews.

I have always wondered how this worked in practice, for there really was no cash economy in Germany immediately after the war. Hilde, a non-smoker, hoarded her cigarette ration to buy goods and services, just as she had done during the war. She had no money, and no budget for buying things in the usual way. She was paid a daily allowance in scrip, the military paper money, for use in the PX and the officers' club, but her real salary was held for her until she required it after she left Belsen. The workers were paid in food and clothes, but no one had a wage or expected one. To apply to an agency for anything meant filling out endless forms and waiting forever. People relied on barter or even the black market. Hilde had become quite skilled at understanding a barter economy, because it had already existed in Belgium and Holland. It never entered her head, she says, to think about money or how to earn it.

Her liquor ration served as currency, too. Officers got ten or twelve bottles a month, my mother remembers, mostly gin. When my father first met her, in the spring of 1946 not long after her return from a trip to Brussels, he found that she had lined up all her gin and whisky in a sideboard in her room. For the first time, it dawned on him that one could do something with one's ration other than drink it. By then he had acquired quite a reputation as an alcoholic, because in his own way he was a naif, much less adept at managing in this survival economy than Hilde was. Despite her skill at hoarding her liquor ration for trading in supplies for the day care center, however, Hilde had learned that she was no delicate female when it came to boozing. The British consumed a lot of alcohol as a matter of routine, and to her amazement, she discovered that she could drink her male companions under the table. "You must have a hollow leg," they told her. My father, for example, describes a party on New Year's Eve, 1947, at which she consumed a great deal of champagne, apparently without ill effect, while my father and the British officers around her, habitual drinkers all, became gradually comatose.

Her new skill was exhibited in a surprising way when she tracked down the Dupuis and went to visit them for the first time after the war. She thinks, but is not sure, that the visit occurred sometime in the autumn of 1945. She had found their new address in Lustin-Gare, the village to which she had come, posing as a Dutch nurse, just about two years before. The Dupuis's beautiful house on the Meuse in Rivière had been burned to the ground by the Germans, who had suspected them all along of Resistance work, during the terrible retreat of 1944. After all they had been through, Hilde's visit turned into a prolonged celebration of their mutual survival. Mme Dupuis insisted that she buy a ring for Hilde tout de suite, right away, so that she would never forget the moment of their reunion, and my mother still wears it, a delicate confection of sapphires and diamonds.

The Dupuis also celebrated with food and drink, as only they knew how, and when Hilde told them that she had acquired a reputation for containing her liquor since she had last seen them, they plied her with absinthe, the French liqueur which at that time still contained its legendary toxins. Hilde drank two full glasses after dinner – loathsome stuff, she says – and then announced with dignity that she was going to rest for a bit. The family watched her walk carefully across the living room, making sure to place her feet one before the other, and mount the stairs to her room, where she passed out for a couple of hours. Then she re-emerged, fresh and sober and none the worse for wear. They exclaimed in admiration, but my mother has never touched the stuff since, nor, it might be said, much of any other liquor, either.

When my mother talks about the reunion with the Dupuis, I still hear the rejoicing in her voice. The simple fact of survival was a miracle. There were small miracles every day. She corresponded regularly with Otto Frank, and they saw each other on the occasions when she got to Amsterdam. This was easy enough, since Otto still lived with Miep in the Hunzestraat, just a few doors away from the Scholtes. During the summer of 1945, on one of her first visits to Amsterdam, he had placed a small volume, bound in red-checked cloth, in her hands. As she leafed through it, he explained that Miep had found and saved Anne's diary.

They talked through their tears. Otto explained that he was consulting his friends as to what he should do. He felt so weak, so bereft, not really up to anything. But some of the survivors who had known the family thought he ought to make the diary known to the world. Anne herself seemed to express such a wish. Perhaps he could make a contribution that way, feel that he was fighting the barbarism that had wrecked his life, and keep the memory of his family alive. Did Hilde think that he ought to publish the diary? Yes, she said, it would be marvelous. There would be a record of what had happened. It would be a way for young people in future generations to understand what they had all gone through.

Otto invited Hilde to think of him as a father, and told her that he would think of her as a daughter. From what I have read since, Otto found great comfort in the paternal role. In Auschwitz, he advised and protected Sal de Liema, a young man in his bunk, and thereafter stood in a similar relation to many lost young people. Even so, his relationship with Hilde was special, because she was the same age as Margot, had been her best friend, and looked so much like her. The two fathers had been friends, too, and it was natural that they should take up an intimacy that usually belongs only to families. That was how I found Otto when I came into the world. I was closer to him than to any of my natural uncles or grandparents. My parents eventually asked him to be the executor of their wills and guardian of their children.

These moments of reunion were snatched during brief leaves. Most of the time, Hilde was preoccupied with her little charges at Belsen. It was difficult to get food for them in enough quantities, and frustrating to see the British officers so well-fed when the children needed more milk. It was in the early weeks of the existence of her day care center that she first encountered Max Goldberg, a young doctor from Switzerland who was working for UNRRA. He had arrived in April after caring for Polish soldiers at Fallingbostel for several weeks. He had been given the rank of lieutenant colonel and was the camp's Public Health Officer.

Max arrived at Bergen-Belsen almost exactly a year after Hilde first drove through the gates. He had been sent first to Fallingbostel, he thinks, because his papers said that he was a Pole from the district of Minsk-Masowiecki. Thus, according to UNRRA logic, he was the citizen of an Allied country. He thinks too that his mysteriously high rank was a function of his supposed citizenship; after all, he was newly out of medical school, with little direct clinical experience. His superiors in Paris reasoned further, most likely, that he could speak Polish to the soldiers at Fallingbostel, and that would be nice for everyone; besides, the prisoners there were due to be shipped back to Poland soon, and his stint would be over.

Max saw things rather differently. He had, in fact, been born in Switzerland, the country that he had never left until UNRRA shipped him to Fallingbostel at the age of twenty-five. His *father,* Moritz, had been born in Minsk-Masowiecki and even he, Moritz, had lived in Switzerland since the age of sixteen or so. But the

Swiss don't grant citizenship on the basis of birth. By the time World War II broke out, it was too late for Max's parents, who were naively undereducated about such matters, to apply. As my maternal grandparents in the Netherlands had discovered, the prospect of floods of refugees changed immigration policies in most countries overnight. On his own, Max was considered an unsuitable candidate for citizenship because he was a Jew at a time when many Swiss sympathized with their Nazi neighbor, and also because the leftish politics of his youth displeased the authorities.

He had applied to UNRRA in July 1945, but was not assigned a post until March 1946. The delay was an example of the bureaucratic red tape that Hilde and her colleagues were so skilled at avoiding. When his papers finally came through, he set off by train for Paris – having been strip-searched and delayed overnight by suspicious French border guards, despite his military accreditation – and hence to Fallingbostel. But before getting to his assigned post, it took ages for him to get out of Paris and then out of Arolsen, near Hanover, where the British army of occupation was headquartered. "The town was badly damaged and all the hotels were occupied by British troops or organizations like UNRRA," he writes. "Because I had officer's rank I was in comfortable circumstances. Nobody seemed in an awful hurry to do anything. I became a little impatient and tried to find out when I could start working." My young father, who had joined UNRRA out of a burning guilt that he had been safe while Jews in other countries suffered, found himself first mired in bureaucracy, and then ministering to non-Jewish Poles, former forced laborers for the Reich, for a short time. The Poles were about to be repatriated, and had only minor ailments which he treated in a dispensary. "I learned how to say 'Where does it hurt?' in Polish," he writes. He heard the Poles express their hatred of the Russians, their traditional enemies, who by now dominated Poland and had Stalin in charge besides, and their resentment of the British, too, who were sending them back to their homeland; but the work was otherwise frustrating, not least because it was difficult to communicate with the English speakers around him. My father's spoken English now is flexible and sophisticated. He is, besides, a fluent and witty writer, and prefers writing to speech when I ply him with questions. It's hard to imagine that his English was once halting, and the source of endless comic misunderstanding. "Though we had a lot of English grammar in school, speaking was another matter again," he writes. He envied other Europeans whose English was better than his: "I remember a Danish man who used multisyllabic words like particularly, or definitely or absolutely, with such ease I was sure I would never be able to speak like that."

His English was soon sorely tried. When the Poles finally left, Max asked for and was granted a transfer to Belsen, and arrived there on April 6, 1946. He was puzzled by the frosty reception he got at first. He didn't know that rumors had been flying that a Polish doctor was arriving to become Public Health Officer at the camp, and that this doctor was anti-Semitic – after all, Poles were always anti-Semitic, weren't they, if they weren't actually Jewish? My father's last name apparently did nothing to dispel this impression. The rumor seems to have originated with the Jewish Committee, headed by Joseph Rosensaft (to whom my father always refers by his nickname, Yossel). The bad advance press was hard on Max, at first, because the Jewish Committee consisted of ten or twelve extremely capable people who had enormous influence over public opinion at Belsen. As my father says,

...some of them were old Zionists, idealistic and extremely dedicated and straight as arrows; others seemed opportunistic and lined their own pockets; others did a lot of good for the people but didn't forget their own interest. Rosensaft was the master of them all. He was a smart, foxy man, who understood the political tensions underlying the conflicting goals of the British Occupation Forces and the inmates of the camp.

Max's rudimentary English did not help dispel the rumor of his anti-Semitism. As he was being introduced around on his first day, he saw a woman pharmacist who was part of the Joint team. He shocked everyone by asking with what was seen as unmitigated rudeness, "Who is that woman?" And when David Wodlinger, the head of Joint in the camp, invited Max to his quarters, saying, "Oh, Dr Goldberg, you must come and have dinner with us," my father said, "Must I?," thinking that this was a correct and polite response until he saw the puzzled faces around him.

These misunderstandings were straightened out quite soon, of course, and the victims of his linguistic mangling soon became friends. Max was understood to be Swiss and Jewish, and people began to like him. I can't imagine how they could have failed to take to him, because in addition to his intellectual brilliance, he has a warm heart and a sort of tender vivacity that attracts people, especially women. Both my parents say, however, that he was moody and depressive in those years, more so than when I knew him as a daughter, though I have certainly seen his moods. He kept getting into hot water because of his naive consumption of the liquor ration, his interest in women, and his faux pas.

I ask my mother if she remembers their first meeting. She says that she was in her room after work one day about a week or so after Max arrived in the camp when a woman colleague of hers asked, "Have you met that Polish doctor yet? He's very anti-Semitic." The colleague was from UNRRA, and not Jewish, and my mother says that she had merely to lay eyes on my father and hear his name to realize that there must have been some mistake.

My father can do better than this. He remembers seeing my mother for the first time. He was walking down the main street of the former Goering Panzer Division, where most of the DPs were now housed and where the hospitals were located, with Dr Spanier, the Holocaust survivor who assisted him. A Jeep came racing down the road with a man from Joint at the wheel, "and sitting beside him was a young woman, wild hair flying in the air, wrapped in an American Army raincoat at least two or three sizes too large; in flying by she waved cheerfully at Spanier," he writes. Dr Spanier, who later did what he could to discredit Max to Hilde, now told him all about Miss Hilde from Joint, and suggested that he come to one of the parties the Joint people held in their rooms after work.

It was at the second of these parties that he first noticed Hilde's pretty knees, a focus of his admiration ever since (and of his daughters' constant teasing). A friend of Hilde's called Ruthie Reichman had a few people visiting in her room, and when Max came in Hilde was sitting on the floor,

> her US uniform skirt slid up a little over her knees and I said to her that she had beautiful knees and that I was really captivated by them as by a beautiful piece of sculpture. To me they had the eroticism of a sculpture over which your hand glides with esthetic pleasure, a certain frisson and a touch of sadness upon meeting beauty. Of course this poetic candor was floated on gentle waves of gin, but in vino being veritas, it is true to this day.

Hilde was not much impressed by this bold overture. Perhaps the gentle waves of gin were too painfully in evidence in this burst of purple prose, but she had to admit that there was an attraction between them. She was even more embarrassed when, during a party in Dr Spanier's room, Max got much bolder. The room was full of people, including many strangers and a Dr Grünpeter, a Rumanian survivor who worked for Joint and who was, unbeknownst to Max, infatuated with Hilde. Max, again soused from his nightly cocktails with the British officers at UNRRA, said loudly, "Hilde, you have beautiful lips, they deserve to be kissed." My mother blushed scarlet, and everyone tittered, my father writes. "So why don't you kiss her?" asked Dr Spanier, and my father "bent down and kissed her and Hilde, I could see, wished to disappear through the floorboards." Hilde was angry, but then she rather liked the kiss, she told him later. From that moment, my parents claim, Max stopped drinking so much and added some of his ration to my mother's. He saw that this mindless imbibing was getting him into trouble, and besides, it made him feel sick with himself; it was self-indulgence in a place like this.

Though they involved alcohol, his first two ambiguous encounters with Hilde were not nearly as disastrous as a third incident that involved no drink at all. I retold the story at my parents' golden anniversary party in October 1997. There was a dance of some kind to which Max went with his friends, and Hilde with hers. At the end, Max offered to drive Hilde home in the Jeep he had borrowed for the occasion. She didn't know that, in addition to being a poor speaker of English, Max had just learned how to drive. There were certain skills he hadn't mastered, but it was beyond his capacity to explain this to her in English.

The Jeep had an old motor that stalled all the time, and Max didn't yet fully understand the operation of the clutch. The passenger door was fastened to the body of the car with a wire that had to be unwound in order to get out. When they arrived at Hilde's quarters, Max sat there with his foot on the brake and the engine running. He wanted to explain why he could not do the courteous thing and help her exit the vehicle, but he just didn't have the vocabulary. So he did what he could. "Get out!" he barked at Hilde. She didn't need to be told twice, despite the torrential rain outside. Not only was she an experienced driver herself, but also she was used to gallant British officers who came round to open your door for you and who saw you safely to your destination. "Never again," she fumed as she flounced, drenched, to her front door. "This man has no manners at all." Dr Spanier let Max know a day or two later that she thought him insufferable.

But she softened when Max came up to her after she sang duets with a French co-worker, a Dr Grinbaum, at a holiday dinner, perhaps a Shabbat, and told her how much he had enjoyed hearing her sing. Things improved even more when they discovered that they had German in common, and Max could stop appearing to be a tongue-tied oaf. My father recalls the moment, because it was such a relief:

> I still remember seeing her at some official occasion. We stood by a window and looked out and began to tell each other about our lives and then we found out we could speak German. Her German was still a little tentative, but after a short while she spoke faultless German save for her occasional affecting Hollandisms. I was astounded at her composure in the face of what she had gone through. She spoke reluctantly about it and the details of her life came out quite slowly and when they came out her pain was enormous. These were moments that bound us together and which began to make me feel that these were ties that couldn't be undone frivolously.

By then, Max had learned that Hilde ran a day care center, and he did what he could to support her. Like the other relief workers, he was shocked by the inadequacy of the rations the British supplied to the inmates of Belsen, and he worked with the Jewish Committee, often on the shadow side of regulations, to improve their diet. He certainly endeared himself to Hilde by supplying her children with three to four times the milk ration the British allotted. He describes how this was done:

Each person had a milk ration card. As the Public Health officer of the camp, I was in charge of distributing those milk rations. Whenever a person left the camp or died, my office collected the card and invalidated it. I found a way to retain those cards, and during the time I was there the amount of milk available to the people, especially the children, was much greater than before. Not too many milk rations were withdrawn, as long as I had control over them. I must say I never had any regrets about having committed this larcenous act.

Max began visiting her at the day care center, my mother remembers, in a tiny convertible Volkswagen Beetle. It had already turned hot, so he kept the top down. When his car showed up in the square in front of her building, the helpers at the center called out, "Miss Hilde, the doctor is coming!" my mother says. They knew something was up, because Max's inspections, purportedly in the interest of public health, seemed to take place with alarming frequency.

Still, it was not uncommon for Hilde to spot Max flying by in a Jeep full of women on the way to an outing or the movies. In her turn, Hilde's rather passive circle of admirers was aroused to action, which consisted mostly of urging her away from this dangerous man. Chief among these was Dr Spanier. Spanier, a German Jew who had been a refugee in the Netherlands, was camp physician at Belsen before Max arrived, and became Max's assistant thereafter. He had left his family in Holland to work for UNRRA. The family had been fortunate enough to survive Auschwitz, and he was one of the few middle-aged members of the team. (Bob Moore has since discovered much more about Spanier's dubious past. He had been head of the camp hospital at Westerbork, part of a privileged class that colluded with the Germans, although he did save some lives and do some good.)

It was he who first told Hilde that Dr Goldberg was Swiss, not Polish, and thus let her know that they had a language in common. He was protective of Hilde rather than erotically interested, or so my mother says. My father takes rather a different view. He describes Dr Spanier as a "satyr" who had a girlfriend in the camp and told dirty jokes more skillfully than anyone my father has met since. But Dr Spanier had heard what he had heard. He thought Max was "a drunken good-for-nothing, who was after all the women in the camp," my mother says. "Well, the women did like him a lot."

"Whatever you do," Dr Spanier told Hilde, "don't you ever marry that man. He's no good for you." By now, Hilde was used to caution. Joe Wolhandler had left for the US before the end of 1945, and even the Alexander brothers had finally returned to England, where Hanns was about to be married. Paul wrote to say that he wanted Hilde to come to London in the summer, perhaps to get engaged. Hilde knew that she was drawn to Max in a way she hadn't experienced before, but the relationship was in its early days. They had known each other for six weeks at most, after all. She decided to take the Alexanders up on their invitation. She could make a rational decision once she'd seen Paul on his home turf. Besides, she could use the opportunity to visit her cousin Marion – the one whom my grandmother had saved from starvation as a little girl – who had lived in Leeds since before the war. Getting to England was a complicated matter involving all kinds of special papers obtained on trips to Amsterdam. Hilde was so short of cash that she borrowed some money from Max to pay the fare.

By the time she had taken a military train to Le Havre, a big storm had blown up in the Channel. It lasted three days. No ferries were running anywhere on the coast. While the authorities waited for the winds to subside, Hilde was put up in a Quonset hut for women officers, and there she had plenty of time to think.

Uncharacteristically, she discussed her dilemma with a fellow passenger, also stranded in the Quonset hut. Should she choose Paul? Should she gamble on the wayward Max? She wasn't sure if he liked her. She wasn't sure that *she* even liked *him*. People were always warning her about him, but still, there was a kind of attraction there that she hadn't felt before. "Follow your instincts," said the stranger.

Hilde spent about three weeks in England. It didn't take her more than a few minutes to recognize that she would never marry Paul. She sensed also that she was resented. The Alexanders were much more German than English. They had arrived just before the war from Berlin, and they were distantly related to the Frank family. Otto Frank and Leni Elias, Otto's sister, who had survived the war in Switzerland with her family, were childhood friends of the Alexanders. The Eliases, indeed, lived around the corner from my father's apartment in Basel, and Max had gone to school with their children. All the families – Alexanders, Franks, Eliases, Goldbergs, and Jacobsthals – had some connection to one another by chance, the classic six degrees of separation.

The queenly Mrs Alexander was the real power in the family. She was not at all pleased at the prospect that the same penniless refugee who had threatened her plans for Hanns had now arrived to do the same with Paul. The twins did not resist her. "They were Play-Doh in her hands," says my mother, her years with small children clearly showing. Nevertheless, Paul proposed, and Hilde promised to think about his offer while she visited her cousin Marion in Leeds.

This visit, too, had its shocks. Her kindhearted cousin had changed in the intervening years. She still had her warm nature, but she had married a coarse man, a furrier who made dirty jokes all the time. He was kind enough to give my mother a beaver coat, though, which she promptly sold to convert into more useable items. The two women took a little excursion to Edinburgh, where they talked the situation over. "Follow your heart. Don't marry anyone you don't really love. It's a mistake," Marion told her. Hilde thought of the wisecracking, meat-handed husband in Leeds, and wondered if Marion spoke from the depths of a bitterness she could never directly admit.

Upon her return to London, Hilde found a letter from Dr Grünpeter. Like Dr Spanier, he belonged to the chorus of Max-detractors, though his interest in Hilde was quite explicit; "he followed me around," my mother says. He informed her in his letter that, in her absence, Max had been going out with a flirtatious young woman who worked for one of the other Jewish relief services at Belsen. She was called Renée, and Hilde disliked her intensely, especially now that she knew that she was a competitor. For the first time, Hilde felt jealousy, just as Dr Grünpeter had hoped. "Don't count on Max to be friendly when you get back," he said. Alas, poor Grünpeter. The messenger never profits from these exchanges. He was left in the dust while Hilde sallied forth to do battle for the heart of the errant Swiss doctor. Meanwhile she told Paul that she couldn't marry him. "I'm heartbroken. I'll never marry," he told her, but six months later he was married, to the woman his mother had chosen for him.

I am delighted that my father's voice has by now joined my mother's in the narration of their courtship and of their life together. It's a privilege to have them both as tellers and witnesses, especially because their ways of remembering differ so much. My mother is a perfect observer. She remembers dates, times and events. My father, on the other hand, has a rather poor memory for dates and times – what happened when – but a marvelous memory for significance, for the total picture. His memory of their emotional life together is illuminated like a stained glass window by the power of his love. On love, he is the authority, the *New York Times* to whom my mother turns to check up on the veracity of what she says.

My father confirms that Dr Grünpeter, "who was mortally in love with Hilde," had tried to do his worst, "not that he was not right!" At the very moment when he got a letter from Hilde in England reporting that she had decided not to marry Paul Alexander because, among other reasons, her feelings for Max were too strong – what courage that must have taken! – my father was carrying on with Renée. Renée had been preceded by a beautiful but stupid English girl, and by a Romanian with a questionable past who was now working for UNRRA and was therefore, my father thought at the time, "officially kosher." Back in Basel, he had been "dating a very pretty, short, slightly pudgy Hungarian refugee with extremely long, shiny hair" who had thought that he had intended to marry her. Friends wrote from Switzerland to say that she was talking of breach of promise, though my father writes that "I searched my mind and conscience and I swear there was never any talk of marriage. But I was given to romantic excesses, and the language of love is a strong language, ephemeral as it may be."

I get the impression from all this that Hilde was quicker to recognize her feelings for Max than he was to recognize his. He says that he wasn't pleased about her going off to England to get married, but he "wasn't exactly stunned" either. By then, they had had a number of searching conversations; these had allowed her to assume a certain frankness when she wrote to Max from England admitting that she felt strongly about him. He had even written to her in mid-August, when he had been on a visit to see his parents in Switzerland. He described his despair about the future: his reluctance to come back to a country where he was not a citizen and wasn't wanted, his parents' insistence that he come back to claustrophobic Basel when his tour of duty ended.

After all these confidences, Hilde no doubt expected that they would be able to talk openly about the many emotions and conflicts that engrossed their waking hours. But instead they had a quarrel when she came back, probably because Max didn't respond as warmly as Hilde had hoped. They didn't see each other for several weeks, during which Max plunged into "a trough of despair and doubt." Hilde had told him that she didn't expect any sort of commitment, but that she wanted to stay with him as long as she could. As for Max, "there was that underlying feeling in me, warning me not to lose her." When Max finally marched up to her room, having conquered his doubts, he found her kissing another man, a casual date who left immediately when Max glared at them. Perhaps Hilde was trying to wash Max right out of her hair, like Nelly in *South Pacific*. At any rate, Max and Hilde were recognized as a couple from then on.

They took their first trip to Amsterdam together, staying in the Doelen Hotel, in the late fall of 1946. Max had already become an emotional support to Hilde and began to help her recognize what she had shut off for so long, during the crisis years of the war. He met the Scholtes, who took to him right away. It was almost as if he were meeting her parents, she says. There was an immediate rapport between Max and the younger Scholte children, Kiki and Kees. Otto Frank and Max became friends immediately as well. Hilde was reassured by these responses.

Not everyone was so impressed. In May 1946, Jo had married his girlfriend, Corry, after a short courtship. At her insistence, he had converted to the Dutch Reformed faith, and Hilde had come to the church wedding in her American uniform. Jo had been trying to resuscitate his father's women's wear business, but he was failing, and shortly after he would abandon the firm for a job at KLM. He didn't trust Max, didn't like the fact that he had no financial prospects, and was somewhat snooty about his background. Like the chorus of refugee doctors at Belsen, he warned Hilde against marrying this apparent roué and lefty. "Jo arrived in a big car," my father recalls, "was, as always, completely unreliable as to time, and treated Hilde with condescension and me with undisguised suspicion."

But Jo's was a lone voice in a chorus of approval from the survivors of the war in Amsterdam. Max and Hilde returned, for the moment, to their duties at Belsen in the knowledge that their situation there was temporary, and growing more precarious as the position of the remaining displaced persons improved. My father, in particular, remembers how established a society had grown up there by then, still operating independently of the British authorities and of the hostile country outside the gates of the camp. He describes "a lively black market," with inmates running kosher butcher shops and groceries and selling live fish from tanks built in the cellars of the sturdy stone buildings of the barracks. Occasionally, my father says, they went a bit overboard. One evening, he recalls,

> I was driving to the camp rather late when I passed one of the ambulances we used to transport people to the Glyn Hughes Hospital nearby. This seemed a bit out of the way for an ambulance. I stopped them and asked what they were doing. Then I heard a distinct sound from the ambulance which I thought at first could be the moaning of a woman in labor but then quickly recognized as the mooing of a cow. They had used my ambulances as cattle trucks! I put a stop to that one, but, frankly, I was more amused than angry. Eighteen hundred calories a day was a stimulant to commerce.

Even if society at Bergen-Belsen was becoming more coherent as the remaining residents began to realize that they were in for a long wait before they could find a country that would allow them in, my parents' role at Bergen-Belsen was coming to an end. They began considering their future. Until Max had become a possible element of that future, Hilde had thought that she had found a perfect solution for her homelessness. Representatives of an American organization, the National Council of Jewish Women, had visited the day care center during the previous year. The Council was looking for fourteen young survivors of unusual achievement whose studies had been curtailed by the war. Full scholarships to study in the US would be offered, but the young women had to promise that they would return to Europe when their studies were completed. Marriage would make the candidates ineligible. No one at the time thought of questioning this condition, nor were many men prepared to follow a woman to another country.

In January 1947, Hilde was told that she had been chosen for the award. At first she was exhilarated. She could go to any college in the United States; she could study anything. At last she could become a pediatrician, as she had always dreamed. The Council proposed that after her demobilization, she should come straight to the US. She expected to leave Europe in August 1947, at the latest. As my father writes, this deadline was a "line in the sand" for the young couple. Should they marry, or should they part?

Max was still unsure. He could not imagine emigrating anywhere, to Israel, for example, nor had he seriously considered America, a country that, as the Cold War began to take shape, he regarded with fascination but also with much suspicion. He had no future in Switzerland, he could already see that, but he couldn't quite believe the evidence of his eyes. He still clung to the hope that, eventually, the authorities would reverse their decision and give him citizenship. Besides, his parents were thoroughly established in Basel, and he had lived there his whole life.

Because of these uncertainties, they decided to be reasonable. They agreed that Hilde should accept the American offer. She was deeply in love with Max, she knew that, but unlike him, she was used to instability, to painful separations, and to loss. She was too proud to put any conditions on his affection. Still, they continued their life together under the shadow of these uncertainties. They had developed little routines. They took day trips here and there, and enjoyed shopping for things within the great web of army territory. Max was touched by Hilde's enthusiasm for small luxuries, the things she had never had, when they made trips to army shops in Hamburg or Bremerhaven. He has told us often of one purchase she made, yellow silk pajamas decorated with parrots and flowers, a lurid contrast to years of military khaki.

They decided, too, that they would take one last trip together. Max would show Hilde the Alps and teach her how to ski. Accordingly, they set off by train in February 1947, but they hadn't counted on a blizzard that lengthened the eight-hour trip from Hamburg to Basel to a nightmarish thirty-five hours. Hilde seemed to have an apocalyptic effect on the weather when matters of the heart were involved. Typically, she remembers some "nice Scandinavians who shared their crackers and cheese" with the ravenous couple. They arrived at my paternal grandparents' apartment just in time for the midday meal. Hilde met Max's parents for the first time, sat down on the sofa, and sank into exhausted sleep. My grandfather Moritz took Max into the kitchen. He had known Hilde for exactly five minutes, but he wagged his finger at Max and told him sternly that this woman was different. If Max treated her as he had treated his previous girlfriends, his name would be mud as far as Moritz was concerned. My father has never quite understood Moritz's insight, which he attributes partly to snobbishness: Moritz, an uneducated Polish Jew, had enormous respect for what he perceived as the superiority of German Jews. But he succeeded in making Max reflect once more on his impending separation from a woman he really loved.

The next morning, Max and Hilde set off for Pontresina, a resort in the high Alps of southeastern Switzerland. It was raining the whole way, a condition standard on ski trips, in my limited experience. As the train rolled along the lake at Zurich, a new feeling of certainty crept over Max. Perhaps the paternal dressing-down, a sort of blessing in reverse, had something to do with this sense of security. Nothing else had changed. They still had no money, no country, and no economic future, but now, at least, he knew that he didn't want Hilde to leave him for America.

"Hilde," he said, "I think the thing to do is to get married." He could see that this solution was not as obvious to Hilde as to him. "She looked at me," he writes, "and I remember that a fine line of perspiration appeared on her upper lip. She wasn't sure. Was I really ready? She didn't think I was really sure either." My mother says that her first response was: "I'll have to think about it. I love you more than I've loved anyone, but I don't know if we can get along." After much discussion, they decided that they would embark on a trial marriage for one year, during which they would have no children and at the end of which they would reassess the situation.

It was a murky time, emotionally and even meteorologically. Hilde found Pontresina "overwhelming, depressing, threatening." She was a flatlander, not used to looming crags and dark, narrow valleys. For her first venture on skis, Max took her out to the hill behind their inn, where she slid directly into a fence and twisted her ankle. A few days after their arrival, Max's younger sister Regi turned up. She was a sulky seventeen-year-old, and Max's mother, never a psychologist, had sent her to get her out of the house. Fortunately, my parents say, Regi got a toothache and had to go back to Basel, but she did nothing to improve Hilde's sinking spirits. My mother thinks that "right after the war, I was quite weakened. My body was not yet in equilibrium. I had had starvation and some deprivation. I didn't have any true emotional support without my parents, even from Max, who was so problematic at the time."

It was Max, I think, whose certainty and joy grew each hour, and Hilde who had a reaction that took her by surprise: depression and even grief. Perhaps this tremendous step made her realize how much she had lost in losing her parents, and how alone in the world she was. She was more optimistic than my father, but also more of a realist. The future was so unclear, and the possibility of celebration so remote, with no one to confide in and no one to give her away on the day of her marriage. And then there was the opportunity to study in the United States. How could she turn her back on that, and throw herself into an uncertain life with a man who was no more secure in his future than she was? No matter how much she loved him, life might be too difficult. He might leave her; they might wander in poverty, or grow bitter under the confinement of a narrow border somewhere.

They returned to Belsen from Switzerland in a pensive mood. Hilde notified the Council of Jewish Women that she was planning to marry, and therefore couldn't take up their scholarship. They went to Joint headquarters in Paris in late May 1947. Hilde was being demobbed, released from service, and Max went along to see if he could get a job with Joint in some new part of the world, perhaps in North Africa, where an office was supposed to open up. He had wonderful references from all kinds of colleagues at Belsen, from officials with Joint and with UNRRA. But Joint, the American Joint Distribution Committee, was closing down its operations in Europe, and there was nothing available. Max took this personally. If only he could have observed what was going on in New York, he would have seen that Joint viewed itself as a highly efficient *ad hoc* organization. It left an area as soon as local people could take over, the way it had done, for example, at Blankenese. But he couldn't know that, and saw his rejected application as another broken hope.

My parents spent about two weeks in Paris, half the time under the spell of its springtime magic, and half the time in despair. "Paris was in the flush of the liberation and a feeling of post-war optimism seemed to put a bright shine on the city, especially in comparison with drab, dark, destroyed Germany," my father writes.

> There were hours when we were a young couple in love in Paris and hours when we felt like human flotsam, thrown upon a strange shore and watching the happy natives with wonder and longing. All the time the immensity of events that had taken place and were still taking place swirled in our consciousness, sometimes like planets at a distance and sometimes like asteroids bearing down on us and threatening to crush us.

They stayed in a small hotel on the Left Bank, and walked all over the city. Hilde had received some pay from Joint, with which she bought a couple of hats and a white suit, now that she was no longer in uniform. They have always remembered their time there together fondly. But the other side, the sense that the rest of the world was moving on while they, citizens of nowhere, were trapped in a sort of no-man's-land, oppressed them; and they never forgot that feeling, either. From Paris, they went their separate ways, Hilde to Amsterdam, Max to Basel. Each of them had to establish some sort of citizenship or identity that would allow them to marry, to work, and to live somewhere. Without their military uniforms, they were just two more stateless drifters. They didn't even have the right to become husband and wife.

During this month of separation from early June to early July, Max and Hilde wrote to each other every day, sometimes several times a day. Max occasionally referred to the sojourn in Paris. In one letter, on June 20, a big day for letter writing, it seems, for both of them, Max referred to "our fiasco in Paris, where we believed that we could conquer harsh realities by sheer force of character." It was hard to believe that you mattered much as an individual when state bureaucracies made things so impossible; when you were considered dead, as in Hilde's case, despite the living, breathing reality of her presence; or were misdescribed and miscategorized through meanness and racial malice, as in Max's. Once the carapace of uniform and military rank was stripped from them, my parents had become as vulnerable as the people they had been taking care of at Belsen. Without nationality, without freedom, without money, it seemed to them that they had survived only to become two more casualties of war.

Chapter 8

Love Letters:
Amsterdam, Basel

As soon as my parents separated, they began writing in the German they now knew they shared. Hilde described her train journey home through the dreary flatlands of northern France. There was always suspense at the borders about the legitimacy of her papers, but she was waved through without difficulty. She wrote with her usual wit about the obtrusive feet of the fat lady next to her and about the different characters of the border guards, but the lowering sky of these provinces of France, which had, after all, been the battleground of World War I, filled her with dread. The landscape reminded her of the loathing she felt for Europe and for all its darkness and death, of her claustrophobia crossing its ominous borders, and of her desire to move on. Then Holland burst upon her. The smiling fields full of greenery and cows, the revolving bridges over endless canals, the bustling cities, lifted her heart with affection for her old homeland.

She wrote to Max late at night, curled up on her bed at her brother's, where Jo and Corry had tried to duplicate her childhood room for her stay, and told him everything that had happened and everything she had thought about that day. She tried to be a good little socialist for Max, earnestly describing the reaction of the neighborhood to a bakers' strike. People expressed "hair-raisingly reactionary" opinions about doing without bread for a day or two, she wrote. But after a couple of pages of boilerplate discussion of the economic conditions under which the bakery workers labored and the prospects for a solution, she added: "Despite the pessimistic remarks above, I had several pleasant experiences today." I have to smile; that is the mother I know peeking through her desire to please my sternly Marxist father.

She reminds me of the story in Boswell's *Life of Johnson* about the man the 18th-century English writer meets one day, many years after he has become famous. This man, a retired lawyer named Edwards, had been a schoolfellow of Samuel Johnson's decades before at Pembroke College, Oxford. He knows that his old chum has become a Great Man. "You are a philosopher, Dr Johnson," he says. "I have tried too in my time to be a philosopher; but, I don't know how, cheerfulness was always breaking in." Cheerfulness, even happiness, had a way of breaking in on Hilde all the time. She enjoyed every moment of the little complacencies of peacetime life, and she was going to be married to a man she adored. The baker's strike couldn't match these realities for color.

My parents have let me see the touching and intense correspondence of that month. It is a document of passionate love, and we all laugh at the idea that this besotted couple really expected the trial marriage to last only a year. I have been allowed to glimpse my parents when they were younger than my own sons. I feel maternal toward the people my parents were then. My mother realized some time ago that I'm much older than her parents were when they were deported. Time has made the generations stand on their heads, and we can't always remember who is the parent and who the child.

I have never known my mother to describe a landscape the way she described northern France to my father, nor have I known her as she was in her brief revolutionary phase of a week or two. Her attempt at Marxist analysis lay across her natural liberalism like an ill-fitting coat, and she soon shrugged it off in favor of more specific and active ways of fighting injustice. She comes across as so innocent, so loving, so insecure about her education, now that she is in love with a ferociously well-read man, that I understand why people found her so adorable. The same wide-eyed enthusiast who argued with her dentist about politics after he had filled her ten cavities, who took simple pleasure in riding a bicycle through the rainy streets of Amsterdam and enjoying a cup of real coffee and a slice of strawberry torte, who found friendly people everywhere and trusted them, was also a whirlwind of efficient activity. She went out every day, diligently retracing the bureaucratic steps that would prove to the Dutch authorities that she had not died, and she made progress. "Now that I know that I'm returning to a world where people live normally, I feel capable of anything and thirsty for knowledge," she wrote my father on June 8, 1947.

In the evenings, there were many people to visit. The tiny group of survivors and their Gentile friends saw each other all the time, talked about how they were going to re-establish themselves, and rejoiced when someone emerged from the almost total devastation of the war. She was cherished and advised by people who had known her since childhood and now pitied her terrible loss. The Mierses, a survivor family, insisted on making a wedding dress for her, though Hilde wasn't particularly enthusiastic about the idea of a wedding in the first place; the young couple had agreed that they would get married in Switzerland, and in a synagogue, to please Max's parents. But the Mierses had known

Hilde since babyhood, and they wouldn't take no for an answer. Hilde wrote that the fittings would start in a couple of days: "And for the first time, darling, I like the idea, because [the dress] is being sewn with so much real friendship and love. They assure me that all of Switzerland will swoon in delight at the sight of it. And I want to have a beautiful dress for you. Do you think it's childish of me to get pleasure out of such things?" (June 20, 1947)

Max, by then, was simply counting the days until they could hold each other once more. He addressed her as *Hildchen*, "little Hilde," as he has always done since, and, like Hilde, he complained continually about a mail service Americans might regard as miraculous, with deliveries three or four times a day, and overnight arrivals between the two countries. "I have had to eat my breakfast eggs without a letter from you," he moaned at one point.

At the darkest ebb of his mood, Max had written Hilde a couple of letters that, to me, seem downright cruel. He condescended to her, correcting her spelling and lamenting her lack of education, and cast doubt on their plans to marry. Hilde, who must have really loved him, responded in just the right tone. She added humorous footnotes to the love letter she had evidently been writing when his bitter lines arrived ("What drivel!" for example, alongside her expressions of affection, and "a few kisses" in tiny handwriting next to her original "many, many kisses"). On June 17, she responded with gallant and cleansing anger:

All right, I admit that the whole situation is not exactly heartening at the moment. But I remember a time when I was six, when Jo and I had to climb through a propped-open window to get into our apartment after school. We ate hot meals only twice a week, because our parents didn't get home from work until after nine at night.

We were alone all day. I remember a time when we sat by the window, just as I do now, but with all the lights out, and listened for the steps of the S.S. who were going to haul us away. I remember sitting in the streetcar with my parents, ready to be deported, guarded by S.S. men. They let us go…one week later my parents were gone. I swam across the Maas…with nothing but my life, and I knew that if I survived this war, nothing worse could ever happen to me.

Max, we were so close to death, to poverty and misery…at Belsen I looked into the faces of the dead, listened to the living dead, as they talked to me with their destroyed, rotting faces, and wondered if they were my parents. Darling, I have no fear of life, nothing scares me any more, understand that. [You're depressed] because it's been a month and you're still unemployed? Because there are stupid governments? But my love, I am alive, we love each other, don't you understand the miracle of that?

Max, though paralyzed by other kinds of guilt, didn't seem to resent the way Hilde pulled survivor's rank on him. On the contrary, he was genuinely moved and convinced by her blaze of righteous rage, which marked the end of his dark mood for a time. "Darling, beloved Hildchen," Max wrote back as soon as he got this letter, "I'm going to write in more detail tomorrow, but I want to get this letter out today by air mail. I just want to tell you that I love you terribly. And I beg you to forgive me for giving such uncontrolled expression to my bad moods. You should know, and I'm sure you do know, that none of these moods can shake my love for you. I rejoice hugely at the prospect of our life together, even if external circumstances don't look very favorable at the moment."

In truth, he was having a harder time than Hilde in many

ways, and had spent much of the first two weeks in Basel in a state of black depression. He turned twenty-seven on June 16, and there he was, unemployed, living in his parents' house, where there were many emotional conflicts. Even his bed caused him sleepless nights. "Here I am in my lonely bed," he wrote with self-pitying humor on June 5, just after his arrival, "back again on this queerly constructed piece of furniture that hardly deserves the name of bed. It's 11 now, and I don't expect to get to sleep until about 2 a.m., when my tossing and turning will have worn me out enough." All his medical school classmates had long since found jobs. He was an odd duck, a non-Swiss, Swiss-born, Jewish doctor, and therefore unemployable. Because so many of his friends were at work during the day, often in other parts of the country, he had very few people to talk to.

As his loneliness deepened, so did his despair. How could he have asked Hilde to marry someone who couldn't even find work? It seemed to him that he was trying as hard as he could: writing letters to the appropriate government departments to establish citizenship, to medical employment agencies, to the Polish government offices in Bern to get them to send needed papers, and so on. But everything seemed to lead to a dead end. On June 12, for example, he copied out an answer for Hilde to a letter he had written to the Swiss Medical Employment Agency. In his letter to the agency, he explained that he had actually been born in Switzerland, and that, despite his apparent Polish citizenship, he was absolutely fluent in the language and customs of his birthplace and had been educated in Basel all the way through to his medical degree. He was hoping for a position in pediatrics, and suggested that, under the circumstances, they might not consider him a foreigner.

In the hideous, formal language that came so naturally to German-speaking institutions, the agency answered that there were already too many native Swiss applying for the kinds of jobs

Max was seeking. Even Swiss doctors had been waiting in vain for these positions. Max would have to find a place in a TB sanatorium, or in a psychiatric hospital, places that were desperate for help and would take (so the letter implied) applicants no one else wanted. It was clear that none of the bureaucrats at the agency had the slightest interest in Max's actual status or qualifications, or had noticed the point of his letter.

The bureaucratic entanglements in which my parents found themselves took up the lion's share of their correspondence. Hilde's status, though complicated, can be summarized in a few sentences. The Dutch Government had apparently issued a statement in newspapers and flyers at the end of the war, urging survivors to come forward and re-register as Dutch citizens or residents. In Amsterdam, especially, the Dutch Resistance had bombed the municipal records office during the war, to keep the Nazis from getting at the names registered there. Now, ironically enough, survivors from the capital had no record that they had ever existed, and they had to re-establish themselves somehow.

Because Hilde had been working at Bergen-Belsen during this period, she had not known about the decree, nor that it had a time limit within which one had to declare oneself, and so she found herself confronting officials who told her to her face that she didn't exist. To prove her existence, she had to find witnesses who had known her since birth: no easy task, since she had been a refugee in Holland to begin with, and was now a survivor of a genocide which had wiped out 106,000 of Holland's 140,000 Jewish residents. These witnesses had to write statements that they signed in the presence of a notary, and then, eventually, they had to go with Hilde to an office in The Hague where they would be questioned and, with luck, believed. Hilde had to find four such witnesses and then process them through the municipal and national bureaucracies. The witnesses were Jo and Zus Scholte and the Miers brothers and their wives. In addition, she needed various documents in order to get permission to enter Switzerland to be married. They consisted of a *visum*, or travel document for Switzerland; a declaration of her willingness to marry Max; and the identity papers comprised in the Dutch *Acte van Bekendheid,* act of recognition. To complicate matters further, the *visum* had a time constraint, and had to be co-ordinated with Swiss regulations on marriage. These included a public declaration of the intent to marry, the banns, which by law had to be announced in Basel. The posting of the banns depended on the *visum*, among other documents, and of course they took time. Compared to the bureaucracies of Europe, the Catch-22 of Joseph Heller seems a model of efficiency and reason. Max tried to hurry the Polish Embassy in Bern into sending papers first to Amsterdam and then to Basel; the only hope of any citizenship for the couple was through Max's supposedly Polish nationality, though he had never set foot in Poland.

Acquiring all these documents turned out to be a full-time job for Hilde. She had to find a lawyer and a notary, and she trotted from office to office for weeks on end. She collected signed testimonials – about her health from her family doctor, about her past life in the Netherlands and her character from her witnesses, about her future status from the Swiss and even Polish consulates, and so on. Eventually, she was declared stateless. This was considered simpler for her than applying for Dutch citizenship, which would take years. She traveled on a crazy quilt of a document, full of stamps from the British Army of Occupation and from all the agencies she had had to deal with. Even I appear on it later as a baby, at that point with American stamps at the port of entry in New York. Hilde was helped, in the end, by the prefect of police in Amsterdam, who was the father of one of her schoolfellows and was full of compassion. Without him, and without the help of the Scholtes and other good friends who were prepared mildly to perjure themselves about how far back they had known her, Hilde would have languished in the Netherlands for much longer than a month. But she had a basic faith in the goodness of the people around her which, incredibly, seemed justified by events, despite the horrors of the years through which she had just come. Gerard Nijssen, a historian researching the background for a television program about my mother, discovered in 2002 that she had, in fact, been granted citizenship in 1946, though no one in the relevant government agencies seems to have realized it at the time. All the agonies described here could have been avoided, had Hilde known.

Max's position was much more deeply embittering, though he had survived the war in safety. His family had been in Switzerland for a relatively long time, long enough not to be considered refugees. His mother, Cilly Sachs, had been born in Fürth, Germany, in 1897 and had come to Switzerland as a toddler around the turn of the century. She was one of seven children of a peddler of limited means and even more limited energy. His wife and children did the work of selling textiles and clothes at country fairs, while he stayed at home and read, as was often the custom in lower-class Jewish families in those days. The four girls were regarded as a burden on whom an education would be wasted, and Cilly was taken out of school at the age of fourteen to help in the family business. This was a pity, because Cilly was a highly intelligent woman who spent her life regretting her limited training and never stopped teaching herself new things, including English. My father has told us about the nights during his adolescence when she retired to bed after a brutal day's work with an apple, a yogurt, and a volume by the social philosopher Herbert Spencer.

When Cilly's mother grew old after the death of her husband, she lived in a nursing home in Endingen-Lengnau, a village inhabited exclusively by Jews until the late 1800s. It was a rural ghetto, my father says, a relic of a Swiss law which forbade Jews to live in cities. The edict was abolished only because the American government under the unlikely leadership of President Buchanan protested in 1860, when American-Jewish businessmen traveling in Europe found themselves suddenly subject to these medieval restrictions. My father's description of this event is confirmed by Swiss historians Jacques Picard and Willy Guggenheim, and by an astounding document from the records of the 36th Congress of the United States. This includes a message to the House of Representatives from President James Buchanan, dated April 24, 1860 and entitled "Discriminations in Switzerland against Citizens of the United States of the Hebrew Persuasion."

The cities of Switzerland began acquiring Jewish inhabitants rather late after having expelled them during the Middle Ages. Jews had lived in Basel, for example, for some time before they were accused of poisoning the wells and causing the Black Death of 1349. As a result, the entire Jewish population of the city, about 600 souls, was burned to death on an island in the Rhine. There had not been much of a Jewish presence in the city, or indeed anywhere in Switzerland, after that, though occasional minor returns and expulsions occurred. Not until Napoleon invaded Switzerland in the early 19th century did Jewish cattle traders, and eventually merchants, appear in small numbers, arriving from Swabia on the north and from the Alsace to the west. At the time of my father's birth, Jews had lived in Basel for perhaps fifty years. They had been granted residency in 1862 and full civic rights in 1872. The community in the 1920s consisted of about 1500 souls, and stands now at about 2000. When I visited the beautiful historical museum of the City of Basel in 1995, I noticed that there was not a single word about a Jewish presence in the city.

By the time my grandmother and my future grandfather, Moritz, found themselves and each other in Switzerland, the country was more tolerant, but still very narrow in its view of foreignness and what we now call ethnic difference. It must have looked awfully inviting nonetheless when my grandfather Moritz arrived during World War I. He came for personal reasons that, for everyone involved in the murderous 20th century, turned political. It was he who had been born in the Polish city of Minsk-Masowiecki, then under Russian dominion, the city that gave my father his improbable rank of lieutenant-colonel after the war. Like many Jewish men from that part of the world at that time, my grandfather Moritz never knew his date of birth exactly, because birth records were used to draft Jews into the Tsar's army for indeterminate periods of a minimum of seven years. Anti-Semitism, both codified and casual, turned military service into a kind of slavery that any sensible Jewish family tried to avoid.

Around 1910 or 1911, when Moritz was about sixteen, he decided to follow his father, who had deserted the family for a woman who lived in Lucerne. Moritz worked for a while for a rag-dealer in Stuttgart, and when war broke out in 1914, young Moritz was interned as a Russian alien. After a year or two of confinement, he and his father, who vouched for him from Switzerland, managed to convince the authorities that he was just passing through, and he was allowed across the Swiss border. When he got to Lucerne, he found himself in more or less continuous domestic warfare with the Other Woman and her sons, although his father was warm and welcoming. That is all I know of what must have been a complex emotional situation.

Moritz spoke Yiddish, but not German. He used to tell us that he learned the basics from street signs. Of course it was not High German he picked up, but the wildly variant dialects of his new homeland. I could hear the Yiddish inflections in his voice when I was a child. Undeterred by this liability, he soon found work as a peddler, and within a few years proved to have a reasonably good head for business. It was at a neighboring textile booth at one of the fairs that he first saw his future bride, and they married quickly in 1917. Cilly's parents were delighted to get rid of her, and Moritz, in fact, had a much better feel for the trade than did her own father. Four children followed: Paula was born in 1918, my father, Max, in 1920, Leo in 1924, and the youngest daughter, Regi, in 1929. The family lived at first in the small industrial city of Grenchen, near the watchmaking town of Biel, where the two older children were born. They survived under conditions of almost continual turmoil. Their hand-to-mouth existence, especially during the difficult 1930s, was exacerbated by Moritz's habit of showing initial flair and energy, and then losing interest in the various enterprises he took up. He loved to play cards with his cronies at the Basel Casino, the same building where Theodor Herzl convened the first Zionist Congress in 1897.

Moritz "never really understood the culture he found himself in," my father says now. "He imitated the style of gentlemen in operettas, and learned poses from popular culture, the way people do now with the movies. He didn't have a clue about how things really worked." That's how I remember my grandfather, in fact. He was a wizened little man who liked to wear a sharply creased fedora on the side of his head, and balanced an unlit cigarette at an angle on his lower lip. By then, the 1950s and '60s, he reminded Susie and me of James Cagney. He was small, but sinewy. Right through his eighties, he liked to flex a bicep for his grandchildren to admire: "Feel that," he mumbled through his dangling cigarette. "The old man's got some life left in him yet, eh?"

It was Cilly who kept the family going, doing all the hard manual labor involved in raising four children on very little money. Both parents rose before dawn and returned after dark with huge wet bundles of wool and underwear after a day of traveling by train around the country to the open-air fairs and markets. My father remembers a moment in 1937 when Cilly and Moritz could not meet the payments on a suite of living room furniture they had bought years before. Bailiffs arrived and sealed up the living room until the payments had been met. That process took another year. At such moments, Moritz took to his bed for weeks on end, rising from his depression only to gamble with friends in the eternal hope that his winnings would lift the family out of debt. Then he returned to quarrel over money with Cilly once more. There was plenty of conflict among the siblings, too, and between parents and children. In Paula's case, there were fights over the endless restrictions imposed on her freedom because she was a girl, and in Max's, over politics, in which he was embroiled from early adolescence. Max felt especially close to his older sister, to whom he felt bound by an intuitive sense of injustice, and to his frail younger brother, who had asthma and eczema and suffered under the conditions poverty imposed. My father has always said that he himself physically resembled his paternal grandfather, Samuel, who was tall, solid and athletic in build: Leo was small and wiry like Moritz. It was a noisy household, with much screaming and hitting. Even when they were merely playing, the boys liked to arrive at the midday meal by leapfrogging over the length of the table, causing the neighbors to pound floors and walls in protest.

When I ask my father about his relationship with his parents, he becomes surprisingly inarticulate for a man who has always loved words. Besides, he is a psychoanalyst who underwent psychoanalysis himself as part of his training. Surely, after all these years, he must have some insight into the emotions which drove this energetic and noisy family. But he has very little to say. He becomes almost sheepish. He says that he and his father fought; that his father was enigmatic to him, a mask, an often hostile, sometimes impulsively loving figure with whom conversation was impossible; that his mother inspired constant guilt because of all the suffering she endured on behalf of her children.

Max was a brilliant student. He was the first in his family to go to college, and then to medical school. But all the while, he says, he felt guilty that his parents "were forced to work in summer and winter outdoors, leaving in the dark morning hours and returning late at night with their heavy packages of merchandise and wet tarps, on rainy days, that weighed a ton. Meanwhile I was sitting in warm auditoria, listening to my professors or plotting political actions with the organization of left-wing students." He feels, now, a deep compassion for them both, for their difficult lives and missed opportunities. More than that, he cannot say.

I can testify to his guilt about his parents, for I saw it in operation until they died, and they both lived to a ripe age. Occasionally, in the early 1950s, we ate up what small savings we had accumulated in America by visiting them in Switzerland, because Moritz had generated a crisis which turned out, upon arrival, not to be one; or, later on, they would come to us and stay for months filled with unexpressed tensions. In my childhood, my father told us about the occasions when he took my grandmother to an afternoon tea dance at one of the department stores in downtown Basel. He did this because he felt that Moritz, with his constant card-playing, neglected her, and that an elderly woman like my grandmother needed some looking after. Not until I was in my thirties myself did I realize that Cilly had been all of thirty-six at the time. By then, she saw herself as old, and acted accordingly. She lived to be ninety, but I never saw a spark of youth in her. Perhaps that kind of extended elasticity requires money, education and leisure, resources she didn't have.

My father's memories of childhood are few. The linguistic shortcomings of his parents seemed to have created a sort of blankness in him. He remembers his bald, vigorous grandfather Samuel very well: running alongside him to the synagogue, delighting in the origami birds he knew how to make. If he was in a good mood, he would make a bird with special pockets, a deluxe version. Samuel was warm and lively – his personality, as well as his physical characteristics, resembled his grandson's – and Max felt an affinity with him. The most traumatic event of my father's childhood, he says, was Samuel's death when a fishbone caught in his throat and became infected. My father was sixteen at the time, the same age his father had been when he set off for Switzerland from Poland, and his grandfather was sixty-five.

While we are on the subject of physical affinities, I ask my father about the mood swings which seem to have been a family trait passed down through the generations. Could there be a physical reason for them, a matter of hormones, perhaps? Characteristically, he dismisses my speculation out of hand. My father has some difficulty with probing conversation, still, after all these years. He cannot resist cutting off points of exploration or connection with peremptory commands.

This habit used to irritate my sisters and me to the point of madness, particularly when his "Don'ts" were couched in the jargon of his profession, with which he was otherwise generally quite sparing. We wondered whether he did this with his patients, but we guessed not. It would have been terrible clinical practice. At home, however, we heard "don't project, don't be hysterical, don't exaggerate, don't be so defensive" from both parents. Such a ploy kept them firmly in control of the direction and the temperature of certain expressions of feeling: our emotions seemed somehow unworthy. This would hardly have mattered in a family as child-centered and loving as ours if we had not had our particular history, but as it was, the habitual belittling of what we felt supported our haunted intuition that we were hollow, small souls in comparison with the heroic and martyred generations of the war. Our weaknesses were symptoms of neurosis, we were told. It wasn't the command to be stoical which bothered us so much; it was the labeling. If you had been called hysterical, nothing you said thereafter could be taken seriously.

I consider my father, growing up amid the anxiety of constant struggle, in a large family whose emotional temperature was always high. I consider that, despite all the talking and shouting, his parents were fundamentally inarticulate, unable to give voice to their deepest thoughts and feelings. They had considerable warmth, but they had both been raised in conditions of neglect. Moritz's mother may even have been mentally ill. My father has always thought that she might have killed herself; but such circumstances never make it to the light of day in most families, and the truth will never be known. Like many bright working-class children, my father educated himself right out of his class of origin and found, to his horror, that he no longer had a common language with the people closest to him. But circumstances larger than the fortunes of his family contributed a great deal too.

Switzerland offered safety, but not comfort. Foreignness and Jewishness kept the family from civic welcome and civic engagement. My father says that the tiny community of Jews in Basel, about 1 percent of a city of under 200,000 people, was mostly self-contained, and that only a few Jews became lawyers, doctors, or professionals with a chance of acceptance into the wider institutions of the city. My grandparents could have done much to improve their position if they had applied for citizenship in the 1920s, when anti-Semitism was not envisioned as an official point of view and the flood of refugees from Germany had not yet begun. But they were too unaware to put in for it then, and as a result they remained foreigners, handicapped by all the Swiss regulations against outsiders. Most of Moritz's friends from Poland did become citizens during that period; it cost several thousand francs, which they managed to save for the purpose. Other Polish relatives came to Switzerland. Some even married Cilly's sisters and brothers, and some settled in the Rhineland, in Germany, where they disappeared during the Holocaust. Many of these relatives were better established in their new homelands than were my grandparents. We laugh ruefully about my grandparents' cluelessness as we discuss their life in Switzerland.

They had to deal with the routine stereotypes of anti-Semitism every day – what my father calls folk anti-Semitism – involving cunning, money-grubbing Jews who only have eyes for the main chance, and yet they contradicted all of these prejudices. They were naive, undereducated people, ill-fitted for business, and with little initiative. Their strengths lay in their basic intelligence, resilience and humor. They were capable of affection, too, but were simply not brought up to the habit of showing warmth very often.

With the rise of the Nazis in Germany, the intensity of Swiss anti-Semitism rose as well. There were many Nazi sympathizers in Switzerland, especially in German-speaking areas like Basel. The German border was right there, a mile or two from the city center. Max, in his early teens, endured constant slights. Sometimes well-meaning remarks from kindly disposed people hurt more than obvious insults like the gross caricatures he found on the blackboard when he came in from recess, or the snubs of the landlord's wife, "who wore the pants in that household," my father says. She subscribed to Goebbels's propaganda rag, *Der Völkische Beobachter*, with its weekly news about getting rid of the scourge of Jewish vermin.

My father remembers two incidents involving teachers, for example, both from his days at the *Gymnasium*, the college-preparatory public high school he attended. My father excelled in literature, history and writing, and he recalls the way in which his teacher, Dr Dietschy, chided his German class more than once for its poor performance on an essay: "Look at Goldberg from Poland, he puts you all to shame." His geography teacher, Dr Vosseler, held a chair at the university. In order to illustrate the difference between an Alpine skull (short and round) and a Slavic skull (long and narrow), he took measurements. Max was chosen as the only example of a Slavic skull in the class, but Dr Vosseler was surprised and disappointed to discover that my father had an alpine skull like everyone else. My father adds that his teacher was not a racist, "just an anthropologist, and actually firmly anti-Nazi." Still, it was painful to be reminded even by people who admired him that he was seen as radically different, though he had lived alongside them all his life.

Nonetheless, he excelled all the way through school, and in fact became rather gifted at turning enemies into friends. He challenged the boy who drew the caricature to a fistfight, which my broad-shouldered father won handily, and before long the boy had confided in him that he was worried about his homosexual desires. I find it amusing that my father clearly had the makings of a doctor of souls in him at that tender age. Later on, as a medical student, he gave lectures on sexuality to his socialist youth group: "I cringe when I think what an arrogant know-nothing I was, fulminating against the repressive bourgeois family," he writes when I ask him about this period, "but it was all pretty harmless...The extent of ignorance about matters sexual was incredible, and was no credit to the Swiss family. They were eager to hear what I had to say, and to this day I believe I did some good, no matter what theoretical hogwash I administered with it."

But most of the time, Max lived in a dissociative haze. He went to high school, and then to medical school. He passed his exams just as the war was ending, and wrote a thesis. He led the raffish social life of a university student, and did what he could against Nazism from his oddly protected vantage point by taking part in various socialist groups. He still lived at home with his parents, as was the custom in that time and city. Inside, he was tormented by this mixture of safety and paralysis. News about what was really going on in the countries surrounding Switzerland was severely restricted, but political feeling ran high. It was strange leading a normal life so near a border largely closed to refugees. Those Jews who made it into Switzerland from neighboring countries were treated badly. The traditional Swiss suspicion of strangers, combined with a simmering pro-Nazi element, especially among the immigration and border police, made them unwelcome. Unlike my native-born father, the refugees, mostly Viennese who arrived after the *Anschluss* of Austria in 1938, were denied all work and access to civic institutions (my father could have worked, but not as a doctor). In addition to this generally tense atmosphere for Jews, there were a few moments of public fright during the war.

The most ominous moment came in 1942, when a manifesto signed by 200 of the country's most prominent academic, business and political leaders was published. It urged Swiss citizens to recognize that a new political era had dawned, and that it was time for Switzerland to join what they called the New Europe, whose leader was Adolf Hitler. The declaration was denounced by the liberal newspapers, and caused an uproar. But until General Guisan, head of the Swiss army, declared that the manifesto appeared to pose an immediate threat to the survival of the democratic Swiss state, it was unclear which way the country would go. General Guisan called for a general mobilization of the Swiss Army, and for a few days soldiers were seen everywhere. The crisis passed uneventfully. Thus, my father writes, "…the savior of Switzerland, and by extension my family, was General Guisan. The 200 backpedaled and were not heard from again. That the Germans, a few months later, were defeated at the Battle of Stalingrad maybe helped a little to shut them up."

There were other scares during the war as well. In 1942 and again in 1943, my father says: "Rumors flew that the Germans were poised to invade. Thousands of people packed up their belongings and fled toward the interior of Switzerland, a laughable enterprise, since it would have removed them from the Germans for just another hour or two. To go somewhere, you had to have a place to go to or the money to rent one, so we, having neither, didn't take off. But for several days, the roads leading out of Basel were clogged for many miles with cars carrying huge burdens of household goods on their roofs; the train stations were overrun. Then the rumors were rumored to be wrong, and everyone returned. Everybody, not just the Jews, was seized by this panic. Subsequently it turned out, according to documents presented as early as the Nuremberg trials, that the rumors were correct. Hitler intended to secure the Gotthard route to Italy, but each time the Russians started an offensive in the East, and he had to withdraw the invasion divisions and throw them into battle on the Russian front."

Fortunately, Switzerland made it to VE Day – May 8, 1945 – intact. A few days later, Max began preparing for his medical exams. He knew, as he went through his thousands of pages of readings and notes, that though he would take the same exams and diagnose the same patients as his Swiss citizen colleagues, he would not get the same medical certificate, and would not be entitled to practice medicine. It was at that point that he applied for a position with UNRRA.

That was the background that had contributed to Max's depression upon his return to Basel from Belsen and Paris in the June of 1947. Now, in early July, with most of the bureaucratic rigmarole behind him, things were beginning to look up. He was really in love, and he was getting married at last. That was quite a lot, as Hilde frequently reminded him, drawing on the psychological trump card of her survival somewhat shamelessly, it seems to me; but then she was only twenty-two.

At the beginning of July he went to Amsterdam to bring his bride back to Switzerland. Even this trip proved complicated. He had to fly rather than travel more sensibly and cheaply by train because, as a citizen of Poland, now a Communist country, he would not be allowed past the border checkpoints on the railways.

Air travel was still in such an embryonic stage that the same rules of passage did not apply, but the extravagant cost of the round-trip ate up most of his limited savings. My parents had a joyful reunion. They even had some privacy the first few days, because Jo and Corry had taken a trip to England. On their return, however, Corry announced that they were expecting friends in two days and that the young couple would have to leave. They had nowhere to go, but as usual kind friends intervened – the Bolt brothers, the partners first of my grandfather and then of Jo, until he left the clothing business altogether, and then the Scholtes. None of these families had any space to spare, but they were gracious nonetheless, just as they had been during the war.

When my parents finally got to Schiphol Airport, Max sat down in the plane only to find that Hilde was no longer behind him. He had to wait, devoured by anxiety and oblivious to the reassurances of the crew. She had been detained by an officious Dutch policeman. Hilde, ever dauntless, asked to see his superior, told him her story, and mentioned the name of her friend, the head of the Amsterdam police. The superior officer's eyes filled with tears as he listened to her history. He apologized profusely, chastised the offending policeman, and escorted Hilde onto the plane, telling her that she should be treated with honor and not with insults. At last the airplane took off for Basel and more complications.

The young couple stayed with Max's parents in their apartment on the Mittlere Strasse, first in a front room facing the University Eye Institute across the street, and then upstairs in the former maid's room (in those days, even poor families had maids). They slept on the same lumpy mattress that Max had complained about in his first letters. That Max couldn't rouse himself to find a new one for his bride is, to me, eloquent testimony to his depression and paralysis of will during their month apart. Max's parents didn't seem to mind that the young couple shared a bed in the weeks before their marriage. Arrangements for the big event began immediately. The civil ceremony was held a week or two after they arrived in Basel. There were witnesses, flowers and a speech by the clerk, my father says. The interview with Rabbi Weil, the Orthodox rabbi of the Great Synagogue of Basel, had taken place a few days after their arrival, but he told them that he was going on vacation and couldn't marry them until late August. They settled on the date of August 24, and the rabbi noted all the details on index cards.

Since the synagogue wedding was to take place so close to the start of the academic year in September, by which time the young couple hoped to be working at some job or another, they decided that they would take a pre-religious nuptial honeymoon. Max's parents raised no objections; they were resigned to his progressive shenanigans by now. "We were married, after all," my father points out. So off the couple went to Arosa, a mountain resort not far from Pontresina, where such momentous decisions had been reached a few months before. (I don't think Hilde remembered at the time that Betty had gone to Arosa on her mysterious solo trip in the 1930s.) They did a lot of hiking, for which Hilde dressed in fetching but inappropriate outfits – white shorts, a big straw hat, and strappy sandals. The sun blazed down, its intensity enhanced by altitude, and soon enough the highly allergic Max developed a sunburn to end all sunburns. "You can readily see from the description of Hilde's outfit," my father writes, "that we forgot to take our brains on this honeymoon. I don't know where we left them." Max's face was covered with cracked, bleeding blisters. He couldn't eat or drink, except cool liquids through a straw. He developed a high fever, and had to spend ten days in bed.

Nonetheless, he recovered in time for the religious wedding. The ceremony turned out to be very formal and very large. My father speculates that quite a few members of the Jewish community of Basel came to see what was so special about the woman the wayward Max had finally chosen to marry. The rabbi, resplendent in white and gold, conducted the ceremony with great solemnity, inevitably provoking giggles in the nervous couple. This became a torment within a few minutes, when the rabbi, in his sermon, described Hilde as the daughter of a distinguished line of doctors from Hamburg. He had gotten his note cards mixed up, and had her confused with someone else. Max and Hilde, shaking with laughter, barely got through the ceremony, and then discovered that one of Max's uncles, deputed to make movies of the scene as they left the synagogue, had used up all the film taking pictures of his second wife, whom he had recently married. In the evening, there was a cheerful family dinner at the apartment in the Mittlere Strasse, which featured the slurping and burping of the relative the family dubbed *Quartofwateruncle*, because of the way he drank huge quantities of bubbly mineral water. Paul Alexander, of all people, turned up at midnight, rather the worse for drink, with a wedding present. The next day Max and Hilde traveled by tram in sultry weather to have their official wedding pictures taken at a photographer's. They were both acutely uncomfortable and look it in the picture, not least because Max's black bow tie was fastened by a straight pin and was in imminent danger of falling off.

Through frequent retelling, this part of their story has developed a well-polished quality. Because they were together, my parents remember such small reversals as amusing distractions from the main event, their married life. Still, reality set in when Hilde started working in the Rheinbrücke department store as a bilingual secretary. With her usual energy, she had found work right away. Max, too, following the advice of one of his former professors, had finally found a job at the Biological Institute. The idea was that he could eventually publish a paper about the research he was doing, and in this way gain some official recognition from the medical and scientific establishments in Basel.

Their optimism increased by the day. Hilde's employers at the Rheinbrücke liked her; the director of the Institute sympathized with Max's plight and seemed eager to help him develop a serious project of his own. The couple had found a pretty two-bedroom ground floor apartment with a small garden, on which they put down a deposit with some of the savings they had left from their work at Belsen.

Max and Hilde never lived in that apartment. On November 29, 1947, the United Nations voted in favor of the partition of Palestine into Jewish and Arab states. In December, Max and Hilde had a visit from a *shaliach*, literally "one who is sent," an emissary from the Haganah, the underground Jewish defense organization based in Palestine. He had got their names from other *shlichim* who had been former inmates of Belsen. The Arab states had already threatened war and there was much terrorism in the Middle East. It was fully expected that the Arab League would invade Israel upon the declaration of statehood in May 1948. Medical personnel would be urgently needed. Would Max and Hilde consider volunteering?

After much thought, Max and Hilde agreed, on one condition: that they would be assigned together to active units, and that they would never be separated. The *shaliach* visited again, in January 1948, and they were sworn to secrecy. They could tell close family where they were really going, but no one else, and they were asked to quit their jobs in preparation for departure, which could come at any time. They found a plausible explanation for their sudden resignations by saying that Max had been offered a temporary position as a fill-in doctor in the countryside. Neither Max nor Hilde was happy about quitting in such a way. Hilde liked her boss, Herr Jakob, who was Jewish, and had become quite valuable to him. But they had no choice as they waited for orders.

They had little confidence in the outcome of the inevitable war for Israeli statehood. The Jewish settlers were badly outnumbered, about 600,000 souls surrounded by hostile nations whose citizens numbered in the tens of millions. The news from Palestine was largely bad, and at home the Jews of Switzerland were fearful. They counseled prayer and financial support, but they were afraid that younger hotheads would rush off to fight, abandoning the security of their position in Switzerland. There was even a meeting of the Jewish community of Basel in one of the beautiful medieval guildhalls in the city center. There, the rabbi and other leaders counseled caution. The "situation," as they liked to refer to it, was dangerous and the outcome uncertain. Max got more and more furious as he listened to what he saw as cowardice disguised as prudence. As he tells it, he finally got up.

> I made my famous or infamous speech in which I rather vehemently attacked the rabbi and the community heads and called upon the young Jews of Switzerland to rise up and go and defend Israel and not listen to the fearful counsel of their elders. Of course I said nothing about our own imminent departure. But the effect was pretty good. I still remember the stunned looks I got from some of the good burghers. I must have looked dangerous to them, maybe as if I were hung with hand grenades and high explosives.

My mother smiled sweetly at him when he sat down as if to say, "yes, that's right, I'm married to this lunatic." But she wasn't sorry, either. She had already begun to find life in Switzerland suffocating, and besides, they both say, she was fearless. She had described herself that way to Max in one of her letters in June, and Max had agreed. "At that point in her life," my father writes, "Hilde had an utter disregard for danger, since she felt that her life had already been destroyed. Her sense that she had been given the chance to live a second life came much later."

I ask her about this assessment, and she says that she was willing to go anywhere and do anything, as long as my father and she were together. She was not particularly interested in security or safety, that was true. The smothering routine of daily life had depressed them both. Since they were still living with Max's parents, they had not yet enjoyed privacy as a married couple. Hilde feared that deadly boredom more than she worried about danger, and so she embarked on the new adventure with enthusiasm. She still has that unanchored quality, the ability to give up an old life, an old possession, as if possession meant nothing at all. This almost yogic detachment, for good or for ill, is a result, we think, of the Holocaust. Not all survivors have it by any means, but it has always been characteristic of my mother. And so she set the tone at the very end of 1947, as my parents prepared to leave for war once again.

Max, too, was glad to be active in the cause of Jewish survival. He describes his existence in Switzerland during the Holocaust as "like living on a balcony overlooking the carnage." Sometimes this metaphor took on a literal power, as when the inhabitants of Basel watched American Flying Fortresses streaming into France and Germany, just the other side of the Rhine. This was probably in 1944, my father says. The planes were so low and so close that he could practically see the pilots from his attic window. Then there had been his experience at Bergen-Belsen, which had immeasurably broadened his understanding of what had happened in the war at which he had had a ringside seat. He had learned a great deal in Belsen, but now he was being called to active combat for the survival of the Jewish people.

Chapter 9

War Again, Israel 1948

THE STORY OF my parents' escape from Switzerland and into combat in Israel is such a good yarn, and so full of brave, sometimes foolhardy exploits, that we children have always accepted it wholesale: idealistic Jews, incompetent Arabs and all. But in recent years it has been harder to separate the heroism of those days and the justice of the cause, though the heroism was real, and the cause had considerable justice, from the myths about the perfect behavior and conscience of Jewish fighters. At this moment, with the advent of new forms of terror, Jews and Palestinians have grown further apart than ever, and the hope of reconciliation seems to have perished in unceasing violence. Perhaps as a result, the heroic myths of the past have come up for re-examination by Israeli historians, among others. In the late 1960s and early '70s, Israel enjoyed a brief prestige in the eyes of the world, unparalleled since. In 1960, Paul Newman played Ari ben Canaan in the film version of Leon Uris's novel *Exodus,* which was itself a sentimentalized rendering of the War of Independence of 1948. The Six-Day War of 1967, the attack on Israeli athletes at the Munich Olympics of 1972, the Yom Kippur War of 1973 and the raid at Entebbe of 1976 had earned almost universal compassion and admiration. In those days, it was easier to think of Israel as David and the Arab world as Goliath than it has been since the two intifadas have so changed the terms of the conflict. It is difficult for Jews scattered around the world, and indeed, for many Israelis, to watch Israel struggle to maintain its good name in an always hostile world, difficult to imagine a way of life fraught with so much fear and violence; difficult to acknowledge that anti-Semitism is on the rise once more, and that the very existence of the state of Israel could be questioned as it has not been previously.

Max and Hilde could foresee none of these developments, of course, as they prepared for their trip to what was still Palestine. Their departure, which had been kept secret from all but family, must have caused my Basel grandparents pain. In early spring of 1948, the young people set out on their adventure, following instructions from the Haganah, the underground Jewish defense force in Palestine. Their luggage was to travel separately while Max and Hilde took a bus to a mountainous and unguarded spot on the French border. There they strolled and kissed their way from Switzerland across the frontier, posing as a courting couple on an afternoon walk, but looking out all the while for observers and for landmarks of their arrival in France. They were supposed to saunter over to the railway station and casually board a train for the next town and from that town, where their luggage and tickets would be provided, to Marseille, but they overdid the strolling and kissing and barely made the train. They dashed down the platform and leapt into the carriage cheered on by the passengers. My father writes: "We certainly seemed to have blown our cover."

Nevertheless they had a smooth trip to Marseille, where they tried once more to be inconspicuous. They had been told how to get surreptitiously to Camp d'Arénas, the illegal training camp of the Haganah, but a taxi driver soon sized them up and said, "*Ah oui, le camp des juifs.*" ("Oh yes, the Jewish camp.") The supposed secrecy of the operation was further eroded when General de Gaulle came to Marseille to give a speech. It was a tense period, police reinforcements were brought in, and because they were short of space, the Jewish residents were told to vacate half the camp to accommodate the police for two weeks. My parents say that the French authorities simply pretended that the Jews weren't there, and everyone got along.

My father describes the weeks in the camp with some amusement. The arrivals were housed in barracks of forty people on army cots, but the married couples among the volunteers could use the bathhouse together when it was their turn in the schedule, which, my father writes, "was an opportunity for marital behavior that met the legal definition of sex." Most people at the camp were Moroccan and Bulgarian, and a few of the volunteers were professional adventurers, non-Jews who went wherever a war was brewing. There was a lot of marching and drilling – without weapons, which the French had forbidden – and much laughter, my father says, because some volunteers seemed unable to tell left from right, and always took off in the wrong direction.

But it was rumored that the camp had the best forgers in Europe working on the documents the volunteers needed to sneak into Palestine. Upon their arrival, Max and Hilde had handed over all their passports and identification papers, and soon they acquired different names, passports, and family members. Max had become a single Frenchman who was on his way to New Zealand with a stop in Haifa. Hilde had a new nationality, a new husband, and a visa for Turkey. In April, they took a bus to the port of Marseille and boarded a ramshackle ship of about 1500 tons called, providentially, *Providence.* They spent ten uncomfortable days on board, preferring to escape their hot and overcrowded cabin in the bowels of the ship by sleeping on deck under the Mediterranean stars, and lulled, my father writes, by the "thumping of the ship's engines and the rush of the waves. The problem was that the crew started to hose down the deck at four in the morning and often we had to beat a hasty retreat ... but this seemed a small price to pay for the wonderful feeling of lying under the illuminated sky in the gentle air of the night." The members of the crew were mostly unkempt Vietnamese, my father continues. "There were all kinds of narrow alleyways leading to mysterious doors and everything seemed to be covered in some kind of decrepit rusty patina from which moisture emanated in unhealthy mists." Helped by generally good weather, an unlimited supply of Algerian red wine and the excitement of being underway at last, the young passengers didn't worry too much about hygiene, heat, or overcrowding. An officer of the ship approached Hilde with an offer of hot showers to which, it seemed to her, "there were unstated conditions attached which she was not prepared to meet," so one shower was negotiated with Max keeping watch outside the door.

Until they were intercepted on the seventh day of the voyage by two British gunships about twenty miles off the coast of Palestine, Max and Hilde had been more entertained than anxious. Only three weeks remained of the British mandate before Israel became an independent state, and the passengers no longer seriously worried that they would be turned back. The internment camps on Cyprus, so important in the tale of the *Exodus*, had already been closed. But British troops could still harass prospective immigrants, and in this they succeeded. The *Providence* was detained for three days, the ship rolling and heaving in place in a relatively quiet sea, and Max's seasickness took over. He and many others spent most of their days hanging over the rails, but not Hilde, who has always been a good sailor.

At the end of the three days, British officers boarded the ship to announce that it had been given permission to land, not at the obvious harbor at Haifa but at Akko, ten miles further north. For the first time, the travelers caught a glimpse of the old-new country of Palestine, so soon to become Israel. They cheered and wept as Mount Carmel rose before them, the white houses of Haifa on its flanks glittering in the sun; they passed the dunes of the bay and the massive Crusader fortress of Akko – another site featured in *Exodus* – which the British had used as a prison for the rebellious leaders of the Haganah and its terrorist rival, the Irgun. The young passengers scrambled down rope ladders into small boats, and ten minutes later they were in Israel. They were hurried onto a long line of waiting buses, because their hosts didn't want to wait until the British changed their minds again, and off they went through a desolate desert landscape. My father remembers that the driver of their bus stopped among orange groves – *pardessim*, in Hebrew, from which the English word Paradise is partly derived – and picked an orange for each passenger. Gradually the long line of buses got shorter, as each group of emigrants was taken to a different destination. Max and Hilde were delivered to Tel Litwinsky, a huge military camp that had been taken over by the Haganah just a few days before.

Tel Litwinsky had been used as a rest and retraining camp for the British Eighth Army during the North African campaign in World War II, but now it was in chaos, because the British had left in haste and without much concern for their successors. The Jewish soldiers there were veterans of the Eighth Army and of the Jewish Brigade, which had fought in Italy in 1943 and had sustained great losses at Monte Cassino. True to British principle in the lands they occupied, the Jewish soldiers from the settlements in Palestine – in contrast to Jewish fighters from Britain itself – could join only as enlisted men, and none of them had been permitted to rise higher than the rank of sergeant. Nonetheless, many of these veterans of World War II became essential officers in the new Israeli army.

My father reports that my parents' arrival at Tel Litwinsky, together with the several weeks following, became a blur of registration, form-filling and office-visiting. During that period, David Ben-Gurion had declared Israel an independent state (on May 14, 1948), and the next day five Arab countries – Egypt, Iraq, Syria, Lebanon and Jordan – began their invasion. The new state had to be organized and the new army mustered. For freshly arrived volunteers like Max and Hilde, that meant a lot of running around. There were not enough weapons; there were not enough training manuals, and the forming army relied on a mix of what had been left behind by the British and on the guerrilla techniques developed within Palestine by the Haganah, Palmach, and other underground defense organizations.

My father says that Israel was a rude awakening for him. When he met medical people who had already lived in Palestine for some years, their usual greeting was: "You came from Switzerland? Here? To this Levantine dump? You must be crazy!" This, he writes, was a shock to his "incompletely suppressed sense of doing something heroic." People were badly behaved in public. They pushed, they shoved, they hadn't learned queueing from their British occupiers, they didn't help old people or the disabled, they hadn't learned table manners, or common expressions like "please" and "thank you." It was not quite what Max and Hilde had expected back in Basel, when Max had shaken his fist at the elders of the community in a glow of defiance. They visited Paula, Max's older sister, and her growing family in a dusty settlement near the seaside town of Netanya, and that was another shock. It was a rough life for people who had been bred in the cities of Europe, even if they had escaped the worst of Europe over the ten previous years.

In early June 1948, Max and Hilde reported to Afula, a town in the Galilee, the north-central region of Israel, where they were to join the 14th Battalion of the Golani Regiment (later Brigade). After another dusty bus trip through a semi-arid countryside dotted with Arab villages, Max and Hilde arrived in the midst of a short but intense air raid. Iraqi planes, they were told, bombed often but inaccurately, because they released their bombs too high up. Sirens screamed, shells exploded all around them, and then as abruptly stopped.

The headquarters of the Battalion were at the Kadoorie School, the best-known agricultural training institute in Palestine. Yitzhak Rabin had been a student there ten years before. The school was nestled in the hills near Nazareth. Almost directly opposite rose Mount Tabor, where so much of the biblical Book of Judges takes place, its rounded height now crowned with a monastery. The campus of the school was beautifully planted with lush trees and flowers, giving it the appearance of a semitropical resort, my father says, but on June 6, the night following Max and Hilde's arrival, the water tower was shelled and destroyed. The main building had already been designated as an infirmary for lightly wounded soldiers; Hilde and other nurses immediately began to set it up.

The officers of the battalion were sober and business-like. Most of them had been raised on kibbutzim, the socialist farming communes of Jewish Palestine, and had been trained secretly in the Haganah and the Palmach, the military organizations which had originated there. Max was handed a stack of old British army manuals on organizing hospitals and field stations under combat, and that was the extent of his training as a military medical officer. He was introduced to his medical sergeant, Amichai ben Dror, who was barely out of his teens but could interpret English and Hebrew, and whose energy and initiative proved invaluable in combat. When Max and Hilde met Amichai again in 1995 on a trip to Israel, their friendship resumed as warmly as it had begun on that June day in 1948.

By now the war had intensified. The Arab siege of Jerusalem had begun with fierce fighting and casualties. Among the most notorious and crucial incidents were the first battles for the police station at Latrun, on the Jerusalem road. Egyptian troops had moved into the Negev desert in the south, and had laid siege to a kibbutz, Yad Mordechai, which was composed almost entirely of survivors from Poland, particularly from the Warsaw Ghetto. So far the defenders of the kibbutz were holding back the Egyptian invaders. Other units of the Golani regiment had already been sent to the defense of kibbutzim on the eastern borders of Palestine, along the Jordan south of the Sea of Galilee. There, tank units of the Jordanian army had crossed the river and were trying to break into the valley of Jezreel. These were the battles depicted in *Exodus*. Later on, settlers at the kibbutz of Degania held the tanks off with homemade Molotov cocktails until the regular units arrived.

The task assigned to my parents' battalion was to halt further incursions by the combined Arab forces in their area. Their commander, Chaim ben Yakov, explained that a force consisting of Syrian and Iraqi troops and irregulars from Jordan were fanning out from Nazareth toward a T-shaped intersection of two roads: the one going north from Afula, and the east-west road which connected Tiberias, on the Sea of Galilee, to Haifa, on the coast. If the Arab forces captured the intersection, Jewish territory would be sliced in half; all settlements east and north of that point would be cut off, and the entire territory of Galilee could be lost.

There was a settlement called Sejera near the intersection, just across the road from the Arab village of Lubia, which was now full of snipers who could shoot directly onto the road and into Sejera. My parents' battalion had been told to occupy Sejera and establish headquarters on its highest point. From there, they could survey the eastern hills near Nazareth and much of the surrounding territory. Their base was to be an old Turkish farm built on the highest hill in the village. It consisted of two sprawling stone courtyards, with wooden galleries running around the second story on the inside walls, and a flat roof with a two-foot stone parapet around the top.

Sejera was a well-known village in Jewish Palestine, with an interesting history of its own. It was here that the earliest Zionist settlers, mostly Russian students, conceived of the collective settlements which later became known as kibbutzim. When David Ben-Gurion, the first prime minister of Israel, arrived as an immigrant from Russia, he took a job as a night watchman at that very farm. Now the thick stone walls of the farm were reinforced with sandbags, and one of the larger rooms was set aside as a front-line surgery for wounded soldiers.

The high command had decided that Lubia should be taken as well. My father says that when you stood at the bottom of the village road, where it connected with the Afula road near the crucial intersection, Lubia looked quite formidable. Like Sejera, it was perched on a steep, rocky hill overlooking the roads below. The attack was to take place the next night, June 7. Toward evening on that day, my father says, the chief medical officer of the Golani regiment arrived at the Kadoorie School. He was Isaiah Morris, an English doctor who had been in the British Army during the war, had taken part in the invasion of Normandy and in the bloodiest of the fighting there, in an area known as the pocket of the Falaise, and had now volunteered to serve in this new war. The doctors agreed that they were already short of bandages, disinfectant, syringes, and morphine and other painkillers, and Dr Morris took off for headquarters in search of more supplies. In the early hours of June 8, Max said goodbye to Hilde and began the short trip to Sejera, only fifteen minutes away by jeep. Once a driver came within sight of the village of Lubia, and even more dangerously, when he took the left turn up the hill between the two villages, he drew fire from the rifles and machine guns stationed there. But they made it into Sejera, where there were already wounded, mostly settlers from the town surrounded by weeping women. Amichai went off with a squad of soldiers, but returned with many more dead than wounded.

The attack on Lubia had gone terribly wrong. Arab forces had infiltrated the town the night before, and the Haganah soldiers, who had expected an easy conquest once the snipers were overpowered, were met instead by overpowering gunfire. Iraqi planes began to attack as well. Trenches had been hastily dug by the side of the road the day before, and soldiers had to jump into them whenever the bombs dropped. There were no air raid sirens here. Indeed, most of the volunteers had been thrown into battle so hastily that there had been no time to issue uniforms or even helmets. Thin-skinned, balding Max didn't even have a hat, and he was still dressed in his grey wool trousers from Switzerland, despite the intense heat. The soldiers of Sejera had to be ingenious with their equipment. The roof of the Turkish farm had only two defenders armed with light submachine guns. They ran crouching back and forth behind the parapet, to give the enemy the impression that there was a battery of machine guns there. The armored cars and tanks were mostly fakes got up to look like the real thing, and marks inside showed passengers where they had to keep their heads down. So soldiers had to use their wits as well as their rather limited arsenal of weapons. The incessant, deafening noise seems to have been an element of terror in itself, quite apart from the random death it brought.

My father says now that he noticed a weird sort of detachment in himself when he first came under fire. He wasn't frightened, but super-alert and calm, and he carried out his duties almost automatically, like a robot. It was a good thing, because his first day in combat was especially terrible. The Haganah soldiers had to retreat from Lubia, Arab troops stationed themselves near the Afula road, and three Iraqi tanks rumbled down from the north and stationed themselves about 500 yards from the road into Sejera. Of the 200 troops assigned to the assault on Lubia, forty had been killed and about 100 wounded. My father says that during that day he had seen dead soldiers everywhere. Many were students from the Technion, the MIT of Israel, who had been hastily recruited. Ignorant but courageous, they had marched straight up the hill into certain death. The medical personnel were moved into the farm where, their commander told them, they would be surrounded, in effect, by the massing Arab troops below. Going down the road to Afula, under the noses of the Iraqi tanks and the soldiers stationed there, would be extremely hazardous; yet it had to be risked. Wounded soldiers had to be evacuated, either to the infirmary at the Kadoorie School or to the big hospital in Afula.

During the night of June 8, the medical team moved up the hill to the Turkish farm in Sejera. By then, Dr Morris had arrived with supplies. It was obvious that there would be heavy casualties when fighting broke out again, and he decided to stay to help Max. As dawn came up over the hills after the very active and noisy early hours of June 9, my father crept up to the roof for a look around. As he gazed west in the direction of Nazareth, his detachment left him and, for the first time, he experienced the cold clutch of fear. "The hills looked as if snow had fallen during the night," he writes, because they were so crowded with Arab soldiers in their white garments and kaffiyas. They were no more than half a mile away. Bullets whizzed by, he ducked, and then, he says, "all hell broke loose." Shells exploded all around, mostly mortars, but bigger ones too, inside as well as outside the two courtyards, and then the wounded began pouring in. When Max returned to the makeshift operating room inside the farm, he had to work frantically. The soldiers had been dug in around the perimeter of the farm and had been hit at very close range. They had terrible head wounds, shredded limbs, and other severe injuries, and Max was restricted mostly to amputations, control of the bleeding, and pain relief. "The infernal noise of explosions went on and on," my father writes in his account of that night:

Occasionally there was a pause and we thought that the attack might have stopped. Then it resumed with the same ferocity. In our room with Dr Morris and three Army nurses, we were constantly busy. There was a lot of pain all around, many moaned, some cried out. Orderlies ran in and out with stretchers, using every letup in the firing to get wounded soldiers into the personnel carriers and drive them off. Finally we had so many wounded that we ordered up a specially fitted bus. It arrived and was loaded; we sent it back under escort of some armored personnel carriers and one fake tank. Later Amichai came back up to tell me that two of the soldiers had died on the bus, one of them bleeding uncontrollably from the stump of his severed leg.

We had a soldier come in with a head wound. There was an entry hole but no exit hole, so the bullet was still in his brain; he was quiet, slightly somnolent. The bullet didn't seem to have destroyed any vital areas, but the head wound was bleeding profusely. Isaiah Morris was bandaging the patient's head, I fastened the strips when they came to an end; he needed another bandage. I turned to the left to pick up a roll from the equipment table, then there was a loud explosion, everything went dark, I was thrown to the floor, out of the corner of my eye I saw Morris sink to the floor, there were cries of pain from the nurses and soldiers. A bright fountain of blood was gushing from my arm. I was calm, dissociated. I pulled some rag from a small table, I wrapped it around my arm as tightly as I could. I had intense pain in my chest and my right abdomen. I thought I might have a liver injury. I got up and dragged myself out of the room and as quickly as I could I limped around the corner to the battalion commander's bunker and shouted that we had been hit and that I thought Dr Morris was dead. Then I seem to have fainted. Amichai told me just recently that I woke up when there was a lull in the bombing and that I said: "Does this silence mean I'm in Paradise?" I don't remember this.

But I remember lying on the floor of a small armored car, which had a number of fake armored plates marked with large chalk crosses which indicated that they were not steel but plywood, and would offer us no protection. The driver's windshield was almost totally closed in by two armored plates, he was looking through maybe an inch of open space. We rumbled down the road and started on the right turn toward Afula, when we began to be hit by intense gunfire, especially on the roof, and suddenly, my heart stood still, the motor stopped. The driver said, I think the motor got hit. The fire intensified and I thought: could it be that I escaped the bomb up on the hill only to be killed being evacuated? It was the first time since the early morning that I felt deep fear; my dreamlike detachment, again, was gone. And suddenly the motor coughed, it began to wheeze asthmatically and we inched forward, turned the corner and were safe, out of range of the Iraqi guns. We came to the gate of the Kadoorie School and the driver asked one of the soldiers to call Hilde down. She came down and she was very shocked, but by this time I felt o.k., having gotten some

morphine, but very weak. She still remembers that I said
to her: "Hello, Hildchen, how are you?"

My mother says that she, too, was working frantically behind the
lines when word came that the front-line operating room in Sejera
had been hit by an Iraqi mortar. Everyone inside was killed or
wounded, she was told. One of the doctors was dead – either the
Swiss or the English one. Hilde thought "not again," and stopped
breathing, more or less, as she waited for news. She was
summoned to come down to the makeshift ambulance at the gate,
where Max's white face looked out at her from the darkness
inside. When he smiled and asked her how she was, she felt as if
the oxygen had returned to her lungs. She hopped into the
ambulance and they continued to the large hospital at Afula,
which was so choked with wounded that the lawn in front was
filled with soldiers on stretchers.

Max got even better care than he might have expected during
his stay. About a half hour after his arrival, a young woman doctor
wandered through the rows of stretchers calling his name. She
turned out to be his former Hebrew teacher from Basel, and they
had a good chat over the next few days as she tended his wounds.
These included considerable shrapnel in Max's arms and lungs.
Some fragments had sliced through the radial artery of his right
arm when it caused the spectacular bleeding my father
remembered. The shrapnel in his lungs, and some of the rest, too,
has remained to this day, since removal would have been too
difficult. Penicillin had only come into use at the end of World
War II and was still scarce, but fortunately it was available for
Max. As for the surprising reunion with Hannah, the doctor, my
parents learned in later years that Israel is a country that
specializes in miraculous reunions. When I was fifteen, we hired
a taxi to take us to Nazareth, and our driver turned out to have
been my father's ambulance driver in 1948. At the airport,

returning to New York, we met Josef Rosensaft. My parents encountered many more such revenants on subsequent trips.

Max had several visitors. The battalion commander came the next day and told him that they had been able to hold the farm, despite heavy losses. He informed Max that he had been injured several hours after a UN ceasefire had been declared and accepted by both sides. A few hours after the catastrophic mortar had plunged into the makeshift surgical theater, the fighting around Sejera had stopped. The Chief Medical Officer of the Army, Dr Schieber (later Hebraicized as Shaba), visited Max because he was the first doctor injured after the official start of the war (a fine distinction, since many doctors and nurses had already died in Arab ambushes in Jerusalem before war had been declared). And about three days into his stay, an exuberant man aged about seventy-five came to Max's bedside. He was sorry that Max had been wounded, he said, but those wounds had changed his own fortunes. He was a retired doctor who had been languishing in the Jewish settlement of Yavneh, near Tiberias. The Army had called him in as a temporary replacement when Max had been put out of service. Working again made him feel reborn, he told Max, and he felt thirty years younger. His hormones had begun to flow again. His blood coursed more quickly through his veins. He was able to make love to his wife again. "Thank you, thank you, thank you!" he exulted as he wrung Max's hand.

The irony of this rejuvenation did not escape Max, who reflected sadly that Dr. Morris had died and that 45 percent of their battalion had been either killed or wounded. But Sejera had not fallen. It would remain one of the pivotal battles in that war. I've been told that schoolchildren in Israel still learn about it in their textbooks. Hilde helped Hannah care for Max as long as she could; after about ten days she returned to the unit. Max was discharged sometime in early August. After a brief furlough in Netanya with Paula, Max and Hilde reported to their battalion's new location, Camp Mansoura at the foot of Mount Carmel. Max had been wounded on June 9. By now it was late August. Another ceasefire was in effect, and there was relative calm for a while.

My parents have always insisted that I was conceived one stifling hot night "in an affirmation of life" in the barracks at Mansoura. The second ceasefire bought them some time to observe and reflect. They learned that the Haganah had begun to punish followers of the extremist leaders Menachem Begin and Yitzhak Shamir. These were soldiers who had enlisted in the Haganah but wouldn't swear allegiance to the new state because they favored conquest of territories beyond the UN boundaries. Their Haganah officers imprisoned them for this disloyalty in the hottest cellars of the hot barracks. The soldiers capitulated after a day or two, but tensions between the two groups had always been high and remained so well into the lifetime of the fledgling state. The issue of boundaries and Arab rights has been traumatic ever since.

The Golani Regiment continued its conquests in the Galilee in a series of battles. Max and Hilde found themselves in better accommodations. For a brief period of a few weeks, they were quartered in a co-operative farming village called Merchavia. They had a room with a farming family from Poland, where they were fairly comfortable. "Every morning," my father writes, the farmer's wife called out to her husband Mottel in Yiddish: "'Have you milked the cows already.' This was not a question but a command."

Despite the idyllic peace of these days, military work was going forward. Max and Hilde set up a clinic for soldiers in Merchavia, where Hilde was chief nurse and Max the medical officer. Each morning my father and his assistant, Amichai, traveled to Megiddo, at the southern perimeter of the area the Golani Regiment occupied, to see to soldiers there. My father writes:

Even under war conditions I appreciated the fact that Megiddo was the biblical Armaggedon and even more that the excavations of fortifications and stables were said to be from Solomonic times. The excavations were done by the British in the thirties, and their outhouses still carried signs: Natives and British. We had an infirmary with stretchers on large marble slabs that were excavated and were said to be part of King Solomon's stables. It gave the work special excitement.

The road to Megiddo, however, was problematic. It was a straight road traversing the whole valley, and was under fire from Arab forces still holding the Mountain of Moab just to our east. The technique was to rev up the engine of the Army truck, then drive at breakneck speed while sinking down as low in the cabin as was possible without losing sight of the road. We got a few bullets to the chassis, but nothing serious happened. In the meantime, Hilde was treating soldiers in the infirmary; while before she had been able to tolerate the various ailments – festering wounds, accident injuries, slow-healing gunshot wounds and infections of various kinds, especially of the feet – she became queasy and one morning somebody came running: "Doctor, doctor, the nurse has fainted." She had morning sickness. She was pregnant.

Although they were technically in the war's second ceasefire period, which had stretched from mid-July into the as yet unforeseeable future, skirmishes and even major battles continued. The army had become much better equipped in the weeks since the battle of Sejera. There, the defenders had two light machine guns and a few mortars in the way of heavy weaponry;

now, modern rifles, machine guns, ammunition and other supplies arrived daily from the Skoda Works in what was then Czechoslovakia.

The Israeli air force, until the late summer of 1948, had consisted largely of little single-engine Cessnas. The settlers nicknamed them Primuses because they made a sputtering noise like the Primus kerosene heaters in Israeli houses. Now American fighter and bomber planes had arrived. They had been bought as war surplus in the United States and had been smuggled out of the country in dangerous night flights. Supplemented by fighters from Czechoslovakia, they changed the balance of power in the air. There weren't many, my father writes, "but those few went a long way."

Meanwhile, the fledgling state had gained some advantages. The Egyptian army had been halted for the moment at Yad Mordechai, the Polish survivors' kibbutz in the Negev desert to the south. The road to Jerusalem had reopened and a wider corridor had been established there. The Golani brigade had conquered the whole of Galilee, including the vital city of Nazareth.

By now it was early September of 1948, and Max and Hilde moved with their battalion of the Golani brigade to Emek Beit She'an, a subtropical valley south of the Sea of Galilee. It stretched from the Jordanian border to the hills surrounding the large town of Jenin (now part of the Palestinian Authority). During the day the soldiers rested in the shade of the orange groves, because Arab troops still held Mount Moab and their snipers shot at anything that moved in the valley below. The commander of the battalion had a little talk with Max and Hilde. The regiment was about to engage in a dangerous maneuver, and he wanted to evacuate Hilde. Max agreed, but Hilde refused to consider that option. "She was going to stay with me. She had almost lost me already and she was not going to lose me again," my father writes. The men capitulated, and she stayed.

Meanwhile, negotiations to establish the boundaries of the new state and to bring the war to an end continued in Jerusalem. The UN mediator, Count Bernadotte of Sweden, hoped to get the new state to give up the Negev and the Arab towns of Lod and Ramallah in exchange for an extended chunk of western Galilee. There was much turmoil in Israel over this prospect; the Israeli government, under David Ben-Gurion, was torn between negotiation and further military conquest to make the return of land more difficult. The terrorist organizations, especially the Irgun under Menachem Begin, refused all compromise. Most affected, of course, were the soldiers in the field, who were often ordered to run desperate, last-minute missions before final negotiations began.

In Emek Beit She'an, the commander of the battalion met his officers at 8 p.m. on the evening of September 17 and read out the new orders from Jerusalem. A major action was to begin at midnight. Troops were to advance from Netanya east, from Megiddo south, and from Beit She'an west, with the goal of taking the west bank of the Jordan north of Jerusalem. That was still a weak point, from which, it was thought, Arab troops could break through and make a run for the Mediterranean. Their own battalion had been assigned the task of blocking Jordanian relief efforts from the east while advancing on the road from Beit She'an to Jenin, on their west. My father writes:

> Medical teams would evacuate the wounded on this road to Beit She'an. This was a suicidal mission. The road to Jenin was cut in a deep gorge surrounded by steep hills and mountains. Troops advancing or evacuating anybody would be sitting ducks. Yes, the commander said drily, it was not going to be an easy task, and we should be ready for a lot of casualties. It was a gloomy few hours. We all knew our unit had been placed in a sacrificial position. We took inventory, checked jeeps and ambulances.

At 11.30 p.m. the commander called another meeting. Headquarters informed us that Count Bernadotte had been assassinated by Irgun terrorists under Menachem Begin. It was now politically impossible to launch this attack and it had been aborted. My relief was intense. Once more we had been saved.

The fighting went on. The Egyptians launched another offensive in the Negev, and it looked as if the Golani Brigade would be shifted south to meet them. As Hilde's morning sickness got worse, Max and Hilde began to wonder about her ability to continue serving in the army, and beyond that, about the future of their newly expanding family. The Golani command found her a position in an infirmary in a convent on the summit of Mount Carmel, a beautiful spot where she had light duties. And after much tortured discussion, Max and Hilde decided that they should return to Switzerland, so that my mother could have her baby under the best possible conditions and so they would have time to think about what to do next. Hilde suffered from the heat as well as from morning sickness, and could not imagine a life in a climate where, at the best of times, she could barely function.

The Commander of the Northern Front, whom they had to see to obtain permission to leave the army, was a former Russian officer with a shaved head. He was a formidable figure who looked like General Timoshenko, the fabled leader of the Russian front during World War II. When they went to his headquarters in Haifa, the commander asked how far along Hilde was. They told him three and a half months. He laughed uproariously and shouted, "Some pregnancy! My wife is eight months pregnant!" "The relevance of this remark," my father adds, "has never been revealed to us, since his wife was not a soldier in the army." But he agreed to discharge both Max and Hilde, and in a few weeks the papers had come through. While their documents were being processed, the war had largely ended. A final ceasefire had been agreed on, though, as usual, last-minute skirmishes continued in the southern part of the country. As a result, my father adds: "before the Golani took part in the defeat of the Egyptians (Golani units were the first to reach Eilat on the Red Sea), the Golani Brigade held a huge, wonderful victory celebration." Max and Hilde made the last rounds of their relatives in Israel, the Polish Consulate gave Max a new Polish passport, and in late December 1948 they left on what my father describes as "an adventurous flight to Geneva on an old DC-9 via Tobruk and Malta."

As for the war: in February, March, and April 1949, Israel signed armistice agreements with Egypt, Lebanon and Jordan (which signed for Iraq as well); Syria did not come to an agreement until July 20, 1949. The war had finally come to an end. I had arrived in Basel in late May. The limitations of life in Switzerland closed in on them once again, and Max and Hilde decided soon after on making their way out of the old world altogether and into the new. They were delighted to learn that David Wodlinger, Hilde's former boss at Bergen-Belsen, would sponsor their immigration to the United States. They embarked at Rotterdam on the SS *Veendam*, and arrived in New York, with me in tow, in March 1950.

Chapter 10

An American in Germany, 1971

AND LIVED HAPPILY ever after, for there my parents' wartime adventures end. Each tale of immigration is very like the next in certain ways: adaptation to a new country, the birth of children, a new life. My parents, like many recent arrivals, became good Americans. They had energy, optimism and gratitude in abundance. They became loyal citizens and, sometimes, informed critics. They were glad to shake the dust – the ashes – of the old world from their shoes, and to rejoice in the possibilities of the new. The fit between the country and my parents was perfect, or so it appeared to me as a child.

Hilde's first job in America, in the summer of 1950, was at a camp on Staten Island for low-income city children. She and I spent a few weeks there while my father started an internship at Bushwick Hospital, in Brooklyn. For that year we all lived together in a one-room apartment in that borough until he found a position at a mental hospital in Rhode Island. Max reclaimed his status as a doctor after retraining in the American medical system. He eventually became a psychiatrist and then, after he was accepted at Columbia University, a psychoanalyst in private practice. As was the custom in the 1950s, and with her wartime past so close behind her, Hilde was glad to stay at home with us, especially after the arrivals of Susie (Providence, Rhode Island, 1952) and Dorothy (Englewood, New Jersey, 1960). She was a wonderful mother, playful and enterprising; our summers were full of day trips involving swimming and picnics. During the school year we sisters had tea and cookies every afternoon when we came home, just as Dutch children did, and we discussed our days with her in a pleasant ritual of decompression. Not many years after Dot's birth, and directly in response to the civil rights struggle, Hilde began working in day care once again, first as a volunteer, then as a professional director of an extraordinary, progressive day care center for at-risk children. When it was founded in the 1960s and for many years after, it served low-income children for free. The center, in Paramus, New Jersey, still thrives. Later, Hilde was part of a group that wrote the standards for early childhood education for the state.

My mother said often that she was "inspired by her feminist daughters" to re-establish a career, but really she was driven, as she had been at Belsen, by complementary impulses: her love of children, her sense of injustice, and her driving practical ambition. She had a calm and equilibrium that gave her great resilience during the many rough times she encountered in her work (those very qualities could be maddening to her more mercurial daughters). She has a way of compartmentalizing pain and conflict that is reflected, I think, even in the way she told me her story. When she came to the reunion with her brother on the banks of the Maas in 1943 after a year of not knowing his whereabouts, for example, she neither revealed nor related any emotion. Her relationship with Jo was vexed, a mixture of exasperation and love, and so she resorted to straight narrative. Of course she had forgotten much, but those feelings about her brother persisted until the end of his life.

Jo had always been hard work for the Jacobsthal family, though he was also loyal and brave. In the war, he was a real hero of the underground, and characteristically got Hilde out of danger and into danger at the same time. In those life-and-death situations, the ordinary complications of sibling conflict became inseparable from the risk. After the war, the confusions mounted. He had joined the Dutch Reformed Church upon his marriage. He and Corry eventually had two daughters, Yvette and Helen, but the early years of their marriage were dominated by his ill health. He was too sick with tuberculosis to travel to my parents' wedding in 1947, and he contracted polio either then or not long after. Despite his infirmities he was able to keep working, and traveled a great deal with his family. I remember their coming to stay with us in New Jersey in 1964 on their way from Nigeria to South America. For much of their protracted stay, my mother was felled by migraine. I remember trying to protect her from Jo's chatty visits to her bedroom. As usual, Jo and his wife could be charming as well as difficult. They showed me how to make Nigerian peanut stew for a school project on international dishes, and Jo played with my younger sisters. Our cousins were not easy guests either, especially because they were close to us in age. The family finally settled in Fribourg, Switzerland, where Jo developed his own market consulting firm and where he joined, and eventually became an elder in, the Scottish Presbyterian church. His daughters knew nothing about his Jewish background until Yvette, visiting my parents one day when she was already grown, asked idly what had made Hilde "convert" to Judaism.

Jo was upset that the truth had come out, although he finally accepted what had happened with good grace. Characteristically, he made light of his polio until it got worse again in old age and immobilized him. My husband Oliver and I visited him near the end of his life, when he was in a pleasant chalet-style old age home in the mountain village of Charmey in the Swiss canton of Vevey. By then he couldn't shake his depression. It was visible in his posture and in the set of his face. He still managed to ask us countless times with great politeness if we were comfortable at our hotel. Like my mother now, he never lost his languages, his recognition of people close to him, or his manners. Hilde admired his stoicism and courage, but couldn't bear the lifelong sense of rejection created by her charismatic brother's changes of identity and tall tales.

I think that we were a lively family. My parents have always been fun. They traveled all over with us, inside the US and abroad. We clambered up mountains and into the sea, cycled and skied, threw parties and generally enjoyed our resurrected lives. Kiki Scholte, the youngest daughter of Hilde's Dutch rescuers, spent a year with us as an au pair in 1955, when Susie and I were three and six and she was nineteen; we have kept in sporadic contact ever since. Despite the help she had from Kiki that year, my slender young mother looks tired in many pictures, where she is setting up picnics, washing out clothes at a motel, or cooking over a campfire. She says that she never minded all the work. I remember my parents as full of energy and good cheer most of the time. I don't think that they ever lost their astonishment at being given a second life. Later, when we had settled in New Jersey, we took advantage of the proximity of Manhattan to feed my father's cultural hunger. We saw every play, every Broadway show, every concert and opera we could: the Balanchine dancers in their prime, Leonard Bernstein with the New York Philharmonic, *My Fair Lady*, *Camelot* and *Hair;* Euripides's *Trojan Women* in a devastating stage production by Michael Cacoyannis; Richard Burton in *Hamlet,* and Peter Brook's *Marat/Sade.*

My sisters are active, agile people, each with many talents. Susie, the dancer, became a hand therapist whose uncanny psychological insight helps her in her own practice in Hartsdale, New York. Dot began her working life in journalism and public relations, but trained in voice for many years and eventually became a cantor. All three of us have had the advantages of an excellent education, long and happy marriages, rewarding work and delightful children. We have our share of conflict, though we are all close. Susie and I, especially, having arrived so near in time to the sad and heroic tales of the war, framed our perceived inadequacies against that impossible standard, and competed with each other for the favor of our charismatic parents. Perhaps our otherwise ordinary sibling rivalry could have been handled better, given such a background. As we got older, we began to think that our parents' self-confidence extended to a kind of bragging about their past, and often about us as well, as if we were golden examples of their successful survival. That tendency softened again over the years. The truth is that we were caught in a sweep of history that none of us could help.

Unlike my mother and sisters, I never felt at home or well-adapted. I cannot quite account for this. Despite my good fortune and rewarding life, the sadness of my parents' Europe re-emerged in me. Perhaps, as the first child in our little household of survivors, imagining the dead was the chore I was unintentionally given. The story was everything, shadowing my growth into my own self. I was cheerful, even joyful, as a child, but something drove me very early to fight against every injustice all the time in the helpless, amateur way in which I still do. Those feelings appeared as soon as I had language. I launched my first petition against a cruel teacher when I was nine, with somewhat traumatic consequences. But fighting for myself was a different story. I shrank from that. It was unseemly, even horrifying – so aggressive, like the wraiths in the camps fighting over morsels of bread. There's no question that the whole sad story diminished the sense of my own rights and wishes. In that way I have to acknowledge that my ghosts have, to some extent, won. Perhaps that is too strong. It might be better to say that I just couldn't let them leave me alone.

For a while, a vague gloom consumed me from inside like some sort of autoimmune disorder, perhaps a side effect of the ghosts, and kept me from writing. Now that I have told the story of my parents' youth, I feel as if the act of writing is like a rope bridge over the chasm of time. The Holocaust grows ever more distant. There are still deniers, of course. "Enough about the Jews," said the bigots who occasionally favored me with their emailed remarks a few years back, when I became embroiled in a controversy about a poet who had published anti-Semitic remarks, "you Zionists control everything, even our sympathy." But mostly people become impatient and indifferent. The Holocaust cannot and should not be understood, but it must be remembered. I had always hoped that *this* enormity, at least, would help prevent others, and that the vividness of these horrors would keep our eyes open, but that alertness seems to dim over the years as does all else. We live in dark times once again. Again there are millions for whom hatred has become a kind of idealism, under whose banner death marches grinning.

The fascination of the Holocaust has not faded. Films and television programs continue to be made and continue to win audiences and honors. Books fly off the presses, though I suspect that their readers are dwindling; newspapers are still full of articles; online sites grow. I know that we all share a prurient curiosity about horror. I worry about whether we are remembering our dead, or making use of their fading reality for something else, something not very honorable. I wonder if the war, with its wonderful stories and the sheer scale of its violence, has not become a storehouse of plunder, a career-maker for those who can find scandal.

My mother herself has been indiscriminate, almost promiscuous, when she's asked to tell her tale – over and over, for the Spielberg archive; the Holocaust Museum; schoolchildren; the occasional filmmaker or writer who calls her; and, incidentally, me. Discoveries about her life still come to light. Dutch public television made a half-hour documentary film about her and the wartime day-care center in Amsterdam. It was screened on May 6, 2003 – the anniversary of the Dutch liberation in World War II – as part of a series they call *Andere Tijden*, Other Times. I met one of the young researchers, Gerard Nijssen, and a producer, Ad van Liempt, in Cambridge, Massachusetts in the fall of 2001, and communicated with them and with the filmmaker, Matthijs Cats, by e-mail and phone. During his research for the film, as I have mentioned earlier, Gerard learned that my mother had been made a Dutch citizen in 1946, and might have been spared all the bureaucratic rigmarole of the spring of 1947. In November 2002, my parents flew to Amsterdam for a weekend to make the film. It was a highly emotional weekend, painful and yet full of meaning.

My mother has had her own expertise in the management of her past. She has always said that it was important that her story be told, but I notice that it has always been told in exactly the same way, whether to the family or to others. Although I have made it my own in some ways, I am still shackled to this twice-told tale, like Harry Houdini without the tricks. I suppose I cannot escape the past, any more than my mother can, and perhaps I, too, have been trying to milk my mother's unhappy history for its glamor. It's almost as if my mother and I have been in some sort of race, even now, for the telling of it.

My experience with the weight of the past makes me think about all stories of suffering, and of destinies cut short by acts of unimaginable cruelty. I think of how those stories, from the United States and from around the world, eclipse my own slight history of trying to fight such injustices, when with others of my generation I tried to do what I could. But my moments – of joining the civil rights movement at fourteen and the anti-war movement at fifteen, of a traumatic three years at Cornell University from 1967 to 1970, during the height of the violence there, of marching and demonstrating before it was fashionable and after, too – don't make as good a narrative, dramatic though they often were.

I have a tale just the same about my first reconnaissance mission into Germany. I was very young, just twenty-two.

Having studied German literature in college as a way of understanding my family's story, I was preparing at Princeton for a Ph.D. in Comparative Literature. My German was spotty, the language of someone who had stopped speaking it in childhood, and I thought I ought to spend some time improving it. I had spent a summer in Switzerland, the country of my birth, as an undergraduate, but that had not really helped my German enough. So I got myself a summer fellowship to work in Germany for the summer as a *Praktikantin*, a sort of practical nurse, in a hospital in Kiel, a port city on the Baltic and the capital of the northern province of Schleswig-Holstein. I thought that it would be easier to deal with any former Nazis I encountered if they were flat on their backs. There were objections from some of the farther-flung members of our clan, but my parents were enthusiastic. They reminded me, as they always did when risk was involved, that this was an adventure.

I arrived at the general hospital in June 1971 with an over-packed suitcase in each hand. The building had only three or four storeys, giving it a squat look, and it was built of yellow brick vaguely reminiscent of a public convenience. The day was hot. I was shown to a room on the nurses' floor. It contained a bed that folded out from what appeared to be a gigantic chest of drawers. Lying in it, I felt as if I were in a half-open coffin; the top of the cupboard hung only a few inches from my head. The room was harshly tiled like the corridor outside, though it had big windows, a clock radio, and a bookcase for the few volumes I'd sent on ahead. I was supposed to share a bathroom with the other student nurses down the hall. I hardly ever saw another soul and guessed that most of them were away on their summer break, or lived at home or with their boyfriends. After the required physical and a TB vaccination with a roomful of infants, I was told that I had been assigned to the private ward of the head doctor of the hospital, on one of three shifts. These started at 6 a.m., 2 p.m., and 10 p.m. The morning shift was pure torture. I was not really functional at that hour without coffee, and had two and a half hours of duties before I got any.

For my early-morning ineptitude, and for much else, I was roundly chastised by the head nurse, Schwester Martina, a short, gaunt, scowling red-headed woman with a very loud voice. She began by informing me that the job into which I had been plunged normally required six weeks of training. She knew, in addition, that I was here to learn the language, and *she* wasn't going to waste her time explaining things. They had a schedule to keep to, and they didn't have time for teaching incompetents. Anyway most things were self-evident, and I would just have to find my way.

That's how I came to make my mistakes. I couldn't fold the linens correctly, or make hospital corners, and sometimes misunderstood the schedule. Neither Schwester Martina nor her staff seemed to understand that, though my German was quite good, they used specialized nursing words unknown to me. Like many people when they meet a foreigner, they treated me as if I were perverse or hard of hearing. So they carped and bellowed. I had constant run-ins with my angry little boss, though five minutes of explanation would have solved everything.

I was obtuse about the real reason for her hostility, and that reason was class. Clearly, the American girls who had done this job before had not felt as foreign to the nurses as I did, although

my German, they admitted, was superior. Previous students had
been better prepared for the practical tasks they were to perform.
I concurred that practicality wasn't always my strong suit. But
more than anything, I gave out signals that the nurses couldn't
read, and certainly I couldn't read theirs. I didn't know how to
behave in a properly subordinate way. I was used to reasonable
discussion. Hierarchy, which counted for such a lot in this world,
was pretty much invisible to me. Here nurses deferred to doctors
and women to men.

I began to get an inkling of how things stood when the
patients asked me what I wanted to be "when I grew up," and I
told them innocently that I wanted to be a university professor.
This was greeted with roars of laughter. In Germany at that time,
women rarely taught in universities, and "professors" (or full
professors, in the US) were all men. The patients loved my hubris;
it was a good joke. I didn't know that I was being impertinent,
and I stumbled from blunder to blunder with the best intentions
in the world.

I was genuinely puzzled. I don't think Schwester Martina
knew the true depth of my naïveté. Though the ward was a
rougher world than I was used to and people could be hard on
one another, they weren't generally malevolent. My colleagues had
sometimes clumsy names: Frau Roggensack (rye sack), Fraülein
Schnack. The youngest nurse, Liselotte, became a friend
eventually, and after a while I was invited to spend my weekends
with her and her husband, Wolfgang. But Fraülein Schnack, who
was some sort of secretary on the ward, took a special interest in
me right at the beginning. She invited me out for *Kaffee und
Kuchen* my first Sunday afternoon off. We walked through the
windy, green-roofed streets to a tea-room in the center of town,
where we sat surrounded by large middle-aged women eating
several pieces of cake each. Now I understand how one arrives at
such a state at a certain point in life, but at the time it struck me

as another sign of German decadence. I was alert for signals of covert violence and anti-Semitism. Mentally I was like a street-fighter in a dark alley, crouched down ready for all comers.

I had decided long before that I would declare my Jewishness as openly as possible. I couldn't bear to be in disguise in this country, and wanted badly to test my courage. If I expected to learn interesting things about Germany that would never surface otherwise, I thought, I had to put my cards on the table right at the start. And that hunch, it turned out, was right.

Poor Fraülein Schnack was to be the first person in Kiel to hear that I was a Jew. I tried not to think of her as an old maid – my feminism pursed its lips at the thought – but it was hard to find another way to think about her. She fit the stereotype so perfectly. She was about fifty, and seemed elderly in a way that I like to kid myself into thinking women aren't any more. She fluttered and fussed, and wore middle-aged clothes and a hat. She had wrinkles, and faded, badly hennaed hair. I had already gathered that the nurses regarded her with contempt, and that she was kept in her position by some sort of special arrangement. She had latched onto me because I was too green to know how she was looked upon socially, and perhaps because I, too, regularly displeased the despot at work.

"I know I seem a little – well – a little strange sometimes," she said as soon as the Black Forest cake arrived. "I'm on disability, you know – a pension. I've had it for oh, about twenty-five years now, since I was a young woman, and why? All because a box fell on my head. Bad luck, wasn't it? I was just standing there in the supply room, and a big box fell on my head, and…and I just haven't been the same since."

I clucked sympathetically and asked Fraülein Schnack what life had been like before the fateful box had met her skull. Her eyes grew soft and radiant as she remembered the war, a time when she had really been needed. She had worked the switchboard in an important institution – was it under the supervision of the army? Was it at the shipyards? She remembered the camaraderie, the gaiety under fire. Kiel, a major port, was terribly bombed, but the young people gallantly carried on under the life-and-death stress of battle. "You felt that you were essential, that you were doing something important," she said. She sounded exactly like people I knew later in London who talked with the same nostalgia about the Blitz. I could understand it, too. It was "an adventure," as my parents so often said, for people who were not particularly political and for whom the intrusion of Allied bombs had been exciting. Social conventions melted, and young people lived in groups, full of restless energy and teased by the erotic closeness of death.

I wondered if she had had a boyfriend. Yes, she blushed. He had been in the army, and they had been engaged. But he had been killed on the Russian front. He had been missing for a long time, and she had lived in suspense. The news of his death had come after the war, when German prisoners began trickling out of the USSR. "I knew then," she said, "that I would never marry. That it was the end of that hope for me."

Kiel was full of Fraülein Schnacks. At that time, only twenty-six years after the war, its effect on the German population was obvious. Middle-aged women far outnumbered men on the streets, and there were fewer young people and children than I was used to seeing. The box that hit Fraülein Schnack had contained loneliness, sorrow, boredom, shame and sexual frustration. What doctor had allowed her to believe that her eccentricities had been caused by a perhaps fictional thwack on the noggin? I was astounded that she seemed completely innocent of psychotherapy. Kiel was further from the centers of civilization than I imagined. But of course, I reminded myself, it had been purged of Jews. There were probably no psychoanalysts left in the whole province of Schleswig-Holstein, and no one to help her see that that the blow might not have caused all her symptoms.

Then she asked me what had brought me to Kiel, "our little city," I remember she said. I explained, and then I took a deep breath and said, "and in a way, I'm visiting my past. I'm Jewish, you know, and my mother was born in Berlin. So this is a big experiment for me. Some people in my family didn't want me to come." There was a moment's silence; then she said, as so many people did during that summer, "but you have blond hair and blue eyes. You don't look Jewish." I felt my natural didacticism rising in response to this. I was a living lesson, an experiment I was conducting with myself as guinea pig. I felt daring and curious, and also slightly ashamed. I detected a certain smugness at having surprised my addled tablemate – the triumph of causing moral discomfort – and it was a little too satisfying. Certainly it was too easy.

Instead Fraülein Schnack surprised me. She told me about a Jewish friend of hers who had fled to Chile before the war, made a comfortable living, and had since returned to Kiel after Salvador Allende's Marxist government came to power in 1970.

"The odd thing was that she had lived in the Red part of town," said Fraülein Schnack. "Kiel had a lot of Communists in the old days, you know. There were a lot of riots against the Nazis in the old workers' area around the port. But it was all smashed flat by the Allies – funny, isn't it? She couldn't find a trace of her house when she came back. Still, she was glad to be home. Germany was the only civilized place, she told me. She liked all the social services, now that she was growing older."

So there were Jews who had willingly returned to Germany! I had imagined quite a different conversation. But I discovered a pattern in Fraülein Schnack's reaction that never varied. Every German I spoke to had had a Jewish friend, sometimes a *good* Jewish friend, and every one deplored what had happened, and portrayed himself or herself as an innocent bystander. To hear them tell it, there had been no Nazis in Germany, only friends and neighbors wringing their hands.

The patients told me many such stories, once I got to know them. I talked with them while I administered *Verordnungen*, or "prescriptions," which were comforting rituals like footbaths and massages. I got on very well with my charges, to the annoyance of Schwester Martina. They called me *die kleine Amerikanerin*, the little American, and let me administer the weird routines of the hospital with good grace. In this world run by women, where the only men were doctors who appeared like gods once a day from behind clouds of harrumphing authority, daily and weekly rhythms went on uninterrupted by any challenge. Not all of the procedures made sense, but since the head of our team was half-crazed, this was not a summer for questions. Our patients were mostly elderly and suffered from a variety of afflictions. Although they were all covered by the comprehensive health insurance that Bismarck had introduced to Germany in the 19th century, the better-off patients had private rooms and sometimes substantial privileges. But the medical care itself, good or bad, was perfectly democratic as far as I could see.

The patients loved these ministrations, and relaxed during them. Many of my best conversations took place then, or during odd moments of the day when a break in my duties gave me a few minutes to chat with those well enough to enjoy the intrusion. The greatest enemy for those pre-exercise-as-much-as-possible days was boredom. This was an internal medicine ward, so patients were not generally recovering from surgery. They mostly had long-term ailments like heart disease, stroke, and diabetes. It was a relief to have the chance to do something useful for actual patients, instead of being shouted at for the way I folded sheets.

But death, of course, hovered in the background. It seemed right to me that I should meet it for the first time in this place. The Jewish poet Paul Celan had described death as a master from

Germany, and it was fitting that a child of the next generation should see that master brought down to a proper scale, one body at a time. Indeed, death came anticlimactically to a young man on our ward. He was no older than forty, perhaps much younger, but the ravages of lymphoma had wasted him and turned his skin a bilious yellow, and by now it was hard to guess his age. My job, as youngest nurse, was to keep him supplied with large pitchers of iced lemonade, which I made for him from fresh lemons whenever I had the chance.

The young man sweated buckets hourly, and we changed his sheets several times a day. The lemonade was an attempt to slake the raging thirst brought on by dehydration. There was no high-tech equipment in his room, not even an I.V., as I remember. I couldn't understand why he wasn't made more comfortable, and I spent as much time as I could checking on him and sitting with him for a few minutes. Then, entering one afternoon with yet another installment of lemonade, I found him dead. I knew instantly, by the way his color had subtly changed to a sort of vellum, the shade of medieval manuscripts, and from the way his poor body lay against the pillows; he had thrashed such a lot before. I had spoken with him only an hour or two earlier. I called one of the senior nurses, and burst into tears. For once, my colleagues were gentle and sympathetic.

"We had forgotten that you probably hadn't seen a dead person before," said Liselotte, the young nurse who had befriended me, "or we wouldn't have sent you in there so often. We knew it would happen any minute. The first time is always hard." I was relieved of the rest of my shift for that day, and lay shaken on my coffin-like bed, annoyed with myself for reacting so strongly. Just think how much death my mother had seen when she was my age, I thought. What kind of softie was I, anyway?

The social complications were even more instructive than the medical ones, though much harder to understand. I got into trouble with both nurses and doctors one day when the *Chefarzt*, the chief doctor, came to lunch. He talked to me a lot. He wanted to practice his English, and he was fascinated by all things American. He informed me that he was an avid reader of *Reader's Digest*. That put me into a terrible position with the other nurses. I had been struggling to gain their acceptance, to learn the rules and to enjoy the jokes, and I had made considerable headway. Just a few days before, I had even been invited for a night out with the nurses at a disco. This was the sort of place I wouldn't have been caught dead in in the US, but I was thrilled to be included.

The disco had been bathed in pink, stroboscopic light, thickly hazed by customers' cigarettes. The nurses sat around our table smoking, drinking and talking in a grotesquely animated way, frightening off (I thought) the very men they were trying to attract. I was petrified at first because I have never been much of a dancer, but at the first chord of German rock music, I relaxed. The music had a sort of country-western-Bavarian beat impossible to describe, and a chorus consisting of mangled Anglo-German: *"Baby, zieh' die Hotpants an"* – "Baby, put on your hot pants." I knew that my dancing couldn't possibly be worse than the music, so I wiggled around on the dance floor. After all, I was *American* – that had to offer some sort of advantage. To my amazement, men did come up to dance with me, and with the other nurses, too, once we were separated from the chattering flock at our table. Without exception, the men ground their pelvises against me whenever they could, inflamed, no doubt, by the lyrics of the song. It had been fun. For a few hours, I had felt a part of things, all barriers down. I hoped that the social situation at work would get a bit easier as a result.

Now, back on the ward, the head doctor had appeared and was speaking English, as if it were a code, to the most junior woman there. I couldn't deflect him, either: the rules of hierarchy and gender were too powerful, and he didn't recognize my tactics.

My silence, unusual for me, was what he expected from a young woman awed by his presence. So he plowed on remorselessly, haranguing me with his views on the American divorce rate and Steve McQueen. Meanwhile Schwester Martina glared at me from the other end of the table, and the other nurses, half of whom were in love with the *Chefarzt*, looked down at the table in an ominous parody of nursely respect. I was sure they would all fall on me as soon as he left the room.

To my horror, the *Chefarzt* began a defense of the war in Vietnam just as we were about to get back to work. I forgot where I was and argued with him for a minute or two. The shocked silence deepened. I had forgotten that one never, *never* argues with the *Chefarzt* about anything, especially when one is a young woman on the lowest rung of hospital society. I realized my mistake too late. The nurses stood up to go, bowing respectfully to the *Chefarzt* as they filed out. The doctor waved them all through the door, and then said to Schwester Martina, "Leave the American girl here for a minute. I want to hear the end of what she was saying about Vietnam." His request was the death-knell for me socially on the ward, but I was relieved to be able to talk to someone in a normal way for a few minutes, and we argued about the war while Schwester Martina seethed. I was caught in an impossible situation, but I still cringe now at my youthful self-importance and cluelessness. I came from a doctor's family, after all. The *Chefarzt* was about my father's age, and awe didn't come into the equation for me. I doubt very much, however, that I would have learned as much if I had approached the summer with the tact of experience.

At about that moment, I was rescued by the young nurse, Liselotte. She invited me to spend a weekend with her in her little house on the banks of the Kiel Canal. She and her husband, Wolfgang, wanted to take me on an excursion to a fishing port where we could buy fresh Baltic shrimp on the docks. We could drive through some pretty countryside on the way, and maybe see some friends in the evening. It was midsummer, and I was grateful to be invited out. The evenings were long in Kiel at that time of year. One night we stood on the beach at eleven, watching the last glimmers of sunset lingering over the water.

I liked their house, too. Lying in bed by the guest-room window under the roof, I watched the huge smokestacks of freighters and tankers slide by just across the lawn. I liked the deafening honk of the foghorns, the mix of land and sea. I liked the way even the most unorthodox Germans had a serious breakfast ritual, involving a fully laid table, a soft-boiled egg in its cup, and an array of artfully displayed cheese and cold cuts. I had grown up with that tradition, but it was comic and touching to see it observed in the clutter of an otherwise disorderly household.

I had come to appreciate Liselotte because of her kindness to the patients. She had an admirable way of clucking sympathetically when they complained. Her compassion provided a welcome counterpoint to the insulting yelps that passed for conversation among the nurses. I didn't recognize at first that she lacked a sense of humor. This deficiency, which she shared with her husband, contributed strongly, I surmised, to the collapse of understanding between them later on. I remember Liselotte standing next to me as we gazed down at the naked body of a skinny old man who, though paralyzed from the waist down, still played the roué with us. He liked flirting with his attendants, the younger, the better. Sometimes he simply grabbed a passing hand, patted a buttock, or told an unseemly joke, but of late he had taken to tossing his hospital gown nonchalantly aside, leaving his lower half exposed like a withered Matisse odalisque. Such a simple ploy required our bustling to his bedside to cover him up again, which he much enjoyed.

I seem to recall that we were bathing him. He must have been unconscious or asleep, or Liselotte could never have said what she assuredly did say. She clicked her tongue in the sighing, sympathetic way which I, ever the graduate student, associated with the novels of Thomas Mann. "Tja," she clucked, "will you look at that." She waved her hand sadly over the geezer's shrunken genitals. "So small, poor man. Isn't it interesting that he makes such a fuss over women when his thing is so little." I murmured dutifully that size had nothing to do with it. "Yes, I guess that's so," Liselotte sighed. "You should see the women who come to visit him. And how he talks about his conquests. But still, I think it's interesting." Her voice trailed off, full of feeling. Liselotte's philosophy of sex was generally entertaining, particularly because her tone was always tinged with melancholy.

Liselotte was a tall, heavy, handsome young woman, about four years older than I, and Wolfgang, her husband, was diminutive. On first glance, they looked like Jack Sprat and his wife. Wolfgang's beard and mustache were disturbingly well-trimmed, and he wore steel-rimmed glasses: he fit the stereotype of the German university student. His appetite for sex, Liselotte confided, was boundless. He could do it three times a day if she'd let him. She wasn't nearly as enthusiastic, and this difference had caused "problems" between them; at least he thought so. He couldn't understand why she didn't dissolve in orgasms whenever he wanted her to. He had threatened to find a woman who liked making love as much as he did. He already had someone in mind. "And what does he do all day while you're at work?" I asked. "Doesn't he go to the University?" "Not really," said Liselotte. "Besides, it's summer now, no classes. He says that he mostly stays home and masturbates."

Wolfgang had been perfectly friendly to me at first, though I had noticed an inordinate number of references to sex. On Midsummer night, we had danced at a street fair, and he had approached me more directly. Subtlety wasn't a strong suit in that world. He had shimmied his shoulders in a suggestive way, glinted his lenses at me, and murmured in English, "Let's fuck, baby." He didn't seem to mind my rejection; he was good-natured enough, and seemed quite used to it. None of this seemed to come between Liselotte and me. She appeared to be resigned to his constant attempts to lure other women into bed. I heard later from Liselotte that they had divorced. She went off to nurse in Malaysia, and he dropped out of sight. I found him repulsive, but I was amused at the couple's resignation before what they saw as his inevitable sex drive. Had they asked me for advice, I might have suggested that Wolfgang get a job. They were still fond of each other, and tender, despite the obvious disintegration of their life together.

After that weekend, I practically moved in. The talk when I was there was of their vacation on a small sailboat through what they always referred to as "the Swedish islands." I never found out which islands they meant, but they were planning the voyage on their sixteen-foot yacht with another couple. I could hardly imagine a more horrible holiday. During the course of many trips to the dock to fit out the little boat, I got to know their friend Eckhardt. He was a fellow student of Wolfgang's at the University, studying biology, I think, although he didn't seem to know or care anything about the subject. He looked as Aryan as any man I have ever seen: he was six-five, long-boned and jawed, blond and blue-eyed. His hair and the pouches under his eyes drooped a little, giving his looks a touch of the basset hound. He was handsome, though not, under normal circumstances, the sort of man I was drawn to. But I was in Germany on a quest, and he met the requirements of my darkest erotic fantasies. I had the same effect on him. I was the only Jew and the only American that any member of that crowd had met.

There was much discussion of my Jewishness after I had made my obligatory statement of identity. At the hospital, once they knew, my fellow nurses declared that I looked "exactly like Golda

Meir." Golda Meir was not exactly an ideal of physical beauty, much as I admired her; at the very least, she was forty or fifty years older than I was. If I rejected the idea of resembling Golda Meir, I'd have to admit that I was "the spitting image of Barbra Streisand." That was certainly a more flattering comparison. Still, these two were the only Jewish women whose faces the nurses had any idea of, and clearly they thought that all Jews looked alike.

I don't think I told the nurses about being a Jew in quite the direct way I had planned at the outset. I had developed a little caution after my encounter with Fraülein Schnack. My identity came out unexpectedly for all of us one particularly bright Sunday morning when I went into an elderly lady's room to wake her up, as usual. "Good morning," I said as I opened the curtains. "It's going to be lovely today. The sun is already hot." Just then church bells began ringing, the peals chiming in one after another, from all parts of the city center. "Isn't that a beautiful sound?" I said. "It fits the morning perfectly." The old lady agreed, and then asked, to my astonishment, "Are you Protestant or Catholic?" I was not about to abandon my little campaign: honesty was the best policy, wasn't it? "Well, neither, actually," I said. "I'm Jewish." The lady stared for a moment, as if to draw breath, and began screaming at the top of her lungs. "Get out of here, get out of here, you lying devil! I won't be touched by Jewish hands, I won't! How dare you come into my room! Get out!" I beat a hasty retreat, and summoned the other nurses, who flocked to the room. The screeches could be heard all over the ward. Beneath my shock and dismay, a small voice laughed: *at last, someone who tells the truth.*

The nurses came and reported. To their credit, they were as shocked as I was, perhaps more. The woman was unstable; they had known that from her medical records. She had some kind of senile dementia. Apparently she had lost a daughter during the Allied bombing raids on Kiel during the war. She thought that I looked like her, and when I said that I was Jewish, she had imagined that I had assumed the disguise of her dead daughter to torment her. She had apparently held the view for decades that an international Jewish conspiracy had killed her daughter by paying for the planes and bombs over Germany. My blond hair and blue eyes were clearly the work of the Devil, Jewish bankers, and Communists. But now that everything had been explained to her, she wanted to make amends. She intended to make a contribution to the Jewish Orphans' Fund in my name.

I asked if we couldn't just forget about the matter. The woman was old and crazy; I could take care of her, if she wished, or leave her alone if she found that too upsetting. The nurses insisted, however, rightly arguing that my refusal would only set her off again. So I returned to the old lady's room to find her propped against the pillows, looking as calm as she had before her outburst.

"I want to apologize to you," she said. "You really are the spitting image of my daughter. She was nineteen when she was killed. How old are you?"

"Twenty-two," I said.

"Well, you see how mistakes can be made, you're not so far apart in age," the old lady said. "How can you possibly be Jewish, the way you look?" I said nothing. "Of course, you do have the nose. My daughter's nose was straight."

I tried to take refuge in the quasi-professionalism I had developed during the weeks of Schwester Martina's shouting, and busied myself folding towels with a skill that surprised me.

"I have nothing against the Jewish religion, you know," she went on, undeterred by my silence. "The chant of the rabbis is beautiful. If only the people weren't such scum."

At that point I made for the door. I couldn't bear to hear another word. I thought of my gentle grandparents, my sunny, generous-spirited mother and her day-care children, my father who treated psychotics for free. "She's ill, she's mad," I told myself through gritted teeth. "Be patient. You must get through this."

"Wait, wait!" she called. "What about the money for the Jewish Orphans' Fund?" I stopped. I drew a deep breath. "You should talk to Schwester Martina about that. I have no idea. I'm not a representative of the Jewish people. But I don't think any such fund exists. Don't you remember that there are no Jews left in Germany? Don't you remember why?" And I left.

Or so I remember that climactic moment, from which I emerge word-perfect. I have chanced a guess that my memory matches reality this time, or I would have felt worse about the encounter in succeeding years. I felt sorry for the half-crazed woman even as I despised the racism that had given shape to her dementia. For the first time, I understood how my mother could have pitied the stragglers from Hitler's army whom she met as they crawled their way out of his invincible Western Wall.

This event caused Liselotte to reconsider her own relationship to the German past. She and her friends had never been trained to reflect, but she told the group the story of my encounter with the madwoman, and we had many earnest discussions on the subject. The young people told me that they had not studied World War II in school, and as for the Holocaust, it had not been mentioned, either at home or in the classroom. I was surprised at this, because I knew that schoolchildren in bigger towns were taken on tours of former camps nearby. Bergen-Belsen was near Hanover and Dachau near Munich, for example. In Schleswig-Holstein, evidently, the authorities had not thought such an education important.

My friends were generally aged between twenty-five and thirty, and not one of them had much idea of what had happened during the war. But they began to pay more attention to their language and way of thinking. Liselotte, with a stricken face, caught herself referring to the *Jude* of their little yacht as they stocked it with supplies for their sailing holiday. That was the nautical term for the ship's quartermaster; they'd never considered what it meant before. Wolfgang pointed out that the term for a flaw in a wall you were painting was *Jude*, and then, of course, there were all the old references to Jews and money: don't try to Jew me, stop being such a Jew over a few pennies, and so on. I was amazed that the language had not been purged of such idioms, and so were they. But why should we be surprised? I asked. There was no one left to offend.

We began talking about their childhoods. They were just old enough to have been born during or within a year after the war. The first memory, for all of them, was of fire. They described a house burning, flames shooting high into the sky, and a feeling of absolute terror. They could recall the smell of soot, which was mixed for them with the panic of flight. The consistency of this first image among the young people was itself terrifying to me. Most of them were refugees from further east, people who had packed up and fled as the Russians entered their towns, and their memories were either of Allied bombing raids, or of Russian rage. They remembered being crowded onto boxcars as they fled west, and not having food or water. They vaguely recalled deaths on the way. They were too ill-informed to recognize the irony of their experience. Until I asked them, they had never talked about their early years.

They hadn't noticed, for example, that they had another common memory from those years: the absence of fathers. Many of them had been born while their fathers were fighting on the Eastern Front, in the USSR as it was then. Some of those men died, and others remained in prison camps for up to ten years. Those who returned were strangers whose attitudes contained an odd mixture of Nazi rigidity and the trauma of sufferings endured behind barbed wire. The veterans found that their families had been headed by women for so long that the society they re-entered was a kind of matriarchy.

Eckhard told me about those years in most detail. By then I was living with him in a peeling, white-painted shack he called, romantically, "the garden house" because he rented it for almost nothing from the friend whose back yard it occupied. There were gooseberry bushes in front that produced huge, pink-tinged, translucent fruit; pink roses spilling over a trellis; and inside, the most colossal mess I had ever seen. I felt daring and liberated living under such conditions. Besides, I was cheating on my untrustworthy boyfriend back in the States, and felt curiously free of guilt. My fling only confirmed what I had not, until then, been quite able to admit to myself. I was ready for Eckhardt in many ways.

He was utterly wrong for me, of course. That was part of his charm. There was the language, first of all. He insisted that we communicated perfectly, that he had gotten to know me well, that my inadequacies in German were minor. He was not a linguist, and so he couldn't notice my own feeling that I was not myself in the reduced vocabulary of this foreign tongue; that my gestures, my words, everything, were false, or at best a spectral representation of what I really was. I wasn't sure that I understood him, either, or recognized what he meant to say when he spoke to me. The limitations of language were catastrophic for me, but also exhilarating. I felt like an 18th-century baroness at a masquerade, like someone wearing a casque and domino, and playing at erotic games which my daylight self would never countenance.

There were some delightfully loony moments. Eckhardt, if he is still alive, will probably always credit me with the introduction of garlic into his diet. He was so limited in his experience of life, at twenty-eight, that even this humble herb, common in Germany, was a revelation. He took to it as if he were on the vampire hunt of the century. One night when we were both naked in the summer heat of the shack, he stood me on his rickety coffee table, twined a few pink roses from the trellis into my pubic hair with the care of a window-dresser preparing a dummy, and capered around me waving a wine bottle and shouting, "*Knoblauch! Knoblauch!*" ("Garlic! "Garlic!") like a cannibal from some B-grade movie. Despite my embarrassment at finding myself nude on a coffee table, I decided that goddess of garlic was better than goddess of nothing. There was something touching in the way Eckhardt expressed his liberation from something, or into something. He galumphed his long body into exhaustion, his white skin satiny with sweat as he collapsed upon the none-too-clean sofa.

We took trips together. On the couple of weekends I had off, we tooled through the countryside in his battered little car – a Beetle, or a Deux-Chevaux, I don't remember which – and disregarded the normal rhythms of day and night. Once we went to Hamburg and strolled in Sankt-Pauli, the red-light district. The hawkers shocked me, though I pretended not to be shocked. "Come in, come in," the hawkers shouted at Eckhardt, never at me, "we'll put on a show that'll make your girlfriend wet!" Eckhardt, to his credit, never suggested that we actually take in the delights of that sinful street. Unlike Wolfgang, who oozed prurience, Eckhardt had a sort of sheepdog innocence.

At dawn we looked over the beautiful harbor of the Elbe and joined the prostitutes for breakfast. We drove back to Kiel, sleeping in a cornfield by the roadside for a few hours. I had never engaged in a simple act of trespass like that before, and it was in every way uncomfortable. I watched, impressed, as Eckhardt slept, his long narrow body coiled among the stalks and over the stubble like a great Nordic snake. We went to Lübeck and looked at Thomas Mann's ancestral house, and on the way back we passed through farms and small seaside villages in the lakeland that the locals called the Switzerland of the North. The black and white timbered houses of the countryside reminded me of England. It was a peaceful, prosperous landscape. The past seemed completely erased from it, and I saw it anyway through the golden haze of sexual adventure. I felt fatally softened and too forgiving, as if I had dozed off in the Land of the Lotos-eaters.

We talked constantly, though in the German I thought of as so limiting. Like the other members of our little group, Eckhardt had become fascinated with Jews and with his own childhood, which he had never thought about much before. He told me that his father had been gone for a full ten years. He had been "a guest of the government of the great Soviet Union," as Eckhardt put it. When he came back, Eckhardt had been afraid of him. He was tall and stern, and he gave off an air of silent disapproval. When he wasn't quiet and watchful, he was violent. Eckhardt's mother changed, too. The playful cuddling and confiding chats in her bed came to an end. She drew back, became anxious, and shouted more. Eckhardt had always felt that his father's return marked the end of his childhood happiness.

There was one incident in particular which Eckhardt remembered as decisive. His pet rabbit died. Eckhardt, grief-stricken, decided to give it a proper funeral. He put the corpse into a shoebox, dug a grave, and lit candles, just the way he had seen the priests do in church. He stood before the grave with his prayer book, draped in his mother's lacy shawl, and was beginning the service for the dead when he was hit on the side of the head. His father had come up behind him unobserved.

"This is blasphemy!" his father shouted, and he kicked and stomped on the candlesticks and the other things Eckhardt had arranged. He swept up the shoebox and dumped the rabbit's body into the garbage. And he beat Eckhardt with his belt for daring to take the Lord's name in vain.

His father had been a history teacher in a school before he had been conscripted, and history teachers who sympathized with the Nazi cause had been Goebbels's shock troops among the young, the core of the propaganda campaign to win converts in the rising generation. He had never renounced his fanatical belief in the Führer. His return from the Russian Front was the beginning of a new regime of military discipline for Eckhardt, of rigid timetables and savage punishments. It had been a relief when his father died quite young of heart disease thought to have been brought on by the long years in Soviet prisoner-of-war camps. There had been no question of love between them.

Despite a body and face that suggested an ancestry of marauding chieftains, Eckhardt was a timid man. I watched him tenderly as he told me the stories of his childhood. I thought of the rabbit he had been prevented from burying. He had never become a confident adult. His rose-covered little house was like a burrow, from which, quivering, he poked his elegant nose now and then. Experience frightened him; the larger world frightened him; and he looked upon the turmoil of the times we lived in with a removed perplexity.

When he saw me off on the train at the end of the summer, I knew that I would never hear from him again. He just didn't have the energy. I sent him a card with a big heart by Jim Dine, the fashionable artist of the moment, but he never replied, and soon after he disappeared from Liselotte's circle. She told me that he had become deeply depressed, and that she had lost track of him. I was sorry. I wondered if our idyll in the garden house hadn't made things worse for him. He had been so unself-conscious, so remote from himself and from the emotions and objects of the world, that perhaps I had only caused him pain in the aftermath of our separation. Or perhaps our adventure hadn't mattered much to him, and his habitual sadness had closed over him again like the lowering German sky. I would never know.

At the time, I hadn't cared to explore the summer's mental territory all that closely. How had I ended up in the garden house with the son of an ardent Nazi? If other American girls made leather-jacketed bad boys their objects of longing, I had apparently taken on something much darker, a child of Hitler, even if my Aryan turned out to be more mouse than menace. The trip into Germany was supposed to be a fact-finding expedition, lit at its vanguard by the torch of truth. Instead, though I had learned and experienced much, I had also found my own shadow.

I read a book that summer that was making the rounds of the German bestseller lists. It was called *Die Unfähigkeit zu Trauern*, in English, *The Inability to Mourn*, and it was by a married couple, the sociologists Alexander and Margarete Mitscherlich. I found it helpful as I negotiated my way around the various kinds of madness and memory that I encountered in Kiel. My experience matched its central finding – that Germans had simply repressed what they could not bring themselves to feel. I had witnessed so much emotional distortion that I wondered what would happen to the country in the coming decades.

For the time being I had made my own sort of peace with Germany. The demons of my imagination had been replaced by a population of real faces: Eckhardt and Liselotte, Wolfgang and Fraülein Schnack, the patients, the head doctor, Schwester Martina, and the rest. I, too, had denied what I had done and felt, at least in the rose-covered garden house.

But I found that the summer in Kiel, where I had confronted the frightful past at home in its own country, was not enough to quiet my ghosts for long. Nor could I solve the problems of the world by being a daughter so dutiful that I faced my parents' history instead of my own. As I grew older, I would have to begin the process of exorcism over again.

Epilogue

AT PRINCETON, a few months after my Kiel adventure, I met Oliver Hart, a Londoner who was studying economics. We married in 1974 and went straight to England, where we spent the next decade. Most of the time we lived in Cambridge, where our two sons, Daniel and Benjamin, were born in 1977 and 1982. Oliver was a lecturer at Cambridge and then a professor at the London School of Economics. For some of that period I taught at the University of Essex and later had a research fellowship at Trinity Hall, Cambridge. Oliver was an only child. He wanted to return to England because his own charismatic parents were growing older and he thought that he should stay close by. As it turned out, they both lived to a great age; Oliver's father died at the age of 106. In 1984 we returned to the United States when Oliver was appointed a professor at MIT. I became an associate professor of literature in the same place, but my years there were unhappy, and I failed to get tenure. Oliver soon left for Harvard, where I also teach. We are the grandparents of two little brothers who live near us, and the daily enchantments of a happy life have, to some extent, soothed my family ghosts.

But not completely, since a large part of my life has been devoted to mourning the grandparents I never saw, the cousins, aunts and friends I never met. As I get older and the necessary narcissisms of youth erode slowly in the recognition of time lost and the personal certainty of death, the pain has not diminished. When I was young, it was the horror of massive violence, especially against children of my age, that hovered over me, waking and sleeping. By now the sense of the loss of specific people has grown as well. My sisters share this sorrow. We see our parents as grandparents, we become grandparents ourselves, and we recognize what we've lost in a way that we couldn't have known as children.

The ghosts affected me in another, more difficult way for someone growing up in the striving United States. My ambivalence about my place in the world, and especially about my right to whatever success meant, made it difficult for me to know what I actually wanted. As a child, I was torn between writing and science. I thought that I would grow up to be a poet for sure, and perhaps also a doctor or virologist. Ambition was easy in the abstract. My father, of course, had wanted to be a writer, but he was happy in medicine and hoped that I would follow in all his footsteps, phantom and actual. I knew in a way that I was living out some of his fantasies, but I also loved those disciplines. Had it not been for my clumsiness in the dissection of my fetal pig, Cleopatra Bacon, in my junior year of high school, I might have gone in for medicine in a serious way. But when I sliced through her ovaries without having noticed them at all, I thought it was a warning about what I might do to humans some day if I became a doctor.

I wrote a great deal of poetry then and found joy in it. I even wrote my way out of a short breakdown the summer between my freshman and sophomore years at Cornell. I was enrolled in the Six-Year Ph.D. program, a concoction of the Cold War and the

Ford Foundation, which proposed churning out students with doctorates in six years from their entry as undergraduates. It was a crazy notion and put our little group under immense pressure. My arrival had been preceded by a terrible fire that had killed nine people in our dorm the year before, and was accompanied by increasing political and racial tensions on our campus and in the country. I was taking courses that summer when a beloved mentor and friend, Matthijs Jolles, died suddenly on the very evening that I'd invited him to dinner at our dorm. He was the head of the German Literature department, a non-Jewish refugee from Nazi Germany who understood exactly why I was studying with him. It turned out that he had committed suicide that night, though I didn't learn this until many years later. At any rate he was a precursor, a kind of pre-ghost, for what I dreaded most: the death of my parents, especially that of my father. Those years were unusual in their violence and turmoil, but also in the close relationships that developed, at least in that place, between students and teachers.

The breakdown was a sort of watershed. I wrote less poetry and eventually almost stopped, though never completely. I was glad in 1970 to leave the Six-Year Ph.D. program for graduate school at Princeton. At first its quiet quadrangles were a relief after all the tumult at Cornell, but it was a stiff and pompous place. Our professors were few, male, and jealous of their position. The students were intelligent and sometimes even intellectually exciting, but so docile in this little power structure that I felt out of place once again. I struggled there at times. I was over-reverent toward intellectual authority myself and intimidated by the ferocious evangelism of French criticism, then in full flower; but I felt some contempt for its abstractions and evasions. Literary criticism didn't answer the questions that haunted me. Nonetheless, since I was frightened of competition and of failure and easily bowled over when things went wrong, I lost confidence and stopped in my poetic tracks.

After I married Oliver, it took me a long time to complete my doctorate on Richardson and Diderot, which I eventually published with the help of my Cambridge fellowship and the intellectual encouragement of friends and colleagues in England. Oliver was a driven, disciplined thinker, always immensely encouraging but quite a different animal from me; I admired, and still admire, the qualities in him that were most difficult for me. Though I was quite good at the study and teaching of literature, my heart continued to be divided. There I was, fighting on the barricades for women's rights, arguing with the men in the universities who thought I couldn't be married and have a child and also continue thinking and writing; and yet I was such a mouse inside. I shuddered at academic arguments because of their aggression, and couldn't easily let myself find the expressive freedom I'd had as a girl. What a funny little feminist I was, in the end: so hobbled when it came to fighting for myself. I smile to think of it.

Finally, later in life, I am able to talk about such things through a narrative that will never be my own story. Practically all the people in it have died, some since the writing began, but many long before that: Zus and Jo Scholte; Otto Frank and his second wife, Fritzi; the elder Dupuis and one of their daughters; my mother's old friend from Joint at Belsen, Joe Wolhandler; and my uncle Jo. My parents still live at home in New Jersey, and my sisters and I have been lucky enough to have them all this time. I realize now that my father was a far less comfortable immigrant than my mother. He has always said that he lost his native language when he came to America, and he mourns because, at ninety-four, he cannot travel once more to Switzerland to visit Basel and his remaining family, nor is he likely to see his beloved Alps again. His nostalgia is as active as my mother's has always been absent.

My mother has Alzheimer's disease just as her brother did, and my father takes care of her. Perhaps it is a good illness for someone who has never suffered from nostalgia, but instead from the precise recall of terrible detail. She sits in a streak of sunlight from the garden each day, sunnily forgetting more and more, though never the names and faces of her children and grandchildren; the great-grandchildren are a little vaguer. The mention of a small child can still make my mother smile. She never tires of hearing about our little grandsons. But we daughters can't talk with our mother as we once did. That person has gone, leaving behind a loving mother-child. She is eighty-nine now, almost immobile because the disease has weakened her, but in otherwise sound health. My father has heart disease, hearing loss, and painful arthritis, but he is surprisingly cheerful in the difficult job he won't relinquish to a stranger, and as warm, intellectual, and argumentative as ever. They delight in each other, and joke and hold hands. My survivor-mother remembers to say to my father, over and over: "Did I ever tell you how much I love you?" They will be heroes until the day they die. In New York in April 2013, they were honored once more as members of the dwindling remainder of the *Machal*, the foreign volunteers who fought in Israel in 1948.

Many years intervened before I went to Germany again. In 2001, just six weeks after 9/11, I visited Munich with Oliver. It was the first trip to Germany I had taken since my summer in Kiel thirty years before. We were guests of a university where Oliver was giving a public lecture, and I was far more comfortably housed than I had been all those years ago. Germany's openness to its past had continued to develop in exemplary ways since the 1970s. Its Jewish population had increased from fewer than 30,000 the summer of my first visit to a little over 200,000, most of whom were immigrants from the former Soviet Union.

One night in one of those *gemütlich* Bavarian beer halls that I wouldn't have entered for the life of me a few decades before, our host and his colleagues talked about the repercussions of 9/11, and especially about the invasion of Afghanistan by the United States. "I am a pacifist," said our host, a man with a beard so straggly that I couldn't imagine why he bothered with it. "I am always against violence, and I'm against the invasion despite the twin towers."

I gazed at him and remembered the companions of my summer in Kiel thirty years before, the children raised by their mothers in the absence of soldier-fathers who were either captured or dead. I had wondered, since my time in Kiel, if being brought up largely by women had helped to make that generation more vigorously anti-war than its American counterpart; many Germans were against war at all costs, no matter how many contradictions such a position might lead to. Perhaps single mothers had more to do with their pacifism than feelings of national guilt. Whatever its cause, I was glad to see it. Reminders of the old Germany were everywhere, as my husband and I found when we visited Dachau concentration camp on a suburban train that runs from the Marienplatz, in the center of town, almost to the camp gates. Snow began to fall out of a lowering sky, and an American couple on the train chatted to us about an uncle in Dachau they were going to see. They meant the pretty, comfortable little town that surrounds the camp with its cafes, parks and day-care centers. The name had lost its horrible power for them, I suppose: another example of the tide of time rolling out.

It was cold in Dachau, and the buildings in their grim symmetry seemed familiar from a thousand photographs. The camp was shockingly close to Munich. The museum there now made it clear that the Nazis had never tried to hide that fact. There were blown-up front pages of local and national newspapers from the 1930s, announcing the establishment of the camp, what it did and where it was. We visited the cell blocks, the punishment wing, the watchtowers, the crematorium, the monuments to the various groups imprisoned there. It was freezing, and the bunks were even colder than the air outside. The snow fell steadily, icing the walkways and dusting our hair, and we were grateful to the weather for making the visit as difficult as possible. It made the work of imagination easier.

Perhaps it has all become too easy. We know at once too much and too little. All words lead to the emptiness of Dachau; all words make a suburb around it. And therefore we can allow Cambodia and Rwanda, Bosnia and Congo, Zimbabwe and Sierra Leone, Sri Lanka and Sudan and Syria; Stalin and Idi Amin, Saddam and Mao. What did Hitler do to us? It's as if there can be no more tragedy, or comedy either, no passions of any kind; only the fence around a museum where the suffering faces have long since vanished. When I stood at Dachau, I felt the shroud of darkness descending on me through the sharpness of the frost. It was the darkness I had felt since childhood, that even the hard light of noon could not penetrate; that neither writing nor talking, nor song nor prayer, had been able to lift. I thought of my family, meeting up at a strangely related event a few years back.

In the late summer of 1999, my mother learned that the United States Holocaust Memorial Museum was sponsoring a weekend conference the following January called "Life Reborn." The meeting was to center on the period directly after the war, when the concentration camps slowly emptied of survivors and then became holding centers for displaced persons from Eastern Europe. "Your father and I plan to go," my mother said on the phone. I was amazed. My mother had refused to attend any such event before. My parents asked my two sisters and me to join them. Now we found ourselves confronting the first reunion of the original nuclear family of five, without husbands or children, since my marriage over twenty-five years before. A conference of Holocaust survivors was an odd venue for a family reunion. As the day approached, I grew more and more apprehensive.

I had let myself in for a multilayered, potentially explosive mix of emotions, my inner voice scolded, and to what purpose? I had been trying all this time to outgrow and to understand the villainous past, to transform it into something I could make use of. I was a middle-aged woman, no longer under the spell of the manipulations and outshoutings, the rivalries and disappointments, of childhood. By now, I told myself, I should be valiant and experienced enough to face up to such things. It was only a weekend. Was I not exaggerating, being hysterical? But I could see that I was already talking to myself in my father's voice and falling into a familiar relationship with my mother, placing myself, in imagination at least, in the role of chronicler, protector and sometime rival. My mother's story would always come first; my father's critical remarks would always sting. It was going to be a drama, without a doubt.

The sheer size of the hotel, a Marriott in the Adams Morgan section of Washington, DC, near the National Zoo, and of the crowd, nearly 900 people, not counting the harried and scurrying staff, did much to calm my anxieties about what I had thought might be a small, intense gathering of haunted souls. It was odd, indeed, to read the crammed name-tags on the shoulders of the well-dressed elderly. Like all proper résumés, they started with most recent place of origin and went backward in time, as in: "FRIEDA LEVINE, Santa Barbara, Toronto, Tel Aviv, Cyprus, Bergen-Belsen, Auschwitz, Chelmno, Warsaw." This pedigree had remarkable effects on small talk. In such a group, the hail-fellow-well-met heartiness of recognizing a stranger from the same home town always had a twist. "Oh, you were in Gross-Rosen? The man over there, no, not the bald one, the tall one talking to the bald guy, he was at Gross-Rosen. You want to meet him?" The conference-goers seemed downright festive. They were glad to see each other, curious to know who still prevailed through sheer survival over the forces of darkness. Over fifty years had passed, and a new millennium was about to begin. The general unreality of such a meeting during the transition from one century to the next contributed to a mood almost of gaiety. Everything ran late, everyone talked in the hallways or in the elevators. On one crowded elevator, my sister Dot remarked that the afternoon had been emotionally draining. We weren't sure that we could face the series of seminars scheduled for the next day without a break. I suggested a walk in the morning: "First the zoo, then Bergen-Belsen." The whole car erupted in laughter; all the passengers were in on the joke.

The thread linking all the goings-on at the conference, official and unofficial, had to do with recognition or rediscovery. The moment in the elevator had an existential rightness that everyone understood, but some people had come in the more literal hope of finding a familiar face. A folding screen in the registration area was soon covered with notices. Does anyone remember a woman called Tanya, last seen in Lodz, April 1940? the Liebowitz family of Vienna is trying to locate...could anyone tell me what happened to Rosa my mother, Samuel my father, my cousins, my sister, my rescuer, my friend, last seen at Theresienstadt, at Dachau, at Bergen-Belsen, in Poland, in Czechoslovakia, in Italy, in Shanghai, in Paris, in Berlin? My mother shook her head, looking at this improvised kiosk, which every day grew more leaflets like a tattered tree. "Imagine, they're all still hoping," she said.

But this crowd didn't seem very susceptible to illusions. I thought about what they had been through as I looked around. Many had survived the camps themselves, and many had made their way from the USSR or Poland into the postwar communities the camps had become. All had migrated to America and the majority had migrated more than twice, to the Far East, to Latin

America, to Israel, before arriving in the US. Now these survivors were surrounded by attractive children and grandchildren who seemed, in the mass, to share the same quality of vitality as their elders. I was looking at the luckiest of the lucky, and within that tiny group, the strongest of the strong.

The most significant and painful moment of the conference came, for me, when I walked through the Holocaust Museum on my own. I had only an hour, which was all I thought I could bear, though the staff recommended staying for three. I decided to race through, trying to take in the architecture and the crowds, and perhaps skimping on the images I already knew so well. I had heard that the museum had brought one of the original deportation boxcars back, and I wanted to know if it resembled the boxcars that had chugged so mercilessly through the nightmares of my childhood.

The wisdom of this high-speed strategy was soon apparent. I almost ran past the images of the 1930s and of the rise of Nazism, wept at the display of the murder of handicapped children in Germany, hurried past the bricks of the wall of the Warsaw Ghetto, and then, almost before I knew it, I raced up a short ramp and came to a halt in the darkness of the boxcar. Just as my grandparents might have done, I thought: before they knew it, they were locked in infamous shadow. For me, it was quiet, empty; for them, full of screams, groans, smells, despair. But I had been here before. Everything about the boxcar – its apertures set high in the planked wall, the wooden floor, the dimensions, the darkness – was as familiar as if I had taken the journey myself, except that, as in a dream, the boxcar was silent. I fought a wave of dizziness, and propelled myself onward to the display of the death camps, where there was a model of a gas chamber and a room with its bunks transported from Auschwitz – all familiar, as if I had been there too. I had read too many books, I suppose. The museum seemed to embody the journey my own mind had made.

I tried to separate myself, to look around at the pressing crowd. I was gratified to see so many people passing slowly by, coming in apparently endless numbers, speaking every language and representing, as far as I could see, every racial and national group the world could offer. I thought the visitors were courageous. There were conference people going through as well, most of them survivors, judging by their age, and for the most part they appeared dry-eyed and dispassionate. Perhaps they were as frequent visitors here as they were attendees on the Holocaust conference circuit, or perhaps the veil of fifty years had protected their hearts, or perhaps they had shed all their tears long ago.

Eventually I became aware of a wailing sound behind me. It was as loud as an ambulance, approaching as I rushed on, and out of curiosity I slowed my steps. Surely, I thought, this is another second-generation child. But the noise came from a young African American girl, perhaps seventeen. She could hardly walk for grief. She held out a hand touching the grey wall for support as she lurched along. She was with three friends, all in tears as well, and the noises came from her unselfconsciously, as if she were not surrounded by hundreds of people.

I was moved and almost relieved by her sorrow, because I had felt frighteningly isolated in this world, very much the way I had felt in my nightmares as a child. It was overpoweringly awful to be reminded that this nightmare was the reality. Most of the time, during my waking life, I could pretend otherwise. Even my mother, even the survivors of worse sufferings, did that. But the girl's cries helped. For me, this had been a walk through the world of my ancestors, and for her, a moment of fellowship, perhaps, in which she learned that prejudice and racial hatred are goblins that take on many shapes and colors. And surely knowledge is power. That principle had kept me from despair, despite the contradictions of experience. Sometimes I could not keep grief or a sense of human failure from flooding my heart. At other times, when people who didn't have to care did care, I was encouraged and grateful.

There were such people at the conference. A group of young Dutch historians from NIOD came with a video camera and grave, attentive faces; they attended every session until, exhausted, they suggested we repair to the bar, where we talked and drank, and they smoked. Later, in 2003, they made the program about my mother that was aired on Dutch television. I was amused when I saw how respectfully they listened to everyone, no matter how tedious the tale. When I tore my hair in mock exasperation and mouthed "What, another prayer?" the Dutch visitors had to endure everything politely, without comment. They reminded my mother of the young people who had smuggled babies out of her day care center at the beginning of the war, and who rescued survivors at its end. They reminded my father of some of the people he had met in Amsterdam when he went to retrieve my mother to marry her. And they reminded Susie and me of the young Europeans we had met at the Anne Frank Conferences that we had attended in the late 1960s, when Otto Frank still presided and the battle for international understanding seemed the most erotic undertaking in the world.

In that summer of 1969 we argued with each other in seminar rooms like a little UN: we had translators in glass booths, earphones, the works. Sessions were conducted in three or four languages, I forget exactly how many, but I could listen unimpeded to the Germans, who constituted by far the largest group of participants, though closely followed by English-speaking contingents, and then by the Dutch, and then by a scattering from all over the world. In the evenings, we danced closely with handsome young men who were much more forward than their American counterparts. I remember an auburn-haired Wolfgang who breathed the lyrics of "Michelle" into my ear and then kissed me hotly, right on the dance floor, and the marriage proposal from a Nigerian student, and the whispered urgencies of an officer in the German army, here to make sure that the United Nations Bill of Rights was respected among his men, and that the history of the Holocaust was taught. My sister developed a close relationship with Frits, a Dutch student leader, and drank too much beer, and fell in love a little, I think, as we all did. There was something irresistible about the combination of youth, passion, internationalism and Sixties idealism. The war in Vietnam was at its hopeless height, and the Europeans constantly challenged us about it. We had to keep reminding them that we were against it too, and could not speak for President Johnson or the Joint Chiefs of Staff.

I went to my first Anne Frank conference in 1967, in the summer between high school and college. Susie attended the one two years later, when I went for a second time. During the first conference, the rest of the family was also in Amsterdam staying with friends, and my mother and I had a bitter quarrel with Otto Frank. We didn't speak to him for a couple of years after. I remember it vividly. We met him one morning in a café in the Kalverstraat, a pedestrian precinct adjoining the Dam, the royal palace. We drank our delicious Dutch coffee, and before we knew it, we were arguing.

We hadn't known until then that Otto supported the war in Vietnam. He took the standard cold war view that Communism had to be stopped no matter what. My mother and I were dumbfounded, and we attacked. We were angry and intolerant then. We carried images of the war in our heads: burning monks toppling over in vast, transparent flames, burning children, deforested hillsides. We could not believe that our beloved adopted country could engage in such a war.

We were convinced of the rightness of our cause and fresh from demonstrations and picketing and endless conversations about anti-war candidates whom we could work for. We were wrong to be so hard on Otto. He was already an old man then, though he had a dozen years of life ahead of him, and our relationship was too precious to waste several years in silence and bitterness. In 1969 Otto changed his mind and condemned the war, and we slowly came into contact again. But our relationship was never quite the same. By then, he was too old and too famous. He probably felt that we had betrayed him somehow, and I think we had. His last years were swept by greater bitternesses as well: an attack by neo-Nazis on the authenticity of Anne's diary, which forced him to take the whole matter to court to prove them wrong; a lawsuit by Meyer Levin, who claimed that Otto had broken a promise to him to when he authorized Frances Goodrich and Albert Hackett, instead of Levin, to dramatize the Diary. Levin had even accused Otto of being an anti-Semite, of subverting his daughter's memory. (Lawrence Graver has written a book on the controversy called *An Obsession with Anne Frank: Meyer Levin and the Diary*, and there is some discussion of it in Carol Ann Lee's biography, *Otto Frank*, but I draw on family memories here.) In later years I was ashamed that my mother and I had been so self-righteous over Vietnam, but the times then felt desperate. The very experiences the two old friends shared also drove them apart. The moral stakes were high for them both.

All these memories flooded back as I looked into the candid eyes of the Dutch historians. There was something slightly ludicrous about my episodic and fundamentally shallow connection to the Netherlands, and particularly to Amsterdam itself, but my sisters had it too, and it went back to the Dutch songs and heroic stories of my mother's childhood and adolescence. Our knowledge of Dutch life had developed out of a summer visit here and there and occasional conversations with one family friend or another. What we knew of Dutch mirrored my mother's almost absurdly sunny personality. We had learned mostly words of praise, which in our limited experience constituted at least 50 percent of Dutch conversation. We told the Dutch historians at the conference that if you could say *heel mooi, heel lekker, heel gezellig, heel gelukkig,* all variations of *very nice,* you'd survive in Holland for quite a while. And wasn't that our mother all over, we said, turning to one another, the woman who described everyone as *very sweet* or *very lovely,* no matter how often we winced? Perhaps she had retained the view of the world of a small girl new to Dutch, the world of *heel mooi,* despite everything that had happened to her?

We of the second generation often seemed more embittered than our elders, and this apparent paradox came through quite clearly when survivors' children spoke to the general session on the Saturday night of the conference. Second-generation representatives had organized the event, and almost all of the speakers and their contemporaries in the audience were born exactly in the period that was its focus. But they had a degree of reticence I also understood very well. As long as their parents were alive, they had to keep a respectful distance from the power of original memory. They – we – were all Prince Charles, playing dutiful second fiddle to Queen Elizabeth, our parents' generation.

One speaker, the novelist Melvin Jules Bukiet, read from the foreword to a collection of writings aptly entitled *Nothing Makes You Free* (since published in 2002) by Holocaust survivors' children, whom he called the G2 generation. I felt ashamed that I was neither among the contributors nor among the speakers. What had I been doing all the decades of my life? Had I been fleeing something when I chose the academic path for which I was unsuited by temperament? I had persisted in the ups and downs of academic life for many years, writing about my beloved Enlightenment novelists and *philosophes* while others, evidently, had stayed closer to home, historically speaking, and now had their place on the podium to show for their filial loyalty. I felt a little jealous as I sat in the sea of folding seats and listened to a person who might have been, should have been, me. Bukiet was a wonderful writer, full of insight. His lacerating rage took me slightly by surprise; not that I was a stranger to rage, far from it. He saw himself as a rearguard fighter, almost a ninja, protecting his parents, appropriating the tattooed number on his father's arm as his own, shaking a fist in the face of the leaders of guilty nations and shouting, in the words with which he closed his reading, "Look what you did!"

It was a relief to hear such an articulate voice speaking of burdens which we had not dared to talk about with one another: the crushing sense of guilt, the obligation to be socially responsible, the knowledge that we could not live up to the promise of our miraculous postwar birth. We were all haunted by memories to which we were not entitled. He remarked that, perhaps because of our ghosts and our vague guilt, we G2ers tended to work for philanthropic organizations, or in the medical professions, or as writers – neatly covering the professions my sisters and I had chosen, as we did not fail to notice.

But the points of difference were also great. He seemed less melancholy than furious, less paralyzed than ready to take up the sword of combat. I was puzzled by his aggression, since by now it was a kind of shadow-play. Did he think that our parents could have prevailed by shaking their fists, or that he was stronger against the old nightmare than they had been? My ambition, unlike his, had been throttled in some way by the deep conviction that nothing really mattered, and certainly not my own destiny, a matter of pure chance after all. I thought that all Holocaust survivors' children had such heebie-jeebies, such nearly constant attacks of meaninglessness, but apparently this was not so.

When my sisters and I finally went to the Sunday morning panel on Bergen-Belsen with my parents – the one that had been the subject of my little joke in the elevator – the audience consisted partly of older people, survivors or former relief workers for American Jewish organizations, and partly of younger people related to them. Elie Wiesel was there, and Eric Nooter, one of the Dutch historians, showed slides from his archive of scenes from the camp. Members of the audience cried out when they saw a familiar face. Before even my parents noticed, I recognized my handsome twenty-six-year-old father in an old picture, frowning in concentration as he examined a bare-chested adolescent boy. This caused a little flurry, and my father was asked to stand up and acknowledge the applause of the group.

My parents were pretty much the only European-born relief workers in the room, and that put them in an unusual category. I didn't know whether to be embarrassed or pleased when my mother, caught up in the exhilaration of having met a now middle-aged child she had cared for, leapt to her feet to claim her own role in the rehabilitation of Belsen. She was in a number of slides, but because she had been so young at the time, barely twenty, and so foreign, she had not really been given the credit she deserved for her work. She seemed determined not to be overlooked again in favor of Americans who had defined identities and roles as social workers with this or that Jewish charity.

For the first time, I could see that tensions must have existed all along between the triumphant, well-fed, slightly smug Americans who arrived on the heels of the troops of liberation, and the Europeans, who had been caught in the monstrous machinery of Nazi destruction and had survived. Language itself was an issue. The English-speaking Americans couldn't talk to the people they were helping, unless they had some Yiddish in their backgrounds, while the multilingual Europeans spoke in a patois of tongues, all incomprehensible to their liberators. Instead of letting the old people discuss these things and make connections to their memories and to each other, a rather prim woman of my age cut them off as they tried to speak, and an academic, who had not been told the nature of the event, began to read a dry paper and nearly wept when she realized her mistake. She was Joanne Reilly, an intense and generous-spirited young Englishwoman whose work on Belsen helped me to visualize life in the camp when I began to write my own book. The panel, in a way, mirrored the uncertainty we all felt about how to situate ourselves in the wake of the Holocaust, even after so many years. We didn't know whether to study it, or to write about it, or to reject it, or to allow ourselves to indulge our mixed emotions. We were still caught, it seemed, in the confusion of postwar Europe.

I had known that I wouldn't be able to stand such intensity for long, and had planned to leave by noon that Sunday, though the conference would continue for another day and a half. I gazed at the people around me. Many of the participants, the regular conference-goers, had become used to looking at their younger selves, as my father had just looked at himself, without shock or perhaps much reflection. The important thing was the atmosphere of rescue, the sense that they were still pulling survivors from the wreckage. Even now, feeble voices could be heard, voices that had to be answered, outstretched hands that had to be grasped. You never knew whom you might meet at one of these events. "I was there, I know!" members of the audience shouted when some fact was disputed. Perhaps they were also saying: "This terrible experience has to count for something, doesn't it? It can't mean nothing. I must make it have meaning." That was the task to which all of us had dedicated ourselves, in one way or another: to make this unpromising history yield up some meaning that would help us, and help the rest of the world, limp into the future.

We children of survivors tend to be too serious by half, perhaps because we were raised by people who couldn't help looking back. Our parents, the survivors, cannot quite recover the full humanity of their dead: their quirkiness, their playfulness, an annoying way of scratching a head, a sweet turn of phrase, laziness in the morning, dozing after dinner, a characteristic gait, a need to argue over even the smallest thing, a lisp, a love of cars, of movies, of books, of the tango, of betting, of cigarettes, of jazz, of opera, a knack of rubbing your shoulder blade just where it's tight, a habit of drinking coffee cold, no sugar, and tea hot, not too strong; all those millions of specialties that separate the vibrant living from the piles of corpses heaped up in those tauntingly unforgettable pictures. The fear of forgetting the reality of the long-lost dead makes our survivor-parents cloudy with guilt, and us insubstantial, somehow, vaporous in their eyes. When they return to themselves they snatch at us with eager arms, worried that we too might evaporate.

When I look over what I have written, I am struck by the metaphors of insubstantiality I have chosen. For what did the Nazis tell the Jews in their death camps? That the only way out was through the chimney; that they were to become smoke and be dispersed forever. The Nazi code name for that unspeakable operation was *Nacht und Nebel,* Night and Fog. It is horrifying to think that the murderers might have succeeded, even metaphorically, in vaporizing us who survive, and surely that is not so. Reality tells us otherwise, and the justice of history brings us to life again.

But our melancholy knowledge has, perhaps, turned many of us into *Luftmenschen, air people*, useless dreamers, fantasists, people whose feet don't quite touch the ground. We are beings who, as a character says in Kafka's short story "The Country Doctor," "have no overview." The world, for us, is always in crisis, and we feel the shadow of violent death always on us. We were born in its chill, even when the sun shone. We feel our unreality acutely in the good fortune of our growing up in this opulent country, where we have been educated to make choices freely. We feel we're not quite entitled to that fortune, because of the chill that never leaves us, and so we work hard and are grateful. But we do notice the gaps, the gusty air that keeps us from feeling entirely at home, the *Luft* that blows through our bones and the bones of our parents.

I think all this as I look down at the monuments of Washington from the airplane that will bring me home to Boston. For the moment, I am a *Luftmensch* indeed as I fly into the blueness above the clouds. I leave behind my parents and their generation, who are still at the conference and still marveling at the connections they have made. I close my eyes and try telepathy, the only means I have at the moment to tell them that I rejoice in them. Their growing old is a triumph, their children and grandchildren (and later, great-grandchildren) spread around them like a tribe. Perhaps, even in the new age of terror that began almost with the new millennium, they will be able to imagine the future without immediate fear. I look back to Walter and Betty, Paula and Herta, through closed eyelids here on the Shuttle between the big cities of the East Coast, and I smile. I know that if they could, they would smile back. Fate has made them forever the age I am now. They will grow younger and younger as I age, and I can't help feeling that I know them differently from the way in which my mother knew them. I have tried to understand them, to raise them at least a little from their bed of ashes, or from the sky into which they vanished, to make them live again in the imaginations of their descendants; and imagination, in the end, is all we have. Imagination brings us closer to reality, us *Luftmenschen* of one sort or another, more than anything.

Perhaps that's what Abraham meant when he said to his God: *hineh-ni*, here I am. He might have meant that he was all attention, that he was paying attention as hard as he could. He must have been an imaginative fellow, to hear his one god speaking to him out there in the desert. He was spared the burning of his only son, that time. He was rewarded as no Jew was after that. Still, I try out Abraham's simple words, to see if I have any right to them. I don't think so, and his god has never spoken to me; but I can think of no others. They are so short, so easy to say, and speaking them is the best, perhaps the only thing I can do for my family of dead and for those who live still. *Hineh-ni,* here I am.

Notes

American Prologue: Mother and Daughter

Page

1   The mental hospital was part of the State Institutions at Howard, which included prisons, reformatories and a state farm; see www.bhddh.ri.gov/MH/

Amsterdam: July 1943, Dawn

17   Letter in author's possession from Dr R.C.C. Pottkamp, a historian in the Information and Documentation Department at NIOD, February 11, 2002, containing a typed contemporary description of the raid. See also Bob Moore, *Victims and Survivors: The Nazi Persecution of the Jews in the Netherlands, 1940–1945.* (London: Arnold, 1997), 104.

Chapter 1: Berlin

21   I haven't found a precise backing for my mother's claim that Jewish soldiers were sometimes segregated in the First World War, but photographs do suggest that this was true in my grandfather's case.

There was, however, an infamous Jew Count (*Judenzählung*) in the course of the war. It was ordered by the German government to determine how many Jews were serving on the front line (on the assumption that Jews were cowards), and it shocked the community. See Saul Friedländer, *Nazi Germany and the Jews,* vol. 1. (New York: HarperCollins, 1997), 73–75.

23   One of the documents from Dr Pottkamp (NIOD), above, is a list of former German war veterans "eligible" for deportation from Westerbork camp in the Netherlands to Theresienstadt, in then-Czechoslovakia, which was supposed to be a less murderous concentration camp than the others. Walter is credited with two medals from World War I, the Iron Cross first class, and the Iron Cross second class.

Marriage certificate, Berlin 1919 (in author's possession).

Chapter 2: Berlin and Amsterdam

31   My mother's description of the secular nature of Dutch, and Dutch Jewish life, is confirmed in *The History of the Dutch Jews in the Netherlands,* ed. J.C.H. Blom et al. (Oxford and Portland, OR: The Littman Library of Jewish Civilization, 2002); section by J.H. Blom and J. J. Cahen, "Jewish Netherlanders, Netherlands Jews, and Jews in the Netherlands, 1870–1940," 256–7. See also See Chaya Brasz, "Dutch Jews and German Immigrants: Backgrounds of an Uneasy Partnership in Progressive Judaism," 127, in *Borders and Boundaries in and around Dutch Jewish History,* ed. Judith Frishman et al. (Amsterdam: Uitgeverij Aksant), 2011.
See Chaya Brasz, 137 fn. 50. Brasz points out that about 4000 German Jews arrived in the Netherlands before 1933, for economic reasons rather than because of persecution, 134. Most Jews came through the Netherlands on their way somewhere else. In 1940, there were 16,000 German Jews in the country, 135. Bob Moore puts the number of "full" German and other foreign Jews in the Netherlands at about 22,000, or 15 percent of the total Jewish population, in *Victims and Survivors: The Nazi Persecution of the Jews in the Netherlands, 1940–1945* (London: Arnold, 1997), 213.

Chapter 3: My Mother Comes of Age

39   For an idea of Nazi intimidation in the March and November 1933 elections in Germany, see the *Manchester Guardian*, November 13, 1933, "All Germans rounded up to vote" (online). Saul Friedländer, *Nazi Germany and the Jews*, vol. I, 12.

40   Walter Jacobsthal is named as the synagogue's chairman until 1937 in Dan Michman, *Het Liberale Jodendom in Nederland, 1929–1943* (Amsterdam: Van Gennep, 1988), 116. Michman also cites some of Walter's letters to and from Lily Montagu – my husband's great-aunt – that survive in the American Jewish Archive at the Hebrew Union College in Cincinnati, and of which I have copies. Walter is discussed as well in Chaya Brasz, 136, who also mentions (and includes a picture of) Otto Frank at the Synagogue's postwar re-founding, 128. Michman and Brasz offer detailed accounts of the tensions between Dutch and German Jews, especially during the establishment of a Liberal/Progressive/Reform movement in the Netherlands. One example of many: Michman, 106. My mother's testimony also appears in Carol Ann Lee, *The Hidden Life of Otto Frank* (New York: Viking Books, 2002), 40.

41   There are many accounts of the founding of Otto's firm. Carol Ann Lee interviewed my mother on this point in *The Hidden Life of Otto Frank*, 39. See also Melissa Müller, *Anne Frank: The Biography* (New York: Henry Holt and Company, 1998), 43–4. For pictures of the firm, see *Anne Frank Beyond the Diary: A Photographic Remembrance*, ed. Ruud van der Rol and Rian Verhoeven (New York: Penguin, 1995), 25, 26, 32, 48–9.

42–3   See Bob Moore, *Victims and Survivors*, 28–36, and the whole of his *Refugees from Nazi Germany in the Netherlands* (Dordrecht, Boston, Lancaster: Martinus Nijhoff Publishers, 1986). Also Dan Michman, *Het Liberale Jodendom in Nederland*, Chaya Brasz, "Dutch Jews and German Immigrants," all of which have accounts of the period; Blom and Cahen, "Jewish Netherlanders, 1870–1940," 281. For the poverty of refugees, see a comment made by a member of the Hague congregation, 131. Two letters from my grandfather, Walter Jacobsthal, to my husband's great-aunt, Lily Montagu, were discovered in 2013 by Elisa Ho, an archivist at the American-Jewish Archives in Cincinnati, Ohio, where many European documents have been deposited. Lily Montagu was a founder of the Liberal movement in Judaism, and the two had met at congresses in London and Amsterdam. The first letter, from November 12, 1937, outlines his private opinion of the tensions between Dutch and German Jews, and most especially between the two Liberal congregations in The Hague and in Amsterdam. Lily Montagu responds with sympathy but not much practical help on November 27, and Walter replies the same day with polite anger, reiterating that the crisis needs immediate attention (copies in author's possession).

On the Kindertransports and efforts made by well-known German Jews, see Naomi Shepherd, *Wilfrid Israel* (London: Weidenfeld and Nicolson, 1984), 146–9. For Leo Baeck, see Anne E. Neimark, *One Man's Valor: Leo Baeck and the Holocaust* (New York: E. P. Dutton, 1986), 60–61; not a scholarly work, but contains some information. Anna Freud only arrived in England in the summer of 1938, but her nurseries cared later for refugee and survivor children, as well as for local children who had suffered in the Blitz or who were evacuees. See Elisabeth Young-Bruehl, *Anna Freud* (Summit Books, 1988), 246f. and 320f.

44   Anne Frank, *The Diary of a Young Girl: The Definitive Edition*, ed. Otto Frank and Mirjam Pressler (New York and London: Doubleday, 1995), 17.

46   Anne Frank, *Diary*, 78–9.

48   There were at least two edicts banning Jewish children from public schools: on September 1, 1941 (October 1 for Amsterdam) and September 1, 1942. See Moore's chronology of Nazi persecution in the Netherlands, 261–67.

49   For a photo of the Wieringermeer Jewish Work Village, see Blom and Cahen, "Jewish Netherlanders, 1870–1940," plate 70.

50   Anne Frank, *Diary*, 99–100. See also Anne's writing on her relationship with her mother, 154–5 and 167–8, among many examples.

55   Charles's Chilean sons, Charles and Roberto Jacobsthal, were found through Facebook, and now there is contact between our family and theirs.

Chapter 4: Invasion, Amsterdam 1940

55   This rumor turned up in the media; see "The Parachute Invasion," *The Times* (London), May 21, 1940. A British memoir relates an

anecdote about two German paratroopers caught shaving in their nuns' habits during the Allied retreat from Dunkirk; see Richard Collier, *The Sands of Dunkirk* (New York: Dutton, 1961), 59. Also Walter B. Maass, *The Netherlands at War: 1940–1945* (London, New York, Toronto: Abelard Schuman, 1970), 32.

Werner Warmbrunn, *The Dutch under German Occupation, 1940–1945* (Stanford, CA and London: Stanford University Press and Oxford University Press, 1963), 7–10. Maass, 30f.

56–7   On "Fortress Holland," Warmbrunn, 8, Maass, 21. On Jewish suicides and attempted escapes through Ijmuiden, J. Presser, *Ashes in the Wind: The Destruction of Dutch Jewry,* trans. J. Pomerans (London: Souvenir Press, 1968), 7–10.

Louis de Jong, *The Netherlands and Nazi Germany* (Cambridge, MA: Harvard University Press, 1990), 22–3.

58   On the quiet after the invasion and installation of German bureaucrats with Dutch cooperation: Presser 10; Maass, 43–8, Moore, 50–3, Warmbrunn, 27f.

According to Maass, 52–4 and Warmbrunn, 89, there were between 33,000 and 50,000 members of the NSB.

On informers, see Ad van Liempt, *Hitler's Bounty Hunters: The Betrayal of the Jews* (Oxford and New York: Berg Publishers, 2005). Originally published under the Dutch title *Kopgeld: Nederlands premiejagers op zoek naar joden, 1943* (Amsterdam: Uitgeverij Balans, 2002).

On protests against the Nazis, see Presser, 19–24, 27–9.

59   Gerhard Hirschfeld, *Nazi Rule and Dutch Collaboration: The Netherlands under German Occupation, 1940–45.* (Oxford/New York/Hamburg: Berg Press, 1988), 32–3; Presser, 11–12, Maass, 54, Moore, 42–4.

61   Warmbrunn, 11, Presser, 11–15.
Maass, 59.

62   On Aryan attestation, Presser, 19–29 (Herzberg citation, 19); Moore, 64–5.

64   On registration of Jews, Presser, 33–9; Moore, 64–5.
On increased measures and violence, Presser, 43–7; Warmbrunn, 107, Maass, 60, 64–5.

65   On foundation of the Jewish Council, Presser, 47–9, Moore 68–70.
On the ice cream parlor fights and the sealing of the Jewish Quarter, Presser 50–3; Moore, 71–3. See also Bernard Wasserstein's

illuminating portrait of a tireless social worker for the Jewish Council. Bernard Wasserstein, *The Ambiguity of Virtue: Gertrude van Tijn and the Fate of the Dutch Jews* (Cambridge, MA and London: Harvard University Press, 2014).

67   On the general strike of February 1941, Presser, 56–67; Moore, 72–3. On *Jewish Weekly* and the publication of edicts, Presser 67–70; on the repressive measures, 82–94. Again, Moore has a chronology of the persecution of Jews in the Netherlands, 261–7.

69   On the segregation of Jewish children in schools, Presser 76–80; Nanne Zwiep, 81; and the Nazi roundup of young people at Wieringermeer, Moore 81–2; Presser, 70. An account by Paul K., a survivor of the Wieringermeer raid, is in *Anne Frank war nicht allein: Lebensgeschichten deutscher Juden in den Niederlanden*, ed. Volker Jakob and Annet van der Voort (Berlin and Bonn: Verlag J. H. W. Dietz, 1988), 62–3. Paul K. also says that he found employment with the Jewish Council after he was miraculously spared from Mauthausen, supporting Moore's suggestion that German refugees worked there in various capacities.

70   On the Final Solution, Presser, 2–3; Moore 75–8. Walter Laqueur, *The Terrible Secret: Suppression of the Truth about Hitler's "Final Solution"* (New York: Henry Holt & Company, Owl Books, 1998), 196–7.

About my grandparents during the Occupation, documents from NIOD in author's possession.

71   On Gerrit van der Veen, Maass, 158.

72   On Jews banned from parks and beaches, Presser, 83. On Jewish star, Moore, 265, Presser, 118f.

73   See again Moore's chronology, 263–7.

I wonder now if Walter thought that he might be able to count on some protection from the Jewish Council, but if so he never mentioned it. On bombing of IJ, communication from Matthijs Cats, a historian working on *Andere Tijden,* Dutch Public Broadcasting.

75   Presser, 128–131; Anne Frank, Diary, 8–9.

76–7   Ticket and Chanukah program in author's possession. On Rabbi Mehler: Michman, 120–22, 124, 139. Anne Frank, Diary, 31. Photo of Franks at Miep's wedding, Anne Frank, Diary, interleaved between 182 and 183; *Anne Frank: Beyond the Diary*, 34.

79   Presser, a teacher at the time at the Jewish Lyceum, describes this scene at the graduation ceremony, which is probably the same one

that Anne and her sister attended on July 3, 1942, Diary, 17, though Anne doesn't mention these incidents; Presser, 142–3.

Anne Frank, Diary, 20. My mother's notice arrived on September 29 1942; document in author's possession.

On raids, Presser 152–3, Moore, 81, 146–55.

80   On "Portuguese" Jews, see Presser, 305–11. On Henriette Pimentel, Bert Jan Flim, *Saving the Children: History of the Organized Effort to Rescue Jewish Children in the Netherlands, 1942–1945* (Baltimore, MD: CDL Press, 2005), 47.

The best history of the rescue of Jewish children, from the *Joodse Schouwburg* and elsewhere, is Bert Jan Flim, chapter 3, 46–72. The website for *Secret Courage* may be found at: http://www .morsephotography.com/suskindfilm/journey_vanderpol.htm. In addition to the Vanderpols' and Morses' work in recognizing Süskind's achievements, see Presser, 281–82; Moore, 173–74, 184–85. Dutch Public Television made a program about Hilde on May 6, 2003, that includes a narrative of events and footage of the sites then and now. It is part of a series called *Andere Tijden* (Other Times), and can be seen (in Dutch) online at http://www .geschiedenis24.nl/andere-tijden/afleveringen/2002-2003/Hilde-Gold berg.html

83   On Joodsche Schouwburg and foundlings, Presser, 163, 174; on mentally disabled children, 179. Flim, photograph of Remi van Duinwijck, 52; on mentally disabled children, Presser, 179. See also http://www.verzetsmuseum.org/museum/en/tweede-wereldoorlog/ digiexpo/byedad/byedad,hollandsche_schouwburg/day_care_centre for more information and pictures. I have learned that Rémy the orphan is the hero of an 1878 French novel, *Sans Famille*, by Hector Malot. I'm grateful to my colleague Susan Suleiman, who mentions *Sans Famille* in her *Budapest Diary: In Search of the Motherbook* (Lincoln, Nebraska: University of Nebraska Press, 1996).

88   This raid on 31 March 1943 was not British, as my mother thought, but a line 7-8USAAF raid that went wrong. See http://www.ww2f .com/topic/49131-usaaf-bomb-rotterdam-march-31st-1943/ and a number of online sources.

94   On the "moving" firm Puls: Presser, 364f, Moore, 105.

96   On Dutch-Paris, see the blog by a young historian, Megan Koreman, at http://www.dutchparisblog.com/. She does an extraordinary job of researching and interpreting archival documents associated with

this network. She has also been generous in sharing materials having to do with Jo. Otherwise see an older and less scholarly history of Dutch-Paris: Herbert Ford, *Flee the Captor*. Nashville, TN: Southern Publishing Association, 1966.

Jo describes his escape to Belgium and the flight from Maastricht, among other exploits, in a not entirely accurate letter that he wrote January 3,1945, to the Dutch government in exile in London. He was seeking Dutch citizenship for Hilde and himself. I have one copy of the letter from Megan Koreman, and another, possibly from the United States Memorial Holocaust Museum, among my parents' papers. For the air war over The Netherlands, see Herman Bodson, *Downed Allied Airmen and Evasion of Capture: The Role of Local Resistance Networks in World War II* (Jefferson, NC and London: McFarland & Company, Inc, 2005), 44.

Chapter 5: In the Ardennes, 1943

100–101 See Bernard A. Cook, *Belgium: A History* (New York: Peter Lang, 2004). Chapter 15, on WW II, outlines these events in almost comically schematic form, 121–31; and Bodson 15–24; Étienne Verhoeyen, *La Belgique occupée de l'an 40 à la Libération* (Brussels: DeBoeck Université), 1994, 37–9.

Bodson, 17, 21, and on ethnic difference (in this case between American fliers and the local population), 120–21. Jewish survival rate in the Netherlands and compared to surrounding countries: Moore, 2. Figures vary somewhat among historians. My figure comes from *Timetables of Jewish History: A Chronology of the Most Important People and Events in Jewish History*, ed. Judah Gribetz, Edward L. Greenstein and Regina S. Stein (New York: Simon and Schuster, 1993), 479.

On the Belgian Resistance, see Verhoeyen, Bodson, and a collection of conference essays called *L'Engagement dans la Résistance France du Nord-Belgique* (Lille: Centre de Recherche sur l'histoire de L'Europe du Nord-Ouest, Université Charles de Gaulle, Lille 3, vol. 33, 2004).

On John Henry Weidner, leader of Dutch-Paris, Herbert Ford, *Flee the Captor,* see above, note for 102. Bodson, 47.

Megan Koreman first made the suggestion to me about Jo's possible work with other networks, such as *Comète, Eva* and *Marathon,* which are described in the books listed here (Bodson, 50–64, for example). Her scholarship is meticulous and thoughtfully interpreted.

102   The agency that organized these children's homes was and is known by the acronym ONE (Office de la naissance et de l'enfance). Its website, at http://www.one.be/index.php?id=histoire-de-l-one, describes some of its work in saving Jewish children during the Nazi occupation.

103   On farmers and food shortages in Belgium, Bodson, 17, 75–6; Verhoeyen, 14–17 and his *Deuxième Partie: L'Exploitation allemande*, 215f. The Nazi pillaging of the highly industrialized Low Countries included every kind of material and manufacture as well as agricultural products.

106   David Delfosse, a writer in Paris whose relatives in northern France were involved with my uncle and with the Dupuis in the rescue of Allied airmen during the war, has written and sent photographs of the Dupuis, and has more information about Jo's heroic activities. He has been most generous with this, and with his support in general.

117   The role of non-Belgian or non-French resisters, and especially the role of women, has been underestimated in what histories there are of these movements. Megan Koreman has noticed this in her archival research. Verhoeyen suggests that women were under-represented because their role in Belgian society was limited before the war, 339, but he mentions only leaders, like Andrée de Jongh, of *Comète* (also in Bodson, 26–7, 50–8), and agents sent from London, 339–40. I suspect that there were many young women like my mother, who were active in risky activities but never documented. In Holland, Maass mentions "girls on bicycles," 218.

There is much more on French women in the Underground. See, for example, Margaret Collins Weitz, *Sisters in the Resistance: How Women Fought to Free France, 1940–1945* (New York: John Wiley & Sons, 1995), with its extensive bibliography. Weitz confirms that "underground movements do not leave written records," 11. Among other neglected memoirs by women who fought with the Resistance is Frida Knight, *The French Resistance: 1940–1944* (London: Lawrence & Wishart, 1975).

118   Louis de Jong, *The Netherlands and Nazi Germany*, 46.

119–20   I have found out a little about the Cartons de Tournai at http://familytreemaker.genealogy.com/users/g/e/n/Wautier-Gendeb

ien/WEBSITE-0001/UHP-Index.html, that mentions some descendants of the family, and on a second website that is devoted to Belgian nobility (under Esquires); http://www.eupedia.com /belgium/belgian_nobility.shtml#Esquire. I cannot vouch for the reliability of either source.

On the Battle of Gembloux. May 14–15, 1940, see many online sources, among them http://connection.ebscohost.com/c/articles /2675769/battle-gembloux-14-15-may-1940-the-blitzkrieg-checked, which refers readers to an article by Jeffery A. Gunsburg in *Journal of Military History* (vol.64, issue 1: January 2000), 97.

122   My mother says that Girl Guides and Girl Scouts sometimes took part in clandestine activities, for which their survival training served them well; see also Weitz, *Sisters in the Resistance*, 110, 172.

126   On Hitler's scorched-earth policy, see Martin Gilbert, *The Second World War* (New York: Henry Holt and Company, 1991), 587.

128   http://users.telenet.be/Atlantikwall-15tharmy/Liberation.htm has a day-to-day account (see September 3, 1944). I am not sure of the source, but the facts appear to be accurate.

I saw an example of the Maquis uniform, threadbare but exactly as my mother had described it, in the tiny, underfunded and dusty Musée de la Résistance in Brussels in 2011.

130   David Verloop: Ford, *Flee the Captor*, 274–75. A letter from Jacques Grenez in my possession indicates that Jo had told Jacques that Hilde was his fiancée, not his sister, and encourages her not to try to make contact with Jo for the moment. I imagine that it was written before Jo's release.

Suzy Kraay and the disaster that followed her arrest: Ford, 247f.

132   Gestapo headquarters were at 347 avenue Louise in Brussels. In 2011 there was a mobile telephone shop on the site.

134   On the Hunger Winter of 1944–1945 and its relation to Market-Garden, see Gilbert, 593; Hirschfeld, 53; Moore, 226–27; Warmbrunn, 15–16.

On Field Marshal Montgomery and his miscalculation, see John Keegan, *The Second World War* (New York and London: Penguin Books, 1989), 436–8; and especially Maass, 205f.

137   On food for starving Holland, see Maass, 237–40; Gilbert, 678–79. On deaths in Holland of Jews and non-Jews, see Gilbert, 746. See Moore's slightly different figures, 259–60. See also Diane L. Wolf, *Beyond Anne Frank: Hidden Children and Postwar Families in*

Holland (Berkeley and Los Angeles: University of California Press, 2007). The usual estimated survival figure of Dutch Jews is 4.8%, as she describes, 95.

Gilbert, 610; Maass, 215f.; Moore, 228.

138–9   On the Battle of the Bulge, Keegan, 439–47, irritation among generals, 438; Gilbert, 618–622.

143   On Dutch reluctance to recognize survivors, Moore, 228–32, Presser, 535; Wolf, 95–9.

Flim, *Saving the Children* confirms my mother's observation that hidden children had a high survival rate, 164.

145   On V2 raids on Antwerp, see Gilbert, 601, 614–15, 653.

Maass points out that the Germans often launched V2s from Holland, 165–66, 221, though aimed mostly at England.

On Montgomery's failure to clear the harbor at Antwerp, see Keegan, 437.

146   Ben Shephard reports this journey in his excellent book on the early days of the medical rescue, *After Daybreak: The Liberation of Bergen-Belsen, 1945* (New York: Schocken Books, 2005), 80.

Chapter 6: Bergen-Belsen, April 1945

148   On the crossing of the Rhine at Remagen, see Keegan, 519–521, Gilbert, 646–52, Maass, 224–25.

On the liberation of Belsen, see *Bergen-Belsen. Historical Site and Memorial* (Celle: Lower Saxony Memorials Foundation/Bergen-Belsen Memorial, 2011), 10.

In March 2013, the United States Holocaust Memorial Museum publicized new research showing that there were over 42,500 camps, ghettos and prisons in the Reich and its territories, suggesting that very few people in Germany could have been unaware of the persecution of Jews and others. *The United States Holocaust Museum Encyclopedia of Camps and Ghettos, 1933–1945,* ed. Geoffrey P. Megargee and Martin Dean. (Bloomington, IN: The University of Indiana Press), 2013.

149   A brief mention of the Western Wall is in Keegan, 438.

For a brief general description of the camp, its location and history, see a United States Holocaust Museum website:
http://www.ushmm.org/wlc/en/article.php?ModuleId=10005224

On the stench, see Robert Collis and Han Hogerzeil, *Straight On*

(London: Methuen and Co. Ltd., 1947), 48. On local Germans' apparent ignorance of the camp, see Leslie Hardman and Cecile Goodman, *The Survivors* (London: Valentine Mitchell, 1958), 45.

150   For typhus signs: Collis, 31; Derrick Sington, *Belsen Uncovered* (London: Duckworth, 1946), 9. The figures for dead and survivors come from the testimony of the British 11th Armoured Division at the USHMM website, but Isaac Levy, the second British rabbi to arrive at the camp, has 20,000 dead: Isaac Levy, *Witness to Evil: Bergen-Belsen 1945* (London: Peter Halban Publishers, 1995), 16.

On Eichmann, see Hannah Arendt, *Eichmann in Jerusalem: A Report on the Banality of Evil* (New York: Penguin Books, 1992), 87–9.

153   April 21 was also the day that the evacuation of sick inmates to the Panzer Training School began, Shephard, 87.

154   All the histories have accounts of the DDT treatments; Sington, 55, is one example. The Imperial War Museum in London has photos of DDT dusting of British servicemen at Belsen in its archives.

On Glyn Hughes and the hospital: Joanne Reilly, *Belsen: The Liberation of a Concentration Camp* (London: Routledge, 1998), 24–6, 178. Reilly's book, along with Ben Shephard's, is among the most thoughtful and authoritative postwar account of the liberation of Belsen. See also Levy, 19, 134f and Shephard, 42f.

155   On daily death rates see Shephard, 53–4.

156   Collis's article for the BMJ of June 9, 1945, with Colonel Johnston's account of the camp, is online at http://www.bergenbelsen .co.uk/pages/Database/ReliefStaffAccount.asp?HeroesID=65&=65 See also *Law Reports of War Criminals, vol. II: The Belsen Trial* (London: Published for the United Nations War Crimes Commission by His Majesty's Stationery Office, 1947), 9–10. www .loc.gov/rr/frd/Military_Law/.../Law-Reports_Vol-2.pdf, *Sington, 35.*

157   On colonial reflexes, Shephard, 194. On women rescuers with the British forces, Reilly, 42–49; Shephard, 82; and on the overpraising of medical students at the expense of women personnel, 130–32.

158   See Shephard on "corpses still alive," 62 and 116. On Lieutenant-Colonel Johnston, see Collis, *Straight On*, 56. Some videos and photographs are available online from the Imperial War Museum in London, http://www.iwm.org.uk/collections/item /object/205133268, and the United States Holocaust Memorial Museum in Washington, DC, http://resources.ushmm.org/film

/display/detail.php?file_num=2709. Also Shephard, throughout but especially 47. Levy, 11-12, Shephard 52-54.

159 Catalog of the Imperial War Museum's exhibit on Bergen-Belsen, *The Relief of Belsen: April 1945 Eye Witness Accounts*. London: Trustees of the Imperial War Museum, 1991, 19–21. Hardman, 31. Collis, 52. On language difficulties, see Leslie Hardman, 21, 24. Hardman spoke Yiddish, and acted with great compassion as an intermediary and advocate for the inmates. He was soon supported and helped by his superior officer, Isaac Levy, the second Jewish chaplain to arrive; see Levy on Hardman's work and exhaustion, 12–14. Also Shephard, 68–71.

160–61 On the deaths of Anne and Margot, see Shephard, 177. Shephard is particularly interesting on the stories of rescuers and survivors after the war and on assessments with hindsight of the quality of the rescue at Bergen-Belsen.

The deaths of Anne and Margot are recounted in many sources. See, for example, Carol Ann Lee, *Roses from the Earth: The Biography of Anne Frank* (London: Viking/Penguin, 1999), 196–97; Melissa Müller, *Anne Frank: The Biography*, trans. Rita and Robert Kimber (New York: Metropolitan Books/Henry Holt and Company: 1998), 261–62; testimony in Jon Blair's film *Anne Frank Remembered*, 1995.

On the dead in Belsen between January and mid-April 1945, see Eberhard Kolb, *Bergen-Belsen 1943–1945* (Göttingen, Germany: Vandenhoeck & Ruprecht, 2002), 43. He gives a figure of 18,165 for the month of March 1945; also Reilly, 17.

On Otto's liberation from Auschwitz, January 27, 1945, Müller, 273, Lee, 187–88, and many testimonies on video and in print, from Otto and his family and friends.

The same accounts, above, also mention Anne's single blanket sheltering her from the cold.

Testimony of Janny Brandes-Brilleslijper in film *Anne Frank Remembered*. See also Shephard, 15 and fn. 10 for this page, 215.

162 Hardman, 74-5.

163 On Bengal Mixture, see Reilly, 40; testimony of John Dixey, medical student, *The Relief of Belsen*, 17; Hardman, 49. Shephard, 104–06, 127. On Human Laundry, Reilly, 36; *The Relief of Belsen,* 23–4, Shephard, 58, 89.

164 On benzene injections, Sington, *Belsen Uncovered*, 78; Collis, 79. On

unfamiliarity and horror of illnesses in the camp, see *The Relief of Belsen*, 15–16; and especially Reilly, 46; Shephard, 107.

Collis, 86; on Lieutenant-Colonel Johnston, again, 55–6, Shephard, 59. Johnston himself testified in a statement included in *The Liberation of the Nazi Concentration Camps, 1945* (Washington, DC: Government Printing Office for the United States Holocaust Memorial Council, 1987), 54–6. According to Shephard, he was too ill to attend and sent a written statement, 186.

165   Hardman, 62. On the AJDC and UNRRA, see Reilly, 104 and throughout thereafter, especially chapters 3 and 5, section 4; Oscar Handlin, *A Continuing Task: The American Joint Distribution Committee, 1918–1964* (New York: Random House, 1964), 92–106. Also Yehuda Bauer, *American Jewry and the Holocaust: The American Joint Distribution Committee, 1939–1945* (Jerusalem and Detroit: Hebrew University and Wayne State University, 1981).

On Jewish Central Committee and Josef Rosensaft, *The Relief of Belsen*, 7; Reilly, 82 and throughout. Yehuda Bauer, "The DP Legacy," 27–8; Menachem Z. Rosensaft, "My Father: A Model for Empowerment," 77–81; Elie Wiesel, "Keynote Address," 84–5. All in *Life Reborn: Jewish Displaced Persons 1945–1951* (Washington, DC: United States Holocaust Memorial Museum, 2001). Levy, 9 and throughout.

166   On the removal of DPs to other countries, see Collis, 101f; Hardman, 88–9; Reilly, 80–108. See especially Isaac Levy, whose book chronicles his persistent efforts to get British authorities to recognize the unique problems of Jewish survivors.

167   Levy and Shephard both describe the rigidity of British rule; Levy 48–67, Shepard, 194.

170–71 On the departure of the Gypsies, Hardman, 74–6.

On postwar artistic performances at Belsen, see the ORT website, http://holocaustmusic.ort.org/places/camps/central-europe/; Reilly, 39–40.

172   Ian Paterson F.R.C.E. obituary, *The Scotsman Evening News*, November 4, 2008.

173   This volume was in its last stages of editing when an excellent book came out chronicling the remarkable wartime career of Hanns Alexander. See Thomas Harding, *Hanns and Rudolf: The True Story of the German Jew Who Tracked Down and Caught the Kommandant of Auschwitz* (London: William Heinemann, 2013). Harding

describes Hanns's role as interpreter for the War Crimes Commission, 174; see also note for p.152 Harding mentions Colonel Leo Genn, Hanns's commanding officer, who was also an actor, 174–6 and fn. for that page, 306.

174 Harding has a slightly different account of Hanns's fiancée, 89–91. Hanns had met her independently, and she was a German-Jewish refugee like him. She had a strong personality, however, as Harding suggests in many places, perhaps most amusingly 220–21.

175 René Pottkamp at NIOD, the Dutch War Research Institute, found the Nazi lists confirming my grandparents' dates of deportation to these camps; copies in author's possession.

176 On Dutch Jews in camps who lacked the survival skills of Eastern European Jews, Presser, 495.

180 On the bombing of the Amsterdam municipal records office by Resistance fighters on March 27 1943, see the online site of the Dutch Resistance Museum in Amsterdam, http://www.verzetsmuseum.org/museum/en/alwayspresent,itinerary _ideas/plantage_area.
See Harding's account of the same spring and the following months of 1945, ch. 12 of his book. Hilde isn't mentioned except perhaps obliquely in a December 1945 letter in which Hanns writes to Ann: "Don't worry about me keeping the Dutch girls warm," 221.

181 Kaddish, *The New Union Home Prayer Book*, 203–04.

Chapter 7: Displaced Persons, Bergen-Belsen

185 Herbert Agar, *The Saving Remnant: An Account of Jewish Survival* (New York: Viking Press Inc., 1960), 94–5, 181f., including an account of General Patton's hostile attitude toward survivors in the American zone, 182. This is a limited and rather rhetorical account of the work of the AJDC.

186 See the film *The Long Way Home*, directed by Mark Jonathan Harris 1997. On Ernest Bevin, see Reilly, 86–8, 96f. On inadequate rations, see Reilly 176–78.

187 On Earl Harrison and his report, Reilly, 89–96. See also online: http://www.ushmm.org/museum/exhibit/online/dp/politic6.htm. Levy 71–2. On Rosensaft, Reilly, 99–100 and the record of his appearance in the AJDC newsletter, *JDC Digest*, vol. 5, no. 1: January, 1946, 8.

188   On the comic similarity between the twins see Harding 128–30, among other examples.

189   On the return of Jews from Eastern Europe, film, *The Long Way Home*; Yehuda Bauer, "The DP Legacy" in *Life Reborn*, 25.

191–2 On the war crimes trial at Lüneburg, *Relief of Belsen*, 27–9.

Though both twins were based at Bergen-Belsen (Hanns much more intermittently), Hilde had not seen him much by the close of 1945. According to Harding, Hanns proposed to Ann in January 1946; 225, was demobbed April 20, 1946; 247, and married Ann, May 19, 1946; 248.

Reuma Weitzmann, "Interview" (typescript), part of a survey of "Holocaust survivors in the Bergen-Belsen Displaced Persons Camps in the British Zone of Occupation" by the Oral History Division of the Institute of Contemporary Jewry, The Hebrew University, Jerusalem, July 22, 1993. Conducted by Hagit Levsky and Chana Kovari; 6–7, and generally the whole account. Handlin, 102.

See also "The Task of Remembering" by Genya Markon, in *Jewish Displaced Persons in Camp Bergen-Belsen, 1945–1950: The Unique Photo Album of Zippy Orlin,* ed. Erik Somers and René Kok (Seattle: University of Washington Press in association with the Netherlands Institute for War Documentation, 2004), 134–39. This essay contains an account of Hilde's work; also see Markon's contribution "Eyewitnesses," which has descriptions and pictures of Reuma Weizmann, 214–15, and Hilde, 224–25. Hilde appears with her staff at the day-care center in a photo, 66–7.

Also Reilly, 178–9.

193   Reuma Weitzmann speaks of Ben Shemen; see its website at http://eng.ben-shemen.org.il/ Ari Shavit gives a dismaying account of the involvement of Ben Shemen in the expulsion of Arab inhabitants from the town of Lydda, during the 1948 War of Independence in his article "Lydda, 1948" in the *New Yorker* of October 21, 2013, 40–46. See also online, http://www.newyorker.com/reporting/2013/10/21/131021fa_fact_shavit. It is a tragic story, and almost unimaginable given the recent experiences of the young Holocaust survivors there. The *New Yorker* article is a chapter in Ari Shavit, *My Promised Land: The Triumph and Tragedy of Israel* (New York: Spiegel and Green, 2013).

197   Film, *The Long Way Home*; Handlin, 97–9.

Interview with Rabbi Herbert Friedman in film *The Long Way Home.*

198 Essays by Erik Somers and René Kok in *Jewish Displaced Persons in Camp Bergen Belsen 1945–1950* (see above) provide a history of the DP camp at Belsen, of the struggles with the British forces in charge, and of the development of a stable community; see esp. 70–2.

199–200 On small number of Joint workers in Europe (65), see *JDC Digest*, vol. 5, no. 2, February 1946, 17.

The same issue of the *JDC Digest* that reports on Rosensaft's speech mentions a $100 million campaign for displaced persons, and millions of dollars' worth of supplies are reported in all issues from this period.

202 Otto as father figure: see testimony of Sal de Liema in Lee, *The Hidden Life of Otto Frank*, 113.

206 On Dr Spanier, Moore, 221–23; Presser, 425.

211 Telephone conversation with Thomas Harding about the relationship between the Elias cousins of Otto Frank and the Alexander family.

Chapter 8: Love Letters

224 James Boswell, *Life of Johnson*, originally published 1791. (Oxford: Oxford University Press, 1987), 957.

231 On Endingen (also called Oberendingen) and Lengnau rural ghettos, see Mitya New, *Switzerland Unwrapped: Exposing the Myths* (London: Tauris Publishers, 1997), 16–17; also Willy Guggenheim, ed., *Juden in der Schweiz: Glaube, Geschichte, Gegenwart* (Küsnacht/Zürich, Switzerland: Edition Kürz, 1982), 21f.

232 New, 17. The message from President Buchanan to Congress, and the hearings that followed, are readily accessible: see House of Representatives, 36th Congress, first session, April 24, 1860.

On Jews during the Black Death, see Heiko Haumann et al., ed., *Juden in Basel und Umgebung: Zur Geschichte einer Minderheit* (Basel, Switzerland: Schwabe & Co. AG, 1999), 12–13; and the first essay, by Werner Meyer, in *Acht Jahrhunderte Juden in Basel* (Basel, Switzerland: Schwabe Verlag, 2005), 26. These sources and others give an exact date, January 16, 1349, when all the Jews of Basel were burned on an island in the Rhine, obliterating the community. See also www.jewishvirtuallibirary.org. My father says that he had always been told that Jews had been nailed into barrels and thrown into the Rhine. Either way they met a terrible fate, along with the Jews of Strasbourg and other cities.

234   On the first Zionist Congress in Basel, see Haumann, *Juden in Basel*, 31–4.

238–9   On anti-Semitism and pro-Nazi sentiment in Switzerland, see Jacques Picard, "Switzerland and the Jews," in New, *Switzerland Unwrapped*, 17–23; and Noëmi Sibold, *Bewegte Zeiten: Zur Geschichte der Juden in Basel von den 1930er Jahren bis in die 1950er Jahre* (Zürich, Switzerland: Chronos Verlag, 2010). The title of the first chapter says it all: "Judenfeindschaft in den 1930er Jahren" ("Jew-Hatred in the 1930s"). See also Shaul Ferrero, "Switzerland and the refugees fleeing Nazism: documents on the German-Jews turned back at the Basel border in 1938–1939," Shoah resource centre, www.yadvashem.org\o._pdf\

241–2   I have found a few references to General Guisan, mostly online, which refer to a mobilization of troops in 1940 and a strategy of retreat to the Alps; the incidents of 1942 come up obliquely. See also the US Office of Strategic Services (OSS) records for 1942–1946 listed among open "Holocaust era assets" in Military Agency Records on the US National Archive website, http://www.archives.gov/research/holocaust/finding-aid/military/other-oss.html, box 111, folder 20. On General Guisan see Jonathan Steinberg, *Why Switzerland?* (Cambridge: Cambridge University Press, 1976), 46–50. Also Klaus Urner, *Let's Swallow Switzerland: Hitler's Plans Against the Swiss Confederation,* (Lanham MD: Lexington Books, 2002).

In August 1942 Hitler referred to Switzerland as "a pimple on the face of Europe." It is well known that Hitler had a plan to invade the country called Operation Tannenbaum. Himmler's records show a plan in 1942 for the *Germanischer SS Schweiz*. I wonder if rumors of this plan may have caused the panic of 1942.

For Hitler's views on invading Switzerland, see many websites, including http://www.pbs.org/wgbh/pages/frontline/shows/nazis/readings/halbrook.html, where Swiss anti-Semitism and pro-Nazi sentiment in the war are not mentioned.

244   For photos of Rabbi Arthur Weil, see Haumann, ed., *Acht Jahrhunderte Juden in Basel*, 176, 205.

Chapter 9: War Again, Israel 1948

249 The revisionist historians who radically challenge the heroic version
of Israel's founding include Benny Morris, Avi Shlaim, Tom Segev
and Ilan Pappé, among others.

253–4 On Jewish veterans and the general organization of the Israeli
military in 1948, see Ilan Pappé, *The Making of the Arab-Israeli
Conflict, 1947–51* (London: I.B. Tauris & Co. Ltd, 1992), 47–52,
particularly 50. See also Benny Morris, *1948: A History of the First
Arab-Israeli War* (New Haven, CT: Yale University Press, 2008), 21.
On the Haganah and its terrorist rivals, Chaim Herzog, *The Arab-
Israeli Wars: War and Peace in the Middle East from the 1948 War of
Independence to the Present* (London: Greenhill Books, 2004)
17–21.

May 14, 1948, is now Independence Day in Israel; see Herzog, who
describes the sound of Egyptian warplanes bombing Tel Aviv in the
background of Ben-Gurion's radio announcement, 46, 47. On lack
of training and weaponry in early June 1948, Herzog 48, Morris, 200.
On foreign volunteers including medical personnel, Morris 85–6.

On the deployment of the Golani Brigade and others, see Morris,
119, 204. See also its website with a history, http://www.jewish
virtuallibrary.org/jsource/Society_&_Culture/golani_brigade.html
On the Kadoorie School, still in existence, see http://www.kado
orie.org.il/Content.aspx?id=59 . Several of its graduates were leaders
of the Palmach.

256 On Latrun, see Herzog, 41f., Morris, 219–231, especially 229–31,
which describes the battle exactly contemporaneous with my father's
involvement at Sejera (see below). The battles for Latrun were part
of the Jerusalem battles and siege, see below.
On the battle for Jerusalem from November 30, 1947 to June 11,
1948, Herzog 38–45 and 59–68; Morris, 208–31 (including the
descriptions of Latrun).
On Yad Mordechai, Morris, 237–39; Herzog, 71–2. On Degania,
254–57; Herzog, 51–4.

257 Morris mentions an Arab knife attack on the young Ben-Gurion at
Sejera, 7.

258 First battle of Sejera, Herzog, 55–6.

263 According to Morris, 264, the truce came into effect on June 11,
1948, though it was accepted by both sides on June 9. Herzog

doesn't give a date, suggesting some ambiguity on the matter. Morris has more on the first truce, 148.

Before the end of the British Mandate, seventy-eight doctors, nurses, students, professors and other medical personnel in a medical convoy were burned to death in an ambush on the Jerusalem Road on April 13, 1948, Morris, 128–29.

264   On Ben-Gurion's disciplinary action against the Irgun, see Morris, 271–72

266   On better weapons in early 1948, including supplies from Skoda in Czechoslovakia, Morris 84, 87–8,117. On further weapons and aircraft from Europe and the United States, 176–77, 206–07.

On conquest of Nazareth, Herzog, 78–9; Morris, 280–81. In mid-July, the Golani Brigade also defended Sejera and took Lubiya in a second round of battles there.

267   On Count Bernadotte's plan for Israel to give up territory in exchange for more of Galilee, Herzog, 87; Morris, 269–70.

268   On the assassination of Count Bernadotte, Herzog, 88; Morris, 312–13.

269   On the signing of armistice agreements, Herzog, 105, and generally his chapter entitled "Summary: The Israeli Victory," 105–08.

Chapter 10: An American in Germany, 1971

284   This line comes from near the end of what is probably Celan's most widely known poem, *Todesfuge* ("Death Fugue"):

der Tod ist ein Meister aus Deutschland sein Auge ist blau
er trifft dich mit bleierner Kugel er trifft dich genau

(Death is a master from Germany his eyes are blue
he strikes you with leaden bullets his aim is true)

From *Poems of Paul Celan*, trans. Michael Hamburger (New York: Persea Books, 2002), 30–33.

298   Alexander and Margarete Mitscherlich, *Die Unfähigkeit zu Trauern: Grundlage kollektiven Verhaltens* (Munich, Germany: Piper, 1967). This book came out in English as *The Inability to Mourn: Principles of Collective Behavior* (New York: Grove Press, 1975).